Torah for Gentiles?

Torah for Gentiles?

What the Jewish Authors of the Didache Had to Say

Daniel Nessim

The Lutterworth Press

THE LUTTERWORTH PRESS
P.O. Box 60
Cambridge
CB1 2NT
United Kingdom

www.lutterworth.com
publishing@lutterworth.com

Paperback ISBN: 978 0 7188 9662 1
PDF ISBN: 978 0 7188 9661 4

British Library Cataloguing in Publication Data
A record is available from the British Library

First published by Pickwick Publications, 2021

This edition published by The Lutterworth Press, 2023,
by arrangement with Wipf and Stock Publishers

To my wife Deborah, my woman of valor,
who has stood by me through thick and thin.

Contents

Preface

The following study is a slight revision of my doctoral dissertation, "Didache, Torah, and the Gentile Mission: A Mediation of Torah for the Church," which was accepted by the Department of Theology and Religion at the University of Exeter in 2019. Importantly, by studying the Didache, I had the opportunity to research Second Temple Judaism, the Dead Sea Scrolls, both the Hebrew Bible and New Testament, nascent Christianity, and Christian Judaism.

While having the good fortune of living in London during the beginning of my studies at the university, I made frequent trips by train to Exeter and back, usually revising my German on the way. At Exeter, I had an extraordinary supervisor and mentor in Dr. David Horrell, Professor of New Testament Studies, who was unfailingly perceptive, challenging, helpful, and patient. Without his help and direction this work may not have come to fruition. We met both at Exeter and, later on, at various annual meetings of the Society of Biblical Literature. I always went away with much to think about, and reasons to refine my argument. My second supervisor, Dr. Siam Bhayro, also made a number of valuable contributions and largely stimulated my investigation into the social situation of the Antiochene community against the background of the Jewish conflicts with Rome.

Another good fortune was my proximity to Tyndale House in Cambridge. While fifty miles away, it could be reached within ninety minutes by car, and proved to be a life saver with its comprehensive resources and warm, studious atmosphere. An hour spent there was equivalent to at least two elsewhere, making it well worth the drive. There I made friends with Dr. Stefan Bosman, a fellow student, and had stimulating interactions with scholars from around the world. In addition I am grateful for the encouragement of Dr. Mitch Glaser and my friend Bernard Miel.

I can't begin to thank my wife Deborah enough, as in some ways she bore the brunt of my studies, and all with good grace. She is an *eshet chayil*, a woman of valor. My aunt Joyce regularly welcomed me into her home opposite Exeter Central station, and one of the joys of my study was getting to know her better. My parents, Elie and Judith, were also a great inspiration, both in my father's example of studiousness and my mother's warmth and encouragement. My employer Chosen People Ministries, and many financial supporters through it, also were key in making my studies possible, including two short sabbaticals that helped push my work forward.

Not to be facetious, I am grateful to the good scribe Leon, who transcribed the Didache in 1056, and no less the constellation of tremendous Didache scholars who have gone before, too many to mention. I think Leon would have been pleased with most of them. Now, thanks to the graces of Wipf and Stock Publishers, I am also grateful for their assistance in making this work widely available.

Abbreviations

1QpHab	DSS, A Commentary on Habakkuk
ACO	Apostolic Church Order (=Ecclesiastical Canons; *Kirchordnung*)
ANF	Ante-Nicene Fathers (1994) Roberts and Donaldson, eds.
Ann.	Tacitus, *The Annals*
Ant.	Josephus, *Antiquities of the Jews*
Apost. Con.	Apostolic Constitutions
BHS	Biblia Hebraica Stuttgartensia
Der. Er. Zuṭ.	Derek Ereṣ Zuṭa
DSS	Dead Sea Scrolls
Clem. Recog.	Clementine Recognitions
Doct. apost.	*Doctrina apostolorum*
Did. apost.	*Didascalia apostolorum*
Ep. fest.	*Epistulae festales* (Athanasius)
Ep. Pet. to Jas.	Pseudo-Clement, *Epistle of Peter to James*
Epitome	Epitome of the Eighth Book of the Apostolic Constitutions
fol(s)	folio(s)
GTW	Greek Two Ways
H	Codex *Hierosolymitanus* (=H54)
Hist. eccl.	Eusebius, *Ecclesiastical History*
Ign. *Magn.*	Ignatius, *To the Magnesians*
Ign. *Phld.*	Ignatius, *To the Philadelphians*

Ign. *Smyrn*	Ignatius, *To the Smyrneans*
War.	Josephus, *Jewish War*
JTS	Journal of Theological Studies
P.Oxy. 1782	Oxyrhynchus Papyrus 1782
SBL	Society of Biblical Literature
Serek	*Serek Hayaḥad* (=1QS, =Manual of Discipline, Community Rule).
Strom.	Clement of Alexandria, *Stromateis*
Suet. *Claud.*	Suetonius, *Lives of the Caesars, Deified Claudius*
Suet. *Tib.*	Suetonius, *Lives of the Caesars, Deified Tiberius*
Xen. *Mem.*	Xenophon, *Memorabilia*
Quis div.	*Quis dives salvetur* (Clement of Alexandria)
Xen. *Mem.*	Xenophon, *Memorabilia*

Introduction

Abstract

THE DIDACHE WAS WRITTEN for a church enduring internal and external social and political stresses. In this environment it sought to establish norms for the individual and the community. Long looked to for insights into the life of the early church, the Didache's reception of the Torah has received significant passing attention, but has never benefitted from an extended systematic analysis. Well received in the early church, it reflects both a first-century and Antiochene provenance.

It is specifically in the context of its Two Ways teaching that the Didache adopted an established topos rooted in both the Torah and other traditions, accessible to Jew and gentile alike, to convey its teaching on the Torah. This teaching was established on the basis of the presumed authority of religious teachers and specifically that of Jesus himself.

On the basis of this assumed authority, the Didache mandated the Way of Life for Christian disciples, laying the foundations of its approach with the double command to love God and neighbor, reflective of the Decalogue, the two tables of the Torah. Tightly bound structurally and thematically to the following Two Ways, the sectio evangelica, a key section comprising known Jesus sayings, shows an affinity to Torah-affirming passages in the Gospels. As a prologue that bears comparison to the Two Ways "yoke of the Lord" epilogue, it places stress on the Torah as mediated by Jesus.

Within the Two Ways material itself, there is not only a marked structure revolving around the second table of the

> *Decalogue, but a series of textual markers linking and equating it in some ways to the Torah as a whole. In this context, its endorsement of the "yoke of the Lord" is a striking Torah affirmative statement which reinforces the commitment to the Didache's teaching that is required of it.*
>
> *It is this commitment to the Torah as applicable to all Christians that is enjoined upon the gentile disciple; the Torah presented in those respects that were deemed to apply to gentiles. Acceptance of this sine qua non formed the basis for induction into the church and participation in its eschatological hope.*

The Didache is one of the oldest non-canonical documents of the early Jesus movement. It addressed a small but rapidly expanding community in an age of socio-political crisis. Composed in Antioch and written from within a Christian-Jewish milieu, its intended audience was primarily gentile. While attention has naturally been paid to the Jewish sources of the Didache, questions remain concerning its underlying presuppositions regarding the enduring validity, applicability, and authority of the Torah, particularly in regards to its gentile Christian recipients.

A constellation of issues remain to be resolved in Didache studies, and an accurate understanding of the role of the Torah in the Didache is a significant, if not the key, factor in many of these. The question as to whether the Didache may have implicitly or overtly sanctioned and advocated conversion to Judaism remains viable for a minority of scholars. Even more, there is the broader issue as to whether the Didache mandates Torah observance for its recipients. While having been partly addressed in a number of papers and short studies, the Didache's reception of the Torah has not been given sufficient attention nor been sufficiently examined, and this study attempts to address that situation.

Imprecision in our understanding of the role of the Torah in the Didache leaves a critical element in the matrix of nascent Christianity undefined; an unnecessary gap in our understanding. Attention to this matter promises a better understanding of both Christian Judaism and its emerging subset of Christianity,[1] not to mention the relationship between Christian Judaism and

1. This work takes a similar position to Philip Carrington, *Christian Apologetics*, 45. Carrington held that when "the Acts of the Apostles, was written, Christianity was still a sect within the Jewish Church" and proceeded to differentiate "Christianity" from "non-Christian Judaism." I would agree with David Sim who states that "the term 'Jewish Christianity' is completely inappropriate for those followers of Jesus who remained true to their Jewish heritage" Sim, *The Gospel of Matthew*, 25. The point is that the term Jewish Christian signifies that the movement was a Jewish variety of Christianity and somehow

the nascent Judaism out of which it was born. Understanding the Didache's reception of the Torah is thus important in the endeavor to gain a richer and more nuanced picture of the historical relationship of Christian Jews and gentiles to the Torah in their first-century communities.

This study has a personal aspect, as the author is a Jewish member of the Messianic Jewish movement, a socially diverse movement of Jewish believers in Jesus' messiahship, that has many gentile adherents. Insight into how the entwined parties, Jew and gentile, related in the early church may provide some insight into how healthy relations may be fostered, and how the Torah might be received in such communities today. In particular, this enquiry has been stimulated by the proposal set forth by Mark Kinzer's bilateral ecclesiology in his book *Postmissionary Messianic Judaism*.[2] In Kinzer's view, the church is a united but two-fold community "containing a Jewish sub-community that links it to the national life and history of the people of Israel, and a multinational subcommunity that extends Israel's heritage among the peoples of the earth without annulling their distinctive cultural identities."[3] It is supposed that if this is so, there might be some indication of it in the Didache, the so-called "window" into the early church.

This study proceeds on the basis that Didache serves as a witness to an early Christian community under the direction of teachers whose world view and "Christianity" were entirely within, not an aberration from, their adherence to what for convenience we term "Judaism." It will be seen that in response to the crises and stresses in Antiochian society in the mid to late first century, the Didache sought to regulate individual and communal life based on the Torah consistently with Jesus' interpretation. Going beyond a discussion of the Didache's well documented Jewish sources, this study proceeds to argue regarding the Didache's reception of the Torah; the function of the Torah in the Didache; and the meaning of fidelity to it for his readership. In the framework of a document ostensibly addressed to gentiles, it will examine the nature and meaning of their obligation to the Torah and the subsequent ecclesiological ramifications of that.

Methodologically, this study will investigate the Didache's reception of the Torah incorporating a socio-historical analysis of the text and data from other relevant literature. This study also presumes that Early Christian

already something other than normatively Jewish, whereas the movement in my view held itself to be the epitome of Judaism, the goal that had been reached in the revelation of Jesus. Thus the term Christian Judaism best portrays this early movement, one that saw itself as within Judaism and having recognized the Messiah of Israel. Mark Kinzer made a similar case for the term Messianic Judaism in *The Nature of Messianic Judaism*.

2. Kinzer, *Postmissionary Messianic Judaism*.

3. Kinzer, *Epilogue Postmissionary Messianic Judaism*, 178.

Judaism is, as is increasingly understood and as Samuel Sandmel presciently suggested, part of "a Jewish movement which was in particular ways distinctive from other Judaisms."[4] As a product of its milieu, its teachings reflect both Judaism and what is generally known of Christian Judaism. Taking into account the social situation of the community, the text of the Two Ways will be examined for indications regarding the Didache's reception of the Torah. This will be apparent both in the redaction of the document, but also via exegesis of key texts within it.

To some degree this work may be suspect of *petitio principii* as it has set out to prove a thesis that I suspected, but did not at the beginning have sufficient evidence to prove. I hope that my research, arguments, and observations herein are sufficient to demonstrate that (with modifications) my original thesis is correct: that as did the Sages,[5] the Didache presumes the universality and ongoing validity of the Torah and applies those precepts that apply to gentiles to the gentile recipients of the Didache. In this is a formula for unity—for the entire community is united, the unmentioned Jew and the gentile, in obedience to God's Law.

After surveying scholarship on the role of the Torah in the Didache so far, Part One of the study (chapters one and two) will establish the nature and development of the text. A short enquiry into introductory matters, primarily being the sources, provenance, and early reception of the Didache, will provide a basis for our understanding of the Didache's relationship with its recipients as described in Part Two. Part Two (chapters three to five) begins with a chapter setting out the peculiar stresses for the church in the region of Antioch, following which an argument for the suitability of Two Ways teaching to the community is made. Chapter five then follows indications within the text which in the context of first-century Jewish religion and the Jesus tradition position the Didachist as a teacher exerting influence from an authoritative position.

Part Three (chapters six to eleven) then argues primarily from the Didache itself to show that the Way of Life is an imperative choice versus the Way of Death mandated for the disciple. Chapter seven relates the *sectio evangelica* (the Jesus sayings of Did. 1.3b–6) to Jesus' teachings on the Torah. Chapter eight demonstrates the close connection between the *sectio* and the Two Ways of the Didache (Did. 2.1–6.2), and Chapter nine demonstrates the emphasis on the Decalogue (and consequently the Torah) in the Two Ways. Chapter ten then studies the conclusion of the Two Ways where the Yoke of the Lord is presented to the disciple as Torah. Finally, in

4. Sandmel, "Parallelomania," 4.

5. Sandt and Flusser, *The Didache*, 267.

retrospect Chapter eleven notes the peculiarity of the Didache's presentation of the Torah—a presentation specifically required for gentiles but with no requirement of conversion to Judaism.

The goal of this study will be to demonstrate that the Didache: a) affirms the authority of the Torah; b) innovatively adapts and applies the Torah to gentiles; and c) aims to unify and prepare one Church for the coming eschaton. Put differently, it answers the questions: Did the Didachist view the Torah as authoritative? Did he view the Torah as applicable to gentiles? If he viewed the Torah as applicable to gentiles, what are the ecclesiological and eschatological ramifications of this?

The research undertaken will substantiate the conclusion that the Didache's teaching is more than halakah. It demonstrates an outworking of its reception of the Torah as properly set in the framework of Christ's teachings and incumbent upon all humanity, thus uniting all who abide by the way of life in obedience to the Torah and reception of its rewards.

This research into the Christian Judaism of the Didache is particularly relevant to the contemporary Messianic Jewish movement as it wrestles with similar questions regarding the co-existence of Jews and gentiles within its own milieu, and the ecclesiological implications of that for its own community and faith today. The historical question as to the role of the Torah in the faith and practice of the gentile convert to the Didachean community is mirrored by the question regarding the role of the Torah in the faith and practice of gentile adherents of contemporary Messianic Judaism.

Part One: **Didache and Torah**

Part One of this study will begin by addressing the history and current state of Didache scholarship in respect to the role of the Torah in the Didache. Those questions regarding its provenance and redaction that bear on the study of its relationship to the Torah will be summarized in the second chapter, with particular attention being paid to the Didache's reception in the early church and the identity of its recipients.

1

The Didache and the Torah: A Literature Review

Introduction

THE *Διδαχή*, (HEREAFTER DIDACHE) or to use its longer (incipit) title Διδαχὴ κυρίου διὰ τῶν δώδεκα ἀποστόλων τοῖς ἔθνεσιν, had for centuries been known to exist, but only as a lost writing, by references and allusions to it.[1] With that background, it is no surprise that Philotheos Bryennios' 1873 discovery and 1883 publication of his *editio princeps* of the Didache was the cause of a mini sensation and a flurry of scholarship. What has followed in the subsequent century and a half has been an inexorable procession of academic work, generally reflecting the interests and attitudes of the scholarship of its day. It will be seen that while some great progress has been made over the decades, the Didachist's reception of the Torah, particularly in respect to his application of it to gentile converts and the implications of that in terms of church unity, have not been adequately examined. Furthermore, where they have been examined, the conclusions reached have not been tenable due to lack of clarity regarding what the Didachist was requiring in terms of Torah observance.

In this short literature survey, particular attention will be given to the intractable issues regarding the Didache's provenance and date and to the almost equally difficult questions surrounding the Didache's redactional development. The positions taken on these issues have a significant bearing

1. Various modern writers provide helpful surveys of direct references to the *Didache* as well as to quotations and allusions to it in early church literature, such as Audet, *La Didachè*, 79–90; Niederwimmer, *The Didache*, 4–17; Sandt and Flusser, *The Didache*, 1–6. In short, the chief ancient witnesses are Pseudo-Cyprian in *Adversus Aleatores* 4, Eusebius in *Hist. eccl.* 3.25.1–7, Athanasius in *Ep. fest.* 39, and *Apostolic Constitutions* 7.

on the views one might hold regarding the Didachist's community and its practices, not to mention the beliefs that those practices might imply. In particular, these issues are critical for determining the relationship of Jews and gentiles within the Didachist's community, and the relevance of Torah to its adherents. The following pages comprise a survey of that scholarship, particularly as it relates to issues concerning the community of the Didache and its relationship to its social and theological milieu.

Excitement and Expertise

Following the Didache's publication, the initial flurry of scholarship applied to it was markedly competent and prescient. Philotheos Bryennios' *editio princeps* provided an introduction, selection of comparable ancient texts, and of course a well-annotated text of the Didache itself.[2] Cautiously and reasonably for his time, Bryennios set the date of the Didache as sometime between 120 CE and 160 CE.

Having been given a considerable "leg up," a flood of popular literature was inevitable. Numerous short tracts were written, in various European languages, typically small in size, in pocketbook form. In such a booklet, Emil Peterson, in fifteen brief pages, hailed the Didache and its contents as a "*berühmten Funde*" comparable to the find of the Codex Sinaiticus.[3] Approaching it with a bit less enthusiasm, Alexander Gordon took just three pages to describe this "relic of Christian antiquity" but then provided his own translation in his little tract.[4] Significantly, he realized right away that "Neither Bryennios . . . nor his reviewers, have called attention to a very remarkable phenomenon. . . . The treatise is not homogeneous. It exhibits at least three distinct strata."[5] In slightly longer format, some twenty-nine pages, J. Fitzgerald provided readers with a copy of the Greek text and translation with the barest of introduction. Taking a minimalist view, he suggested that "the 'Teaching' has no bearing upon any of the points contested among the several divisions of the Christian Church, save one—the mode

2. Sabatier pays tribute to the very first writers, saying of the abundance of literature quickly published after Bryennios' *edition princeps*: "*Il est bon de le reconnaître, ils ont été singulièrement facilités par le commentaires et les prolégomènes dont Mgr Bryennios a enrichi son édition*" (1885, 3). Hitchcock and Brown concurred with Bryennios on the date in their small 1884 tract, representative of so many at the time, titled *Teaching of the Twelve Apostles*.

3. Petersen, *Die Lehre*, 3.

4. Gordon, *Teaching of the Twelve Apostles*, 3.

5. Gordon, *Teaching of the Twelve Apostles*, 4.

of baptizing."[6] Similarly, Gardiner and Cyrus Camp also published notes and a translation. Interestingly, on the basis of its non-Christological and non-doctrinal content, it was their opinion that the work was written for non-Christianized pagans and that it "was written before the Epistles of S. Paul . . . had become known and accepted in the Church."[7] In an initial translation published with notes, Roswell Hitchcock and Francis Brown claimed the document "undoubtedly belongs to the second century."[8] Of all of these preliminary tracts, the most substantial was that of Augustus De Romestin, who at this early date saw the signs of an oral genesis to the work, having "been taught orally and then committed to memory by those who had to teach others."[9] Thus it was that even from the very beginning, opinions were varied regarding almost every aspect of the Didache.

Time for reflection and research contributed to the rising flood, with more in-depth Didache research following soon after. A year later, upon considering the Didache's evident priority to Barnabas, Hitchcock and Brown wrote in their now much expanded study "we shall be inclined to put the date of the *Teaching* not far from A.D. 100."[10] Already in 1885 Paul Sabatier was able to interact with other published scholars, carefully defending the Didache's Jewish and Palestinian origins,[11] as well as the work's priority over Barnabas[12] and placing it "en Syrie, vers le milieu du premier siècle."[13] At the same time, the Cambridge scholar J. Rendel Harris found a significant number of verbal affinities between the Didache and the Sibylline Oracles. He thus came to the conclusion that the Didache had had an influence on the Sybillists: "I think we may remark in each of the immediately preceding instances, that the Teaching has been directly versified by the Sibyllist or Ps. Phocylides."[14] Contrasting his view to that of Sabatier, Harris emphasized the possibility that the Didache in parts harks back to the pre-Christian era. Two years later, Harris was able to greatly expand his comparison of the Didache to other early Christian texts, as was typical of Didache scholarship in general.

6. Fitzgerald, *Teaching of the Twelve Apostles*, 4.
7. Gardiner and Camp, *The Teaching of the Twelve Apostles*, 2.
8. Hitchcock and Brown, *Teaching of the Twelve Apostles*, v.
9. Romestin, *The Teaching of the Twelve Apostles*, 4.
10. Hitchcock and Brown, *Teaching of the Twelve Apostles (1885)*, xci.
11. Sabatier, *La Didachè*, 71.
12. Sabatier, *La Didachè*, 83.
13. Sabatier, *La Didachè*, 159.
14. Harris, *The Teaching of the Apostles*, 11.

In this first flush of excitement, three scholars stood out, and still stand out today. Adolf von Harnack,[15] Philip Schaff,[16] and Charles Taylor.[17] Harnack, accepting the Bryennios MS as reliable argued: "Die Gliederung des Stoffes in der Didache ist eine so logische und strenge, dass von ihr aus das beste Argument für die Integrität des uns überlieferten Textes . . . ."[18] Within a year, he translated the Didache into German complete with commentary and a full prolegomenon discussing the relevant issues of text, provenance, dating, and purpose of the document. His work would have tremendous influence in the years to come, serving as a sort of benchmark for future scholars.

Benefitting from Harnack's contribution as well as the scores of lesser works, Philip Schaff was likewise quite positive about the value of the Didache from a historical perspective. Having carefully analyzed the work Schaff he decided "clearly in favour both of its priority and superiority" to Barnabas, as well as asserting a Syrian origin and a date between 70 and 100 CE. It is with this presupposition that he became the first to address the role of the Law in the Didache, interpreting the Didachist's position as adhering to the Jerusalem Council and James' "law of liberty" (James 1:25).[19]

In 1885, Taylor also weighed in with two lectures, which were published in 1886. Working along a similar vein, he catalogued a remarkable number of Talmudic comparisons to the Didache. Certain of its Jewish composition, he viewed it as "only a skeleton of the fuller tradition referred to in the New Testament as *The Teaching*."[20] This he saw as evidenced by the Didachist's Judaistic approach to the Torah. He observed that the "author, being a Jew . . . set himself to make a fence to the negative commandments from the sixth onward."[21] According to James Heron a few years later, Taylor

15. Harnack and Gebhardt, *Die Lehre der zwölf Apostel.*

16. Schaff, *The Oldest Church Manual.*

17. Taylor, *The Teaching.*

18. Harnack and Gebhardt, *Die Lehre der zwölf Apostel*, 37.

19. Schaff asserts of the Didachist: "He abstains from all polemics against the Jewish religion, and thereby differs strongly from the author of the Epistle of Barnabas. He enjoins the recital of the Lord's Prayer three times a day, in evident imitation of the Jewish hours of prayer. He abhors the eating of meat offered to the gods as a contamination with idolatry, and adheres to the compromise measures of the Council of Jerusalem, over which James presided. He even seems to recommend the bearing of the whole yoke of the law as a way to perfection, but he is far from requiring it or casting reflection upon the more liberal gentile Christians. The whole sum of religion consists for him in perfect love to God and to our fellow-men as commanded in the Gospel, or in what James calls 'the perfect law of liberty' (i. 25)." *The Oldest Church Manual*, 126.

20. Taylor, *The Teaching*, vi.

21. Taylor, *The Teaching*, 29.

provided "the ablest and most thorough discussion of the question we have seen."[22] Such an early date suited Taylor's position that the Didache's origins are from a very early date when the church was more Jewish in composition. In concert with these views, he held that the Didache preceded both Barnabas and Hermas.[23] And if more "Jewish" implied less creedal in those days, it also tied in with the fact that, as Taylor says, "the theology of the *Didache* is the theology which underlies it."[24]

A few years made a big difference in this early phase of research. Following up on his previous publication, Harris was able to expand on his research into the place the Didache had in early Christian literature. Just two years later he was able to produce a substantial work that included comparisons to works such as the Oracles, Hermas, the Apostolic Constitutions, and more. Along with Harnack and Taylor, to whom he paid tribute, Harris continued the dialogue regarding the Didache's source, cautioning the reader that "whatever theory may be adopted with regard to the Teaching, whether we regard it as Jewish with Christian glosses, as Christian, or as a document emanating from some primitive heresy, our judgment with regard to it will have to take account of Hebraisms in style and in thought which colour the book almost from beginning to end."[25] This was echoed by George Allen a few years later, who compared the "directness of the subject matter" to "the grotesque and fanciful manner of other writings of similar date."[26] Thus the inquiry into the Didache's home community was in full swing, and tended to support the concept of a Jewish source. Yet, as Heron told his readers, "there is nothing of a Judaizing tendency in the book, and that though the writer was, in all probability, a *Jewish* Christian, he was certainly not a *Judaizing* Christian."[27] In this first phase of Didache research then, an awareness of the probable Jewish source behind it began to give rise to ruminations concerning the Didachist's application of the Torah to gentiles.

The Lost Decades of Didache Research, 1903–58

Paradoxically, the British scholar who first announced the publication of the Didache in 1884[28] was also one of its greatest critics. In the following

22. Heron, *The Church of the Sub-Apostolic Age*, 57.
23. Taylor, *The Teaching*, 167.
24. Taylor, *The Teaching*, 167.
25. Harris, *The Teaching of the Apostles: Newly Edited*, 78.
26. Allen, *The Didache*, xvi.
27. Heron, *The Church of the Sub-Apostolic Age*, 75.
28. Interestingly, "In England the first notice of the *Didache* appeared in the

decades, J. Armitage Robinson influentially took a minimalist position and cast grave doubts upon the authenticity and early date of the Didache. In 1912, he thus wrote in an article called "The Problem of the Didache" that "he [the Didachist] contributes almost nothing, except doubtful exegesis, to advance our knowledge of the early Christian ministry."[29] A few years later, he had advanced his opinion in this regard to such an extent that he was ready to discard "the almost universally accepted theory of an original Jewish 'Two Ways.'"[30] Robinson was also highly dubious of the antiquity of the text which Bryennios had published (given, of course, the indisputable eleventh-century origin of Codex *Hierosolymitanus* in which it was found). Challenging its early origin and any significant Jewish input into the Didache, he paradoxically left some threads untied. By way of example, he charged that "following his own fundamental principle" the Didachist has changed "the Golden Rule from the positive to the negative form."[31] In light of the fact that various negative forms are preserved in early Jewish literature, it would seem that this would have pointed him towards a Jewish origin rather than away from it.

Nevertheless, some, such as Richard Connolly, stood up for the textual integrity of the Bryennios MS,[32] but this didn't compellingly detract from Robinson's argument for a late date. Others, such as Gregory Dix, supported Robinson's view. Dix, viewing the Didache as dependent on Tatian's *Diatessaron*, dated it as sometime between 175 and 230 CE.[33] So it was that Burnett Streeter finally stated "Unless somebody says something soon on the other side, the case may seem to go [to Robinson] by default."[34] Reviewing cases where Robinson's "school" took parallels between the Didache and Barnabas as proving the former's dependence on the latter, he asked the question begging to be asked, asserting that the opposite was the case, that Barnabas was dependent on the Didache. Then, referring to the *Sitz im Leben* evident in the Didache, he reiterated the earlier date preferred by the earlier generation of Didache scholars.[35]

'Durham University Journal' for February 1884, by Rev. A. Robertson, Principal of Hatfield Hall, Durham." By this 3rd edition of Schaff's work (1889), the *Didache* had already attracted enough scholarly interest for him to devote a full chapter to the Didache literature.

29. Robinson, "The Problem of the Didache," 354.

30. Robinson, *Barnabas, Hermas and the Didache*, 4.

31. Robinson, *Barnabas, Hermas and the Didache*, 48.

32. Connolly, "The *Didache* in the *Didascalia*," 157.

33. Dix, "Didache and Diatessaron," 250.

34. Streeter, "The Much-Belaboured Didache," 369.

35. Streeter, "The Much-Belaboured Didache," 374.

The debate proceeding at full tilt now prompted Frederick Vokes to write in depth in a book titled *The Riddle of the Didache: Fact, Fiction or Catholicism?*[36] Vokes' solution was somewhat novel, and controversial in itself. Concluding on the basis of the literary evidence that it was written "in the last third of the second century or the first third of the third century,"[37] Vokes positioned it on the fringes of the Montanist movement, writing "This will explain many of the problems of the Didache."[38] In short, Vokes represents the difficulties of the time, still not completely overcome, in trying to reconstruct the Didache's place in history while suffering from what was really a paucity of data.

An interesting contrast to Vokes is provided in William Telfer's articles, published twice in the *JTS*. Propounding what he called the "Antioch hypothesis," he suggested that in the Didachist's days "Docetism was moribund, and Antioch had not yet felt the impact of Marcionism and Montanism."[39] Like Vokes, he testified to the contemporary difficulties in regard to determining the Didache's date and provenance. Well into the 1950s however, Robinson's influence was still to be keenly felt in the study of the Didache[40] and the field continued to falter under a cloud of unresolved questions.

Skeptical source-critical evaluations of H understandably discouraged enquiry into its Jewish sources and reception of the Torah. Indeed, Telfer considered it to be "fiction" and believed the direction of enquiry should be to uncover its "plot" as in any work of fiction.[41] It is fair to say that very little of any consequence was written regarding the Didachean community or its beliefs, let alone its reception of the Torah, during this period.

A Change of Tide

The tide of crippling skepticism began to turn with the discovery and gradual availability to scholars of the Dead Sea Scrolls. The tide was turned by Jean-Paul Audet, a Canadian scholar, in a seminal paper entitled *Affinités littéraire et doctrinales du «Manuel de discipline.»*[42] In addition to pointing out similarities between the Didache and the *Serek Hayaḥad* (=1QS,

36. Vokes, *The Riddle of the Didache.*
37. Vokes, *The Riddle of the Didache*, 87.
38. Vokes, *The Riddle of the Didache*, 117.
39. Telfer, "The *Didache* and the Synod," 133.
40. Moule, "A Note on Didache IX.4," 243.
41. Telfer, "The 'Plot' of the *Didache*," 141.
42. Audet, "Affinités littéraire et doctrinales."

=Manual of Discipline, =Community Rule), he reviewed and assimilated the discussion of the previous sixty-five years. His subsequent high quality in-depth review, source-critical analysis, and commentary was the first of its kind since the nineteenth century. Agreeing with Streeter against Robinson, he argued persuasively that "La Didachè est contemporaine des premiers écrits évangéliques."[43] Rightly noting that the "patrie" of the Didache "est déjà partiellement impliquée dans leur date,"[44] he excluded Egypt as a possibility, bringing forth a series of eleven points to prove that the manual originated in Antioch.[45] On this basis, he viewed the instructive form of the Didache as "naturel" and its intent to give "instructions et des directives, sans prétendre, au moins dans la forme, au niveau supérieur de la «loi»."[46] On this basis therefore, Audet's over 200 pages of commentary paid particular attention to the Jewish aspects of the Didache's composition, as in his discussion of the eucharistic benediction of Did. 9 in light of the Jewish mealtime blessings preserved in the Mishnah, namely Ber. 6.[47] Pierre Nautin put it nicely: "Le P. Audet a probablement donné le coup de grâce à la' théorie de Robinson."[48]

While not settling all of the Didache's intractable problems regarding sources and provenance, the new lines of enquiry did accentuate related questions regarding its reception of the Torah and open up new discussions. Vööbus opposed Audet's arguments for Syrian origin, writing that "this view . . . provides no explanation for a very embarrassing problem—the silence about Paul and his work. This makes it virtually impossible for the Didache to have originated in Syria. . . . The logical choice is Egypt."[49] On the other hand he was appreciative of the Didache's connection to Jewish tradition, as he himself saw that the Didache's "[Eucharistic] prayers are shot through and through with Jewish and Jewish Christian features."[50]

In addition to Audet, other French scholars also asserted the Didache's early origins. Thus Stanislav Giet, after surveying various parallel texts, concluded regarding the Two Ways section that "Cette courte mais substantielle catéchèse juive qui se let à travers l'enseignement chrétien des deux voies, devait être assez courante, au moins dans certains milieux, au début du

43. Audet, *La Didachè*, 197.

44. Audet, *La Didachè*, 206.

45. Audet, *La Didachè*, 210.

46. Audet, *La Didachè*, 250.

47. Audet, *La Didachè*, 399.

48. Nautin, "La composition," 192.

49. Vööbus, *Liturgical Traditions*, 14.

50. Vööbus, *Liturgical Traditions*, 159.

premier siècle."[51] Viewing the Didache not as the product of one author, but a document that must have developed and changed over time while still remaining true to its sources, he therefore assigned a variety of potential dates to the various underlying sources. This approach held much promise, but due to its speculative nature could not produce an assured result. Nevertheless, Giet had made a qualitative contribution to the discussion. These developments in French scholarship provided a basis for Willy Rordorf and André Tuilier to combine the best of both worlds. Building on Audet and Giet's contributions, their conclusion was therefore that "il est dès lors évident que nous sommes en présence d'une tradition persistante en Syrie et en Palestine dans les premiers temps du christianisme."[52]

As a consequence, other scholars began to grapple with the text and sources of the Didache. B. C. Butler argued that Did. 16 was based on Luke, or "Proto-Luke," and a form of the Synoptic tradition indistinguishable from Matthew.[53] A year later this was expanded into an enquiry into the Two Ways material, with Butler presciently acknowledging that if Audet was right, "There existed, say about A.D. 30, a Jewish form of the Two Ways theme in Greek dress, as different from the example preserved in The Manual of Discipline as it was similar to B [Barnabas], D [Didache], and LD [*Doctrina apostolorum*]'s examples."[54] About the same time, A. Stuiber, comparing Did. 6.2–3 and its reference to the yoke of the Lord with the *Doctrina apostolorum*, concluded that it was "einen jüdischen Nachtrag zur Zweiwegelehre" and that "Die juden-christliche Interpretation wird dem Inhalt unserer Verse voll Gerecht."[55] In this way, attention to the sources of the Didache was opening the door to enquiry as to its application of the Torah to gentiles.

Didache Studies Revived

What had essentially been a quiet upswing in Didache research was soon to become much more pronounced. In the first phase of this revival, Jonathan Draper completed a dissertation commenting on the Didache in light of the DSS in 1983,[56] and in 1989 Kurt Niederwimmer published

51. Giet, *L'énigme de la Didachè*, 149, 170.
52. Rordorf and Tuilier, *La Doctrine Des Douze Apôtres*, 62.
53. Butler, "The Literary Relations," 283.
54. Butler, "The 'Two Ways,'" 38.
55. Stuiber, "Das ganze Joch des Herrn," 329.
56. Draper, *A Commentary on the Didache*, PhD.

his commentary *Die Didache*.[57] Later published in English as part of the Hermeneia commentary series as *The Didache: A Commentary*,[58] it was to become a standard reference work for Didache students, due to his approach characterized by reasonableness backed up with careful research. As Draper commented shortly after, Niederwimmer's commentary "rightly sets a redactional analysis at the centre of its interpretation."[59] It was along the lines of his own redactional theory that Draper concluded "the *Didache* is the community rule of the Matthean community."[60] With Clayton Jefford's recent dissertation, published as *The Sayings of Jesus in the Teachings of the Twelve Apostles*,[61] here were now three scholars attempting to untie the Gordian knot. The field now became far less individualistic, as scholars began to work more closely with one another.

Redactional issues continued to be important. Presuming that the Didache itself was "an original writing in Greek," Niederwimmer endorsed the views of its origin held by Giet, Rordorf, Tuilier, and others, but rejected the idea of a double redaction as "unnecessary."[62] His own hypothesis was that sometime "most likely toward the end of the [first] century" the Didachist wrote using sources that included a Christianized form of the Jewish "*de duabus viis*,"[63] an archaic liturgical tradition "written or oral," an archaic tradition regarding itinerant charismatics, and a brief apocalypse.[64] While viewing the source of this Two Ways tractate as "purely Jewish,"[65] he provided a complex "purely hypothetical" schema to represent its use in Barnabas, Didache, the *Doctrina apostolorum*, and other early Christian writings.[66]

Jefford, inspired at a 1992 meeting of the Society of Biblical Literature (SBL) in San Francisco, proceeded to edit a volume on the Didache that for the first time drew together the most notable names in Didache research.[67] Primarily addressing the text, and the history and transmission of that text, the volume also addressed some long outstanding issues, such as the interpretation of Did. 16:5—the meaning of the "fire of testing" and the saving

57. Niederwimmer, *Die Didache*.

58. Niederwimmer, *The Didache*.

59. Draper, "Torah and Troublesome Apostles," 349.

60. Draper, "Torah and Troublesome Apostles," 372.

61. Jefford, *The Sayings of Jesus*.

62. Niederwimmer, *The Didache*, 42.

63. Niederwimmer, *The Didache*, 52.

64. Niederwimmer, *The Didache*, 44.

65. Niederwimmer, *The Didache*, 37.

66. Niederwimmer, *The Didache*, 40.

67. Jefford, *The Didache in Context*.

"curse," which Harris had valiantly (and sensibly) sought to elucidate over a century before.[68] As is to be expected in such an undertaking, a variety of opinions were expressed regarding the relevance and meaning of the Didache. Thus, for example, in viewing the Didache as an "epic," Jonathan Reed took it to represent a unified whole, portraying a community "well after the first Roman war" that conceived itself in terms of the epic of the Hebrews,[69] whereas Tuilier found its earlier origins of great value, citing "l'importance des références a l'évangile du Seigneur cité par la Didache pour la solution du problème synoptique."[70]

A year later, a second volume was produced, also under the auspices of the SBL, and edited by Draper. In concluding an introductory review of Didache research, Draper paid tribute to Jefford's volume the year before. Noting that the "collection of essays . . . indicates that the proliferation of methods which have recently been applied to the New Testament are now being turned towards the *Didache*," he continued to contend that "it remains to be seen to what extent these new methodologies will transform our understanding of this much-debated writing."[71] It is in light of this that he suggested that research "into the Jewish roots of the Didache . . . promises to be an important area for further work."[72] True to promise, this second volume did just that, also for the first time involving Jewish scholars in the research process. Thus, Gedaliah Alon's examination of *halakah* in the Didache, previously only published in Hebrew, showed how the Didache's *Halakot* reflected not only Judaism, but Jewish debates current in the first century.[73] David Flusser, likewise, asserted that the passage in *Did* 6:2 εἰ μὲν γὰρ δύνασαι βαστάσαι ὅλον τον ζυγὸν τοῦ κυρίου, τέλειος ἔσῃ expresses views that "are indeed possible within the framework of ancient Judaism" although he did characterize them as somehow "grotesque."[74] Nevertheless, he found a context for this command in Pauline Christianity and the Noahic precepts.[75] This more thoroughgoing placing of the Didache within the Jewish world of thought was carried through by Draper himself, who even

68. Harris, *The Teaching of the Apostles: Newly Edited*, 65–69.,

69. Reed, *The Hebrew Epic and the Didache*, 224–225.

70. Tuilier, *La Didachè et le Problème Synoptique*, 129.

71. Draper, *The Didache in Modern Research: An Overview*, 42.

72. Draper, *The Didache in Modern Research: An Overview*, 42.

73. Thus, for example, Alon compares the command in Did. 8:3 "Τρὶς τῆς ἡμέρας οὕτω προσεύχεσθε" to the "opinion of Rabban Gamaliel against Rabbi Joshua who says that the *Aravit* prayer is optional." *The Halacha in the Teaching*, 179. Originally published as Alon, "ההלכה שבתורת."

74. Flusser, *Paul's Jewish-Christian Opponents*, 209.

75. Flusser, *Paul's Jewish-Christian Opponents*, 210.

saw within the Didache the implication that full obedience to the Torah was expected of the gentile convert. Thus he interpreted the manual, and Did 16.2 in particular, to mean "the Didache allows the proselyte flexibility about the timetable, but at the end of the day, it is required of him/her that he/she become a full Jew in order to attain salvation."[76]

The second phase in the revival of Didache research was marked by the collaboration of Huub van de Sandt and Flusser. For the first time, possibly since Taylor, rabbinic and Qumranic sources were thoroughly consulted and drawn upon. Approaching the Didache from a historical perspective, the authors reflected Niederwimmer's reticence to assert a clear date and provenance, suggesting that "no answer can pretend to be better than a reasonable guess."[77] Nevertheless, they were highly specific in making their "guess" that this should be at the end of the first century, in a rural Christian congregation, in the borderland between Syria and Palestine.[78] In this world, Paul was seen as holding to an established rabbinic position using the Noahide laws as a barrier distinguishing Jews and gentiles in regard to Torah observance,[79] whereas the Didachist viewed "compliance with the Tora" as "the ideal."[80]

This reinvigoration of a historically oriented approach to the Didache with a greater emphasis on its place in the world of Jewish thought was bearing fruit. Van de Sandt and Flusser paid particular attention to the "layers of composition" evident in the *Didache*.[81] A year later, Aaron Milavec brought his own fresh perspective to the table, however, with his "elephant"—a 984-page commentary on the book,[82] and his "mouse"—a much more accessible 114-page analysis.[83] Milavec put forth a different, but intriguing argument for the original orality and compositional unity of the Didache. While his arguments did not sway the majority of scholars, he brought important considerations to light, asserting that "the *Didache* can be shown to have an overall internal coherence that might escape the casual reader."[84] This unity was borne out of his understanding of the Didache as an oral manual taught on a one-to-one

76. Draper, *Torah and Troublesome Apostles in the Didache Community*, 359.
77. Sandt and Flusser, *The Didache*, 48.
78. Sandt and Flusser, *The Didache*, 50.
79. Sandt and Flusser, *The Didache*, 268.
80. Sandt and Flusser, *The Didache*, 269.
81. Sandt and Flusser, *The Didache*, 359.
82. Milavec, *The Didache: Faith.*
83. Milavec, *The Didache: Text.*
84. Milavec, *The Didache: Faith*, 59.

basis by a "mentor/master to each novice."[85] Later that year, in an essay, Milavec claimed that "should Didache scholars come to accept the thesis of this essay, the way would be open for an early dating of the *Didache* and for its interpretation as a well-integrated and self-contained religious system that must be allowed to speak for itself."[86] It is thus that Draper's assertion that the Didache requires conversion, Sandt and Flusser's view that Torah compliance is an "ideal" in the Didache, and Milavec's view of the Didache as an oral teaching further opened the door to deeper research on its reception of the Torah, but this was not followed through.

Marcello Del Verme cited various prominent scholars in his study on the reception of the Didache to suggest that "Christianity and Judaism are finally being seen as fresh and twin developments of ancient Judaism."[87] It is also in his work that the term "Christian Judaism" first properly came into use, a marked conceptual shift from the more traditional term "Jewish Christianity."[88] Challenging previously held assumptions, Del Verme further held that "some institutions present in the *Didache* appear to be a mere adaptation or transposition to the new Christian environment of institutions typically Jewish."[89] Thus Del Verme saw no trace of a "parting of the ways" in the Didache.[90]

Against that backdrop, Alan Garrow's argument for the likelihood "that the author of Matthew's Gospel depended directly upon a version of the *Didache*"[91] underscored the possibilities in this direction. By his detailed and exhaustive redactional analysis, Garrow did indeed demonstrate the possibility that this is the case, leaving Synoptic scholars with an intriguing position to dialogue with. If Garrow is correct, then the Didache is even earlier than generally supposed, and even more valuable as a window into the apostolic church. Nevertheless, a sure conclusion was beyond reach. In arguing that a differing reading in the Didache—for example, Did 8.2c "means either that the author . . . quoted from an eccentric version of Matthew's Gospel which has been lost, or that *Did* 8.2c is not a quotation for Matthew's Gospel at all"[92]—it is not clear how one can determine definitively which author has misquoted whom, or misquoted

85. Milavec, *The Didache: Faith*, 860.

86. Milavec, "Synoptic Tradition in the Didache Revisited," 480.

87. Verme, *Didache and Judaism*, 19–20.

88. Verme, *Didache and Judaism*, 24.

89. Verme, *Didache and Judaism*, 75–76.

90. Verme, *Didache and Judaism*, 87.

91. Garrow, *Matthew's Dependence on the Didache*, 2–3.

92. Garrow, *Matthew's Dependence on the Didache*, 134.

what common source. What is clear, however, is that there is a dynamic relationship between the two texts, one that Didache scholars cannot ignore. Consequently, while Garrow's arguments are intriguing, they have not won the day. Draper, for example, continues to hold to his opinion that the text is "evolved literature, which was in continuous use as a community rule, and hence was continuously edited before being subordinated to Matthew's Gospel."[93] About the same time, Eugene Spivak argued in his dissertation that "the Didachist relied on the Gospel in his work."[94]

The next significant advance of note was a third major volume, based on contributions to an international conference on Matthew, James, and the Didache in Tilburg, Netherlands.[95] Building on the growing realization of the strong relationship between the Didache and Matthew, it made the case that the book of James was also part of the same milieu. Helpfully, Jürgen Zangenberg approached this possibility as one to be tested by the "hypothetico-deductive" method by which a hypothesis is tested by various criteria such as "coherence" in order to determine its value.[96] In the context of Didache research it is of course tremendously useful to have some such framework by which to sort through some of its intractable problems, such as its provenance, that have defied definitive solution. In addition, van de Sandt was able to point to some striking threads that run throughout each of the three documents. Thus, regarding statements in each regarding the Law, he writes "The thinking in Did. 3:1–6; Matt 5:17–19, 21–22, 27–28; and Jas 2:8–11 amounts to exactly the same thing insofar as these passages specify moral norms based on properly interpreted law."[97] While the conference proceedings did not specifically advance study of the Didache in particular, its valuable contribution was to put the Didache in a context, a milieu, within which framework it could be interpreted.

The revival of Didache studies continues apace, reflecting interest in its intriguing subject matter and early date. Popular yet scholarly approaches have been presented in surveys by William Varner,[98] and another by Thomas O'Loughlin.[99] Both have sought to bring the message of the Didache to a wider audience in a thoughtful way, paying particular attention to themes

93. Draper, *The Didache*, 260.

94. Spivak, *A Christian-Jewish School*, PhD, 14–15.

95. Zangenberg, *Social and Religious Milieu of the Didache*.

96. Zangenberg, *Social and Religious Milieu of the Didache*, 75–77.

97. Sandt, *Law and Ethics*, 334.

98. Varner, *The Way of the Didache*.

99. O'Loughlin, *The Didache: A Window*.

within it that could be related to contemporary theological interests and pragmatic interests of the church regarding its praxis.

A fourth major contribution has recently been made by a subsequent SBL volume, this one co-edited by Draper and Jefford. *The Didache: A Missing Piece of the Puzzle in Early Christianity*.[100] The significance of this volume with its twenty-two studies is that it continues to build on previous scholarship regarding the text, the community, its liturgy, its relationship to Matthew, and its relationship to the New Testament and early Christianity. However, the reception of the Torah still receives inadequate attention. This is remarkable for a document like the Didache that includes implicit and explicit references to many of the Torah's injunctions. True to its title, it focuses on the Didache within early Christianity, but that picture is missing much of its background, because without adequate consideration of the role of Torah in early Christianity and the Didache in particular, one is missing a vital component of early Christian life and teaching. As has been seen throughout this survey of literature on the Didache, this has been an ongoing serious lacuna in Didache research that deserves further attention.

Most recently, and demonstrating that this revival is making its way from academia to the popular sphere, is a substantial commentary by Toby Janicki, which has provided an adaptation of its contents for the Hebrew Roots and Messianic Jewish milieus.[101] In a more scholarly vein, Shawn Wilhite's new commentary on the Didache brings a fresh approach with innovative attention given to the Didache's reception of the biblical canon and its theology, treated according to its own internal signifiers rather than the traditional Christian theological categories of later centuries.[102]

The Two Ways and Torah: Paradigms and Prisms

The Two Ways material of the Didache is particularly crucial to an examination of the Didache's reception of the Torah, and various paradigms have been advanced to express its implementation of the Two Ways tradition. However, while many scholars envisage some relationship to the Torah, none of the perspectives on how this is reflected in the Two Ways Section give adequate weight to the Two Ways Section as an intentional enunciation and teaching of it.

Since the Didache's Two Ways lists are prefaced by the *sectio* and lie within a Christian-Jewish work, it is no surprise that in the early years of

100. Draper and Jefford, *The Didache: A Missing Piece*.

101. Janicki, *The Way of Life*.

102. Wilhite, *The Didache: A Commentary*.

Didache research Harnack saw the section as a Christian exposition of the Decalogue, saying: "Es ist übrigens sehr bemerkenswerth, dass der ganzen Ausführung c. I–III der Dekalog in evangelischer Auslegung zu Grunde liegt."[103] A similar and less than glowing perspective is given by Robert Grant, who wrote on the role of the Decalogue in early Christianity. "The legalism of the Didache is pedestrian. It reflects the attempt to synthesize the Law of the revelation on Sinai with the 'law' of Christ on the Galilean mountain; and its author tries to provide a 'fence' for this law—to be sure, a rather low one."[104]

While not ignoring the recognizable similarities between the Two Ways and the Decalogue, attempts have been made to reconcile the Two Ways with another arguable relationship to either Hebrew wisdom literature or Greek ethical forms. Jean-Paul Audet, observing the structure and contents of the Two Ways, took this position in writing "Le *Duae viae* est, du reste, en accord avec son époque lorsqu'il opère le rapprochement de la sagesse et de la loi (1:1—2:7 et 3:1—4:14)."[105] For Audet, while the Two Ways has a connection to the Decalogue, the stress belonged to its connection with Hebrew sapiential and wisdom literature.

This approach is represented later in John Kloppenborg's analysis of the Two Ways, which argues that it demonstrates a "striking transformation" in "which the decalogue has been made into the starting point and the ultimate warrant for ethics."[106] Kloppenborg observes that the Didache uses the Torah not only in the Way of Life, but also in the prohibitions (Way of Death) of Did. 5.[107] This is correct insofar as it goes, but the fundamental perspective that the Didache is teaching ethics, rather than Torah, is incompatible with the text and its frame of reference within the world of Judaism, as is argued in chapter 9.

Kloppenborg's assertion that the Two Ways of the Didache presumes the Torah's authority has not gone uncontested, and Martin Vahrenhorst has disputed his thesis largely on the basis that the existing variants of the Two Ways to which Kloppenborg compared the Didache, all "explicitly refer to the Torah, the νόμος, on more than one occasion" whereas the Didache, he argues, "never does."[108] Taking this view, he turns Kloppenborg's

103. Harnack and Gebhardt, *Die Lehre der zwölf Apostel*, 52.

104. Grant, "The Decalogue in Early Christianity," 8–9. Kloppenborg takes this last sentence to refer to Did. 3.1–6: Kloppenborg, *The Transformation of Moral Exhortation*, 105 n. 71.

105. Audet, "Esquisse historique," 282.

106. Kloppenborg, *The Transformation of Moral Exhortation*, 109.

107. Kloppenborg, *The Transformation of Moral Exhortation*, 100.

108. Vahrenhorst, *The Presence and Absence of a Prohibition of Oath*, 372.

argument on its head and suggests that "it is doubtful if the Didache's teaching should really be described as 'Torahizing.' . . . [O]ne might even be tempted to describe the Didache as 'de-torahizing' those traditions."[109] Vahrenhorst controversially argues that "every trace of an inner-Jewish debate is missing" in the Didache.[110] This statement is dubious, particularly in light of the Didache's repeated references to "hypocrites" and its designation of alternate fast days, which indicate the immediacy of this very debate. Vahrenhorst takes this position in order to support his view of the "Didache as a document that is no longer part of the Jewish framework."[111] It is thus that while Kloppenborg sought to demonstrate a "Torahizing" of the Didache's ethical teaching, observing that there are "features that indicate an intentional 'Torahizing' of the ethical admonitions in the *Didache*,"[112] Vahrenhorst sought to dismantle Kloppenborg's case. Neither position fully corresponds with the data provided by the Didache's use of its version of the Two Ways material.

In a different approach, Jonathan Draper made a case from oral traditions, in his study "Vice Catalogues as Oral-Mnemonic Cues," that as a text the Two Ways "is simply a skeleton, an *aide de mémoire* for the oral instructor."[113] Draper argued that texts that evolve from the performance of oral transmission bear comparison on the basis of their shared mnemonic cues and not merely as comparable texts,[114] leading to his analysis of the Two Ways section of the Didache. This analysis paid particular attention to its thrice repeated catalogue of prohibitions from the second table of the Decalogue as mnemonic "pegs."[115] The study has merit from the perspective of oral tradition, and his analysis with illustrative charts demonstrating the parallel repetitions in the Two Ways Section is helpful, but it was not within the scope of the article's thesis to demonstrate a theology behind the use of the Torah for the section's mnemonic pegs.

Draper's approach is in harmony with earlier approaches, such as Adolf Harnack's, who in his pioneering study held that the Didache was dependent upon Barnabas, and took Did. 2.2 with its prohibitions of murder, adultery, and theft to be a citation of Deut 5:17–19.[116] Later, having accepted

109. Vahrenhorst, *The Presence and Absence of a Prohibition of Oath*, 373.

110. Vahrenhorst, *The Presence and Absence of a Prohibition of Oath*, 371.

111. Vahrenhorst, *The Presence and Absence of a Prohibition of Oath*, 374.

112. Kloppenborg, *The Transformation of Moral Exhortation*, 100.

113. Draper, *Vice Catalogues*, 112.

114. Draper, *Vice Catalogues*, 117–23.

115. Draper, *Vice Catalogues*, 119.

116. Harnack and Gebhardt, *Die Lehre der zwölf Apostel*, 65, 84.

the Didache's priority,[117] he continued to maintain that the Decalogue was the source for the first five chapters of the Didache.[118] Most often, however, while the source is acknowledged, the assumption is that the Decalogue is merely a framework from which to expound ethics. In this regard, Rordorf and Tuilier put the section in the category of Jewish and Christian vice lists that draw upon the Decalogue stating that "Les «catalogues de vices» juifs et Chrétiens qui se rattachent au Décalogue sont innombrables."[119]

In summary, I have argued that significant but insufficient attention has been paid to the relationship between the structure of the Didache's Two Ways and the Decalogue, taking into account approaches such as Kloppenborg's summary of the Didache's "Torahizing" features[120] and Draper's observations regarding the structure of the Didache.[121] Additional understanding regarding the relationship between the Didache's Two Ways and the Torah is possible with more weight and attention given to the very construction of the Didache's Two Ways section.

Conclusion

This chapter has shown how from the earliest phase of Didache study, its Jewish origins were countenanced by numerous scholars, some of those writers setting the Didache as early as 70 CE. During the first half of the twentieth century, both the early date and Jewish origins of the Didache were cast in doubt. Questions regarding its sources led to it being regarded as spurious, or dependent on Barnabas. Such questions were laid to rest soon after the discovery of the Dead Sea Scrolls, in particular the *Serek Hayaḥad*. Most notably from French-language scholars came a rehabilitation of the Didache that once again stressed its affinities to Jewish literature and tradition, confirming its authenticity. This led to a flowering of enquiry in the 1980s that continues to this day.

Today, Didache studies are far from exhausted, despite the fact that, as Draper puts it, "While most scholars of the Didache today take it as an early Jewish Christian or Christian Jewish text . . . those outside of the field are wary of using it in the reconstruction of Christian origins."[122] Specifically, the importance of the Didache to our understanding of the various

117. Harnack, *Die Apostellehre*, 27.

118. Harnack, *Die Apostellehre*, 8.

119. Rordorf and Tuilier, *La Doctrine Des Douze Apôtres*, 148, n. 2.

120. Kloppenborg, *The Transformation of Moral Exhortation.*

121. Draper, *Vice Catalogues.*

122. Draper, *'You Shall Not Give What Is Holy to the Dogs'*, 242.

receptions given the Torah in the early church cannot be casually dismissed. The role of the Torah in the Didache remains a critical facet of that reconstruction that has not been adequately addressed. Without an understanding of the Didache's contribution to what was a crucial debate in the early church, the picture of Christian Judaism and its Torah observant mission to the gentiles remains obscured. It is to issues like this that the Didache still has the potential to speak and illuminate.

2

Text and Transmission

Introduction

Now that we have surveyed scholars' changes in perspective over time, especially as it regards the Didache's reception of the Torah, this chapter will briefly make some observations regarding the manuscript evidence for the Didache, the origin of its crucial Two Ways material, the Didache's redaction, authorship and date, its reception in the early church, and its recipients. This will provide a basis for the arguments to be advanced regarding its application of the Torah to its gentile recipients. To some degree, the points made will in themselves provide evidence regarding the Didache's reception of the Torah.

Manuscripts and Fragments

The reliability of the accepted manuscript of the Didache has been confirmed on the basis of both the manuscript evidence itself and attestations to it in ancient church literature. The following is a brief overview of the most important manuscripts available for Didachean studies, and is presented with a view to demonstrating that trends in its use point to a discomfort with what early Christians rightly perceived as a focus on the Torah in the original. The MS commonly labelled H (*Hierosolymitanus*),[1] copied in 1056 by Leon the scribe, contains the only complete extant text of the Didache. It was discovered in a known codex by Philotheos Bryennios in 1873 dated by the scribe's hand as 11 June, 1056. The codex contained the following:

1. Jonathan Draper and Nancy Pardee however use H54 in their writings, since *Hierosolymitanus* includes its signature at the Greek Patriarchate in Jerusalem as Κῶδ. Πατρ. 54. Harris, *The Teaching of the Apostles: Newly Edited*, vii; Niederwimmer, *The Didache*, 19.

1. fols. 1–32, John Chrysostom's synopsis of the Old and New Testaments,
2. fols. 33–51b, Barnabas,
3. fols. 51b–70a, 1 Clement to the Corinthians,
4. fols. 70a–76a, 2 Clement to the Corinthians,
5. fols. 76a–80, Teaching of the Twelve Apostles (the Didache),[2]
6. fols. 81–82a, Epistle of Mary Kassoboloi to Ignatius,
7. fols. 82a–120a, the "long" recension of the Ignatian epistles (his reply to Mary and twelve epistles to the churches).[3]

Apart from H, there is one fragment of the Greek text that has survived in *P.Oxy.* 1782, dated to the fourth century by Bernard Grenfell and Arthur Hunt,[4] in which are preserved the text of Did. 1.3–4 and 2.7—3.2. The two sheets were originally part of a "miniature volume" of a type "often preferred for theological works"[5] and written in a hand that from its "spelling and division of words" suggested that the writer "was a person of no great culture."[6]

In addition to this, a large Coptic papyrus fragment of Did. 10.3b—12.2a dating from 400 CE was brought to light in 1923 and numbered Or. 9271, the text being provided by George Horner the next year.[7] Comprising Did. 10.3b—12.2a, it has recently been critically examined and translated by Stanley Jones and Paul Mirecki,[8] who have agreed with a number of previous scholars that the fragment is probably the product of a scribal exercise,[9] thus satisfactorily resolving a question as to whether Did. 12.2a is the conclusion of an early recension of the Didache.

Both *P.Oxy.* 1782 and Or. 9271 confirm the accuracy of the text we have in H. However, both texts include material not found in H. The most significant of these, which bears significance for my argument, is that *P.Oxy.* 1782 includes an intriguing clarifying transition constituting the phrase ἄκουε τί

2. A full set of plates for these folios were supplied by Rendel Harris *The Teaching of the Apostles: Newly Edited*, 108–17. .

3. Harnack and Gebhardt, *Die Lehre der zwölf Apostel*, 11.

4. Grenfell and Hunt, *The Oxyrhynchus Papyri*, 15, 12–13.

5. Grenfell and Hunt, *The Oxyrhynchus Papyri*, 15, 12.

6. Grenfell and Hunt, *The Oxyrhynchus Papyri*, 15, 13.

7. Horner, "A New Papyrus Fragment," 225.

8. Jones and Mirecki, *Coptic Papyrus of the Didache*, 49–57.

9. Jones and Mirecki, *Coptic Papyrus of the Didache*, 86–87.

σε δεῖ ποιοῦντα σῶσαί σου τὸ πνεῦμα between Did. 1.3 and 1.4.[10] This gives a soteriological slant to the *sectio* which dilutes the force of τέλειος in Did. 1.4. The term τέλειος is discussed in more detail in chapters 8.3 and 10.3 and substantiates the Torah orientation of the Didache. Similarly Or. 9271 includes a thanksgiving for symbolic ointment.[11] The fact that neither source omits any phrases within its scope suggests that the MS transcribed by Leon in 1056 did not come from a tradition that embellished its source.

Another translation of Did. 8.1–2 and 11.3—13.7 is found in the Ethiopic (Ge'ez) Statutes of the Apostles, dated c. 350 CE in canon 52. In the text and translation provided by Horner[12] there is no significant embellishing of the text as in the Apostolic Constitutions. The only notable change is a transformation of the standard of "living like the Lord" (in which the Lord would be Jesus) to living "the life of God" indicating that at some point before the text was put into Ge'ez κύριος was taken to signify God. This suggests an interesting turn in focus from a Jewish conception of the faith and possibly Jesus as the fulfilment of the Torah (cf. Matt 5:17ff) to one less rooted in Jewish observance. However, in the portions it uses, this insertion from the Didache is a close rendition of the Didache confirming that the redactor had a text comparable to H to work from.

The third, yet very problematic later text of the Didache, is a translation from a Georgian exemplar. While with Niederwimmer it would seem right to say that this version "probably goes back to a recension of the Greek text that is closely related to that of H[54],"[13] it seems far-fetched to put too much reliance on a translation of a text that has been destroyed, as the transcriber Simon Pheikrishvili claimed.[14] Thus Rordorf and Tuilier do not use it in the critical apparatus of their text[15] (also because of its paraphrastic nature). Likewise, Jefford advises caution with the text "especially since the Georgian (if indeed authentic) offers only minor elements for consideration."[16]

In summary, it is *P.Oxy.* 1782, Or. 9271, and the Statutes of the Apostles that provide the comparable information regarding the reliability of H, and

10. Jones and Mirecki, *Coptic Papyrus of the Didache*; Jefford, *Didache: The Teaching*, 5.

11. Jones and Mirecki, *Coptic Papyrus of the Didache*, 52–53. Stephen Gero proposes that Or. 9271 reflects a "Jewish-Christian *(ḥaburah?)* meal practice" which a later Egyptian redactor sought to make sense of. Gero, "The So-Called Ointment Prayer."

12. Horner, *The Statutes of the Apostles*, 193–94.

13. Niederwimmer, *The Didache*, 27.

14. Peradse, "*Die Probleme*," 304–9.

15. Rordorf and Tuilier, *La Doctrine Des Douze Apôtres*, 249.

16. Jefford, *Introduction: Dynamics, Methodologies, and Progress*, 11.

it can be said that they do confirm the text of the Didache. Certain changes in the text, particularly in *P.Oxy.* 1782 and Statutes of the Apostles point to a possible later interpretation of the Two Ways that recast it in a more soteriological shape with less relationship to the Torah. Though infrequent, this may point to the validity of further enquiry as to how the text of the Didache was received and accepted in the early church, particularly in regard to its reception of the Torah.

The Two Ways Source

The Two Ways material is key to understanding the Didache's reception of the Torah, as will be developed in Part Two. In contrast to Did. 6.2—15.4, the Two Ways material in Did. 1.1—6.2 (minus the interpolation of 1.3—2.1) is well attested in literature both prior to and contemporaneous with its redaction. While long suspected, as seen in chapter 1, this connection was not systematically substantiated until Jean-Paul Audet's 1952 study "Affinités littéraire et doctrinales du «Manuel de discipline.»"[17]

Recently William Varner has vigorously voiced skepticism of any relationship. Varner's dispute challenges "anyone to read the appropriate section of 'The Community Rule' (Serek) 3:13—4:26 and find anything that would make one think of Didache 1–5, unless he or she had been preconditioned to do so." However, in arguing his view, Varner has incorrectly appealed to Willy Rordorf as being of this mind. While Rordorf does pose questions "which future research must take into consideration if it wishes to come to solid established results"[18] regarding the provenance of the *duae viae*, he concludes from his questions regarding resemblances between *Serek* and the Didache by saying "one should above all avoid simplistic, unilateral solutions."[19] While Rordorf does not subscribe to a simplistic and direct relationship between Qumran and the *duae viae*, he does not dismiss it. In reality, Varner's is the minority opinion, and an examination of both texts does indeed substantiate the affinity—not necessarily a direct literary relationship—between *Serek* and the Two Ways first asserted by Audet.

Varner's outright skepticism and Rordorf's more nuanced approach serve to highlight the issue regarding the textual antecedents for the Two Ways of the Didache. As is evident in van de Sandt and Flusser's research, this requires an exercise in reconstruction from various other Two Ways documents

17. Audet, "Affinités littéraire et doctrinales." Republished in English: *Literary and Doctrinal Affinites.*

18. Rordorf, *An Aspect of the Judeo-Christian Ethic*, 151.

19. Rordorf, *An Aspect of the Judeo-Christian Ethic*, 152.

in circulation that attest to a likely foundational Greek exemplar.[20] Hypothetically, on the basis of the Didache and the Doctrina, along with Barnabas, van de Sandt and Flusser ventured to reconstruct the original Greek text of the Two Ways section which they called the Greek Two Ways (GTW).[21] It was after surveying the evidence that van de Sandt and Flusser advanced the argument that "the Doctrina [Apostolorum] is probably our best guide to the Jewish Two Ways edition that was most widely known in ancient times."[22] Spivak adds weight to this in arguing that as a derivative of the Greek Two Ways the *Didascalia apostolorum* also testifies to this early source.[23]

In addition to the *Didascalia apostolorum,* a number of early Christian texts transmit this prototypical Two Ways. These are Barnabas 18–21, the *Doctrina apostolorum*, the Apostolic Church Order (=Ecclesiastical Canons) 4–13, the Apostolic Constitutions 7.1–32, and the first part of the Arabic Life of Shenoute.[24] In addition, the Pseudo-Athanasius *Syntagma doctrinae,* which Pierre Battifol dated to the late fourth century,[25] should be included as a relatively accurate rendition. Both Niederwimmer[26] and van de Sandt and Flusser[27] present systematic catalogues of such Two Ways tracts. There are two that stand out however, for Apostolic Constitutions 7 and the Didache share in common their otherwise unique use of the *sectio* (Did. 1.3b–6). Nevertheless even here Apos. Con. 7 is in reality a version of the Didache. Their use of the Two Ways material thus stands as a specifically Christian adaptation of a pre-existing topos.[28]

In summary, the evidence and weight of scholarly opinion concur in identifying the Two Ways material as a Jewish body of teaching. This original source was variably adapted with and without the *sectio* as teaching material for gentile Christians. As will be seen in Part Two of this study, its Jewish source and identity are significant in terms of determining the Didache's reception of the Torah latent within it.

20. Sandt and Flusser, *The Didache*, 55–80.

21. Sandt and Flusser, *The Didache*, 120–39.

22. Sandt and Flusser, *The Didache*, 120.

23. Spivak, "A Christian-Jewish School," 85.

24. Davis, *The Didache and Early Monasticism*, 356–58.

25. Battifol, Études D'*Ancienne Littérature*, 138.

26. Niederwimmer, *Der Didachist*, 77, 19–20.

27. Sandt and Flusser, *The Didache*, 59–70.

28. Possibly, as David Clark casually suggests, an original version of the Two Ways material was used by various "Jewish groups in the Second Temple era" to train gentile "'God-fearers' in the ways of the covenant," thus being formulated to "teach gentiles the basic requirements of serving the God of Israel." *Order and Chaos in the Didache*, 90–91.

Date, Redaction, and Authorship

The introductory matters pertaining to the Didache each have a significant impact upon its interpretation, but as the following paragraphs show, there is a growing consensus—not unanimous by any means—concerning these issues. Most secure among these is the Didache's provenance, which most scholars would now agree is most probably Syrian Antioch. Geographical reference such as to mountains (Did. 9.4), and proximity to hypocrites (2.5; 8.1–2) reminiscent of Matthew's hypocrites all correspond better with Antioch than the other alternative, Alexandria. Without dispute, this study accepts the Antiochian hypothesis. The date, redaction, and authorship of the Didache all deserve further examination however.

The Date of the Didache

While it is no longer in vogue to hold that the Didache is dependent on Barnabas, as discussed in the previous chapter, it has remained difficult to ascertain its date. Nevertheless a developing consensus has emerged that places the Didache in the latter decades of the first century, and a significant number of Didache scholars view it as even earlier. Aaron Milavec thus holds to a date while the Temple cult was still active[29] and even before the canonical Gospels.[30] Alan Garrow argues that at least parts of the Didache lie behind Matthew,[31] 1 Thessalonians,[32] and Revelation.[33] Thomas O'Loughlin is willing to consider even as early as 50 CE.[34]

The provenance and use of the Two Ways material (Did. 1–6) conceivably dates to the earliest years of the church, potentially related to τῇ διδαχῇ τῶν ἀποστόλων in Acts 2:42. Likewise Did. 16 preserves an early eschatological expression as demonstrated by Garrow in his essays on 1 Thessalonians and Revelation,[35] and as Ernst Bammel has argued from comparison with Jewish prototypes.[36] In contrast to Did. 1–6 and 16, Did. 7–15 does not so easily fit with such an early date. This means that the text of H represents

29. Milavec, *The Didache: Faith*, 797–803.

30. Milavec, "Distinguishing True and False Prophets," 118; "The Purifying Confession," 64.

31. Garrow, *Matthew's Dependence on the Didache.*

32. Garrow, "The Eschatological Tradition."

33. Garrow, *The Didache and Revelation.*

34. O'Loughlin, *The Didache: A Window*, 26.

35. Garrow, "The Eschatological Tradition"; *The Didache and Revelation.*

36. Bammel, *Pattern and Prototype.*

a final redaction of two main texts, separated by some years, that at some point had been merged into one.

On the presumption that this redaction occurred when the supplemental material (Did. 7–15) was relatively recent, an observable development in terms of the institutionalization of the church has taken place between the two redactional phases. This can be seen in the striking change of subject matter from the Two Ways to issues regarding community governance in the supplemental material. The Two Ways material belongs to an age of rudimentary ecclesiastical development. No officers are required for the performance of any of its traditions. Whereas the Two Ways material knows only of τοῦ λαλοῦντός σοι τὸν λόγον του θεοῦ (4.1), the later material contrasts with its prophets (10.7; 11.7–11; 13.1, 4, 6; 15.2; 16.3), apostles (11.3–6), and overseers and deacons (15.1).

Draper holds that the Didache belongs to a date by which the apostles, (itinerant ministers rather than the Twelve) were superseded by prophets after the destruction of Jerusalem "as a center of authority for the community."[37] Holding to three main stages of redaction, Draper finds that the apostles are thus represented only in the "earliest stage of the text."[38] Niederwimmer notes in this regard that "the stages of development here are none other than stages in the development of the process of catholicization."[39] In a book as short as the Didache, this is not conclusive, but suggestive of a church still in the early stages of institutionalization.

By the same token, the world of Did. 7–15 with its prophets, apostles, teachers, bishops, and deacons contrasts with the yet later world of Ignatius. Ignatius, also from Antioch, did not seek to institute a church structure as in Did. 15. Rather, he sought compliance with an existing structure. Nor did he contend with a community beset by itinerant apostles, prophets, and teachers, even if, as André de Halleux argues, they are not necessarily all itinerants.[40] In Ignatius' letter to the Ephesians (4.1), he spoke of an established relationship between overseers and presbyters, and urged the Magnesians (3.1; 6.1) to honor those in both offices.

While there is little internal evidence for the date of the Didache, other observations correspond with an early date for Did. 1–6 and 16, particularly in regard to material found in common with the Synoptics.

37. Draper, *Social Ambiguity*, 299, 311; "Weber, Thiessen, and 'Wandering Charismatics'" 576.

38. Draper, *Torah and Troublesome Apostles*, 343.

39. Niederwimmer, *Itinerant Radicalism*, 339.

40. Halleux, *Ministers in the Didache*, 300–303.

The *sectio evangelica*[41] uses much of the same material in common with Matthew and Luke, but does not directly quote either of them. The same is the case with the thrice-daily prayer in Did. 8.2, perhaps more strikingly so as 8.1 precedes the prayer with the words ἀλλ' ὡς ἐκέλευσεν ὁ κύριος ἐν τῷ εὐαγγελίῳ αὐτοῦ, οὕτω προσεύχεσθε·. This leads to the question why the Didache does not follow the text of the Gospels more closely, and the probability that at the time of its redaction the exact formula in the Gospels was not authoritatively established without other competing texts or oral memories. By implication, this evidence tends to a date for the Didache that is earlier than Matthew or Luke.

A similar observation can be made regarding the rudimentary nature of the eucharist in Did. 14, which complements the thanksgivings before and after meals in Did. 9–10. While it was still very unpopular to do so due to the supposed dependence of the Didache upon Barnabas, H. J. Gibbins argued on the basis of internal evidence that the "data point to . . . some time between the years A.D. 30 and 70."[42] Gibbins' prescience in this regard has been borne out, and while 30 CE is doubtful, being the earliest possible *terminus post quem* for these prayers, his research demonstrates that they are not necessarily a later development. Given the well accepted affinity of Did. 9–10 with the traditional Jewish blessings and grace after meals and the account of Acts 2:42 with the disciples breaking bread from house to house in the context of the διδαχῇ τῶν ἀποστόλων, an early date has some support.

In summary, the independence of the text of the *sectio*, the Didache's thrice-daily prayer, and its thanksgivings from the Gospels and its rudimentary nature point to an earlier date than generally supposed for both the earliest material (Did. 1–6; 16) and the supplementary material (Did. 7–15). The fact that its addressed recipients are new disciples and other teachers suggests a date in which the church is expanding and new churches are being established. The minor and rudimentary ecclesiological development observable in the Didache prohibits a second-century date, or even too late in the first century. For the purposes of this study we will therefore accept a date shortly after the first Jewish War, c. 80 CE as the point at which the redaction of the Didache was essentially completed.[43] This forms the basis of the argument for the church's Sitz im Leben in chapter 3.

41. Did. 1.3b–6, as per Niederwimmer, *The Didache*, 68–72.

42. Gibbins, "The Problem of the Liturgical Section of the Didache," 386.

43. In his recent dissertation, David Brown also settles for 70 CE, "The Didache and Traditioned Innovation," 25.

The Redaction of the Didache

The text of the Didache is clearly a composite, but the process of its compilation in a milieu where some were literate, but not all, is not cut and dried. Richard Horsley points out that the "relation between text and composition and performance was necessarily a rather fluid one."[44] Various estimates of literacy in both Jewish society and the Roman Empire have been put forth. Bar Ilan argues for a mere 3 percent literacy rate in the first century, in his article "Illiteracy in the Land of Israel."[45] Bar-Ilan appeals to Soferim 11.2, which gives the rule regarding Torah reading "In a city where only one person is able to read," indicating that this was a possibility. The fact that it was a possibility does not require that it was a likelihood. Such investigation into hypothetical scenarios is characteristic of rabbinic discourse and is reflected also in the New Testament record, as in the case presented to Jesus of the woman who had seven husbands in Matt 22:23–28 (=Mark 12:18–23; Luke 20:27–33). In this light, Bar-Ilan's figure seems conservative and uncertain. Bar-Ilan himself concedes in a note that the 3% figure may be misleading, and that "the literacy rate (adult males in the centers), might be even 20%," a high rate in traditional society.[46]

Uncertainties abound regarding the extent of literacy in the Roman Empire, but William Harris' extensive study into the matter argues that "nothing like mass literacy ever came into being in antiquity"[47] and that figures "not likely to have risen much above 10–15%" are most likely.[48] This accords with Catherine Hézser's estimate that Jewish literacy at the time was well below 10 to 15 percent.[49] With figures like that, the composition of the Didache can reasonably be seen within a context where it, *prima facie*, was written in order to be read, but not necessarily read directly by the disciple. Further it cannot be assumed that all teachers were proficient readers, but it may be presumed that they committed the Didache to memory.

The transmission of the Didache's teaching was thus not necessarily directly from any given text or texts. Its *incipit* (The Teaching of the Lord through the Twelve Apostles to the Gentiles) itself presupposes an oral origin in the words of the Lord. As Horsley describes, "most extant pieces of

44. Horsley, *The Oral Communication Environment of Q*, 133.

45. Bar-Ilan, *Illiteracy in the Land of Israel.*

46. Bar-Ilan, *Illiteracy in the Land of Israel*, n. 29.

47. Harris, *Ancient Literacy*, 327.

48. Harris, *Ancient Literacy*, 328.

49. Hézser, *Jewish Literacy in Roman Palestine*, 496. It must be noted, that what concerns us most is not Jewish literacy, but gentile literacy in view of the Didache's intended audience (as addressed below). This is nevertheless a benchmark.

literature from the ancient Mediterranean—from poetry and speeches to history and philosophy—originated in oral performance and continued to be recited or performed after they were written down."[50] This needs to be considered in light of his observation that such "performances . . . before a community involved in a conflictual life situation meant that the text always had an immediate historical social context."[51] As will be shown in chapter 3, the recipients of the Didache were indeed in a "conflictual life situation" as reflected in the content of the Didache itself, and its content was amenable to amplification and clarification by the teacher. Such extemporaneous exposition of the teaching seems evident with the exception of Pardee's caveat that "the fact that the prayers of the Didache are given in a full form seems to indicate that they were intended to be recited as written."[52]

These considerations illustrate why the redaction of the Didache has proved to be an intractable problem for scholars despite a century of research. Illustrating the diversity of opinion event today, Aaron Milavec envisages a document that "was originally composed orally and . . . circulated on the lips of the members of this community for a good many years before any occasion arose that called for a scribe to prepare a textual version."[53] In fact, he goes so far as to say that the "creation of the *Didache*, therefore, never took place as a composite of written sources that the author produced in a study surrounded by source documents."[54] This is quite a possibility.

Notably, a number of other redactional theories have been proposed. Thus, while not minimizing the variety of the Didachist's diverse sources, Niederwimmer posits a "single redaction."[55] Further, on the basis of his preference for a single redaction Niederwimmer holds that "at the beginning of the second century . . . a Christian author living in an originally Jewish-Christian milieu created, by compilation, a kind of book of rules that is our *Didache*."[56] In contrast, Spivak proposed a three-stage redaction, with an original Christian-Jewish Didache of 1–12 and 16 informed by The Two Ways Tractate and the Gospel of Matthew. Later, this was

50. Horsley, *The Oral Communication Environment of Q*, 144.

51. Horsley, "Introduction," 8.

52. Pardee, *The Didache and Oral Theory*, 328.

53. Milavec, *The Didache: Text*, ix.

54. Milavec, *The Didache: Faith*, 718.

55. Niederwimmer, *The Didache*, 43.

56. Pieter Botha calculates from the *Edictum Diocletiani* that the copy of the Didache would take one skilled labor day, give or take depending on the quality of the work, suggesting that the length of the Didache was suited to its rapid dissemination and use. Botha, *Orality and Literacy in Early Christianity*, 72. See also Niederwimmer, *The Didache*, 43. .

supplemented by Did. 13–14, and yet later by Did. 15.[57] A yet more complex approach is seen in Alan Garrow's analysis, in which he innovatively argued for various redactors with at least the base (earliest) layer of the Didache underlying parts of the Gospel of Matthew. Garrow has reconstructed a redactional history that is both early and complex, and thus sees the text as one "put together in five stages."[58]

Jefford posits that there is a "conundrum" in that "within the Didache there appear to be two types of material: the first type represents the living, working tradition of a community that is geographically mobile; the second type reflects a settled community that has attempted to shape and reshape the first type of materials in an effort to provide its tradition with specific parameters and limitations."[59] While this rests on his supposition that the Didache represents a sort of "Q community" perspective, and that of a community "in motion" from Palestine to Syria, it is evident that there are two types of material separated by space and time; the earlier being Did. 1–6 and 16, and the latter Did. 7–15. Awkward redactional bridges such as Did. 6.3—7.1, and 10.7, as well as the eucharistic thanksgiving in Did. 14 after instructions regarding meals have already been taught in Did. 9–10 suggest an attempt to connect both the two groups of sources, and the various sources within each group.

The Didache evidences a compendium of previously oral traditions organized around common themes. Thus, the Two Ways presents three related vice catalogues in chapters 2, 3, and 5, strikingly illustrated by Draper.[60] Thanksgiving is taught in Did. 9–10, but again in Did. 14. The baptismal instructions include the repetition of the triadic Matthean formula (7.1, 3). Did. 11.1 and 12.1 enjoin similar welcoming receptions for itinerants followed by related metrics by which to discern their worth. While the former instructions are Christologically oriented blessings before and after meals, the latter are more explicitly oriented towards thanksgiving as a form of sacrifice (Did. 14.3). If the Didache incorporates the teaching of the apostles (plural), as its *inscriptio* and *incipit* allow, it is not surprising that similar material is presented in differing voices.

With all the foregoing considerations held in balance, it is reasonable to concur with Steven Fraade who states regarding Rabbinic literature (which like the "Q" source provides a helpful point of comparison) that "it is now widely recognized that literary composition and oral performance

57. Spivak, "A Christian-Jewish School," 25.

58. Garrow, *Matthew's Dependence on the Didache*, 11.

59. Jefford, *The Milieu of Matthew, the Didache, and Ignatius*, 39.

60. Draper, *Vice Catalogues*, 121.

dynamically *interface* with one another."[61] It is likely that the two key phases in the Didache's redaction reflect rapidly developing situations and traditions in the early church that were relevant to its milieu. They are most often identified as Did. 1–6 and 16 as the earlier phase, and Did. 7–15 as the later phase. As there is a general consensus on this, the argument of this study will proceed on this basis.

To summarize, the Didache's sources and origin are bound up with the primitive oral presentation of its teachings in an environment that was both dynamically changing and largely illiterate. Its authorship and redaction; its eventual presentation in writing emerged through that, making it difficult to parse in terms of its various layers and the process of redaction. Nevertheless, two main layers of redaction are evident. This provides context for analysis of the earlier layer representing a foundational phase in the church's life.

The Didachist

The authorship of the Didache is not stated, as in its *inscriptio* and *incipit* the Didache merely makes claims regarding the apostolic source of its teaching. It is often considered the result of a collaborative effort. In this vein Milavec simply refers to the "framers of the *Didache,* . . . pastors poised on the threshold of the end time."[62] Draper likewise argues for plural authorship, citing the "way a community rule evolves."[63] These are reasonable suppositions, but difficult to prove conclusively. As Hermann-Ad. Stempel states, what we do know is that in the categories present in the Didache, as a teacher he was "eine der drei wichtigsten Personen einer christlichen Gemeinde."[64] These three important persons were the apostles, prophets, and teachers. The Didachist, as represented by Stempel, is thus an individual teacher, possibly alluded to in Did. 13.2 (as the διδάσκαλος ἀληθινός) in a similar way to the author of Matthew in Matt 13:52 (as the γραμματεὺς μαθητευθεὶς τῇ βασιλείᾳ) as Ian Henderson suggests.[65]

Since the Didache does not specify its authorship, when the "Didachist" is referred to in this study it is not intended to define a position regarding the Didache's redaction or authorship. In consonance with that, the "Didachist" is simply to be understood as a construct of all the contributors

61. Fraade, "Literary Composition and Oral Performance," 35.

62. Milavec, *The Didache: Faith*, ix.

63. Draper, "Torah and Troublesome Apostles," 349.

64. Stempel, "Der Lehrer in der Lehre," 209.

65. Henderson, "Didache and Orality," 286–87.

resulting in the text best represented by H. For this reason, when this study means to refer to the "Didachist" it also uses the functionally equivalent terms "Redactor" and "Didache."

More identifiable is the Didachist's role as a mediator, not only imparting knowledge of the Two Ways (1.3; 2.1; 6.1) but as evidence of his standing, instructing regarding the validity of other teachers (6.1; 11.1–2; 12.1ff). In two respects, the Didachist conforms to the second line of its own title, which asserts that it represents the teaching of the Lord mediated by the apostles. Firstly, he is wary of other teachers who do not represent apostolic doctrine. Didache 12.2 advises the community to discern which teachers are genuine, saying ἔπειτα δὲ δοκιμάσαντες αὐτὸν γνώσεσθε. Secondly, as André de Halleux observed regarding 11.2 (and similarly appropriate to the role of one who represents the teaching of the Twelve), the Didachist does not "monopolize the *Didache* to his profit" but "orders the community to receive the person who teaches something different as if he were the Lord, provided that this teaching has in mind the building up of the Church."[66]

Standing in the role of mediator the Didachist had a clear agenda for both the community and the individual disciple. The Didachist was faced with the task of reorienting inductees from a pagan context to the "Way of Life." Thus, the "τέκνον" section of the Didache (3.1—4.1) is characterized by a poetic series of instructions to the spiritual "child" being addressed. The disciple is consistently addressed in the second person singular for the first six chapters, emphasizing the personal nature of the instruction, except for a concluding admonition in 5.2, which is quite clearly a transitional interjection between differing source materials. The wellbeing of the inductee is stressed repeatedly, as the consequences of evil traits and behavior are emphasized in a mnemonic structure. In doing this, the Didache has in Milavec's words a "pastoral genius" to it,[67] which he sees as its "systematic, user friendly" approach. The Didachist's agenda for the community is to put those values, traditions, and structures in place that would enable it to prosper and endure crises within and without. He also steadfastly sought to inculcate values that would enhance and preserve the individual.

To summarize, since the Didache's process of redaction is obscure, the "Didachist" can not be identified with certainty other than by "his" role as a mediator of the Didache's teaching. What is more evident is the Didachist's role in the text, framing his material, and providing teaching for the individual disciple and for the community.

66. Halleux, *Ministers in the Didache*, 304.

67. Milavec, *The Didache: Faith*, iv, 803, 846.

The Didache's Early Reception

The wide distribution of the Didache demonstrates that it was well received and gained acceptance in early Christianity. Curiously, however, later manuscripts seem to downplay phrases that, as will be seen later, emphasize the significance of the Torah, suggesting that not all of its distinctives sat easily with the church at large. It is thus that manuscript evidence for the text of the Didache is hardly divorced from its reception in the early church. The way in which church writers cited it, adopted it, and adapted it for their own situations according to their own understandings of their faith suggests that they found it useful and doctrinally acceptable.

A number of references to and quotations of the Didache have been noted in the early church fathers, and attestations to its near apocryphal status are well known. Foremost among these is Eusebius' statement that a book described as τῶν ἀποστόλων αἱ λεγόμεναι Διδαχαὶ (that of the apostles called Teaching) was among the ἀντιλεγομένων, or "disputed" books in regard to canonical status, in contradistinction to those that are the ἀναπλάσματα' of αἱρετικῶν ἀνδρῶν, the "forgeries of heretics."[68] Similarly, Athanasius in his Easter Letter of 367 CE[69] wrote of "books not included in the Canon, but appointed by the Fathers to be read," one of which is "called the Teaching of the Apostles." Niederwimmer, who has provided a comprehensive catalogue of attestations to and quotations from the Didache, points to the possibility that in such lists it may be other documents or just the Two Ways portion of the Didache that some of the writers have in view,[70] but the Greek, Coptic, and Ethiopic translations already mentioned point to the Didache's wide circulation and allow the conclusion that in most cases there is little doubt that the Didache as represented by H is in view.

As might be expected for a book that figures in canonical lists, several citations of the Didache are found in early church literature. Unfortunately, few of these are unambiguously from the Didache as they can also be paralleled by other related documents such as Barnabas or may be quotations of the Didache's source material itself. It is Clement of Alexandria, however, who demonstrates knowledge of the text; his esteem of it; and by quoting from the Two Ways section and the section on thanksgiving meals, the likelihood that he was conversant with the whole of the Didache. Thus in *Stromateis* Clement wrote μὴ γίνου ψεύστης· ὁδηγεῖ γὰρ τὸ ψεῦσμα πρὸς τὴν κλοπήν,[71] almost

68. Eusebius. (*Hist. eccl.* 3.25 [Lake: LCL]).

69. Athanasius. *Select Works and Letters*, 4. (*Ep. fest.* 39 [NPNF])

70. Niederwimmer, *The Didache*, 4–6.

71. Clemens Alexandrinus. (*Strom.* 1.20.100.4).

exactly the words of Did. 3.5: μὴ γίνου ψεύστης, ἐπειδὴ ὁδηγεῖ τὸ ψεῦσμα εἰς τὴν κλοπήν. Showing his familiarity with a later portion of the Didache he also used the eucharistic expression οὗτος (ὁ) τὸν οἶνον, τὸ αἷμα τῆς ἀμπέλου τῆς Δαβίδ, ἐκχέας ἡμῶν in *Quis dives salvetur*,[72] which gives the impression of being a later, more developed form of the Didache's εὐχαριστοῦμέν σοι . . . ὑπὲρ τῆς ἁγίας ἀμπέλου Δαυὶδ τοῦ παιδός σου in Did. 9.2.

It is thus of interest that Origen, slightly later than Clement but also from Alexandria (at least until his relocation to Caesarea Maritima c. 231 CE), also seems to quote the Didache in the phrase, *scientes quod sine deo nihil fit*, or "knowing that without Him no event occurs" (*ANF*).[73] The phrase closely follows εἰδώς, ὅτι ἄτερ θεοῦ οὐδὲν γίνεται in Did. 3.10. The sentiment is similar to Ἐὰν ὁ κύριος θελήσῃ, καὶ ζήσομεν καὶ ποιήσομεν τοῦτο ἢ ἐκεῖνο in James 4:15, which is not surprising for a document that has so much in common with the Didache. This accords with the observation that James and the Didache (and indeed, Matthew) all arise from a context that places ethical admonitions within a God-centered frame of reference.[74] Thus, while Origen's words might be "problematic" as a witness to the Didache, as is Niederwimmer's estimation,[75] it illustrates that the concepts and phraseology of the Didache were known.

Shortly after the completion of the Didache, a variant use of the Two Ways material underlying it was used as the basis for Barnabas 18–21, as noted above. As Robert Kraft notes, while the "motif" is pervasive throughout the epistle, it is here that "he as much as says he is reproducing extant catechetical material."[76] Two characteristics are evident in Barnabas' use of this material. First, he defines the two ways more specifically than the Didache, describing them as ways "of teaching and authority," second, he reframes them not as "life and death" but as "light and darkness."

Barn. 18.1	**Did. 1.1**
ὁδοὶ δύο εἰσὶν <u>διδαχῆς καὶ ἐξουσίας</u>,	Ὁδοὶ δύο εἰσί,
ἥ τε τοῦ <u>φωτὸς</u> καὶ ἡ τοῦ <u>σκότους</u>.	μία τῆς <u>ζωῆς</u> καὶ μία τοῦ <u>θανάτου</u>,
διαφορὰ δὲ πολλὴ τῶν δύο ὁδῶν.	διαφορὰ δὲ πολλὴ μεταξὺ τῶν δύο ὁδῶν.

72. Clemens Alexandrinus. (*Quis. div.* 29.4).

73. Origen. (*De. princ.* 3.2.7. English translation from ANF)

74. Hartin, *Ethics in the Letter of James*, 303.

75. Niederwimmer, *The Didache*, 8.

76. Kraft, *Barnabas and the Didache*, 5–6.

This analogy of "light and darkness," distanced to some degree from the "life and death" of the Didache and Deut 30, is also found in the *Doctrina apostolorum* as *lucis et tenebrarum*. Based on his belief that the Didache was adapted from Barnabas, John A. T. Robinson believed the "life and death" terminology was from the hand of the Didachist.[77] Rather, it just as easily reflects Barnabas' dependence on the Doctrina. However, Barnabas' term "of teaching and authority" is found nowhere else, and the lack of parallels increases the likelihood that this is Barnabas' interpolation.

Barnabas' use of "light and darkness" rather than "life and death" correlates with a reception of the Torah markedly different from that of the Didache. Barnabas is not unaware of Torah in his use of the Two Ways material, but his admonition to "be your own good lawgivers"[78] betrays a fundamentally different understanding of it. The book's heavily metaphorical understanding of the Torah is in line with its interpretation of the food laws of the Torah: "the commandment of God is not a matter of avoiding food; but Moses spoke in the Spirit."[79] No such transformation of the commands is evident in the Didache, which highlights the contrast with Barnabas' use of the Two Ways material they hold in common.

A second notable use of the Didache is found in the *Didascalia apostolorum*, extant in Syriac and Latin, but not in the original Greek apart from various fragments. There one finds a document ostensibly arising out of the Acts 15 council in Jerusalem,[80] yet, as Charlotte Fonrobert points out, without reference to Paul's account of the controversy in Gal 2.[81] The influence of the Didache is found in passages and phrases throughout the work, beginning as early as the *Didascalia*'s first chapter, which reflects Did. 1.2's command to love one's neighbor and proceeds to reference the Decalogue and certain of its commands in a manner somewhat similar to Did. 2. A further connection between the documents in terms of the reception of the Law is found in *Did. apost.* 26. R. Hugh Connolly has highlighted the *Didascalia*'s exposition of the phrase τὰ σημεῖα τῆς ἀληθείας (Did. 16.3) as related to the letter iota, the first letter in Jesus' name. This is the letter (yod in Hebrew) that in Matt 5:18 Jesus said would not pass away from the Law.[82] While reinterpreting the iota mystically as a reference to

77. Robinson, *Barnabas, Hermas and the Didache*, 46–47.

78. Barn. 21.4 (Ehrman, LCL).

79. Barn. 10.2 (Ehrman, LCL).

80. *Did. apost.* 24.

81. Fonrobert, "The Didascalia Apostolorum: A Mishnah," 489.

82. Connolly, "The *Didache* in the *Didascalia*," 152–53.

Jesus himself,[83] the *Didascalia* nonetheless affirms Jesus was bearing witness to "the Ten Words and Judgements."

The *Didascalia* underlies much of the material in Apost. Con. 1–6, and although the Constitutions present it with substantial amplification and commentary, the Greek text of the Didache forms the basis for Apost. Con. 7. It is thus that to a lesser or greater degree, Apost. Con. 1–7 are all influenced by the Didache. Apostolic Constitutions 7 is generally dated towards the end of the third century and includes substantial amendments "to bring it into harmony with the contemporary church."[84] Presumably because it rendered its presentation of the Didache at a date further along the so-called "parting of the ways" there is a noticeable softening of admonitions that will later be argued as indicative of the Didache's positive reception of the Torah.

This is particularly seen in Apost. Con. 7.2, where the Way of Life is described as ἣν καὶ ὁ νόμος διαγορεύει, thus clarifying that while the Way of Life is appointed by the Law, it is also distinct from the Law. This emphasis is carried through a few lines later when Apost. Con. 7.2 completely omits the phrase καὶ ἔσῃ τέλειος (Did. 1.4). If, as will be demonstrated later, perfection is a concept related to the Didache's reception of the Torah, its neglect in the Apostolic Constitutions, combined with its distancing of the Way of Life from the Law, denote a departure from the Didache's instruction. Such a departure is confirmed in Apost. Con. 7.19 which reads as "For if thou dost not turn out of the right way, thou wilt not be ungodly.[85] This is a starkly different statement than that of Did. 6.2 "If you are able to bear the whole yoke of the Lord, you will be perfect." In this departure from the text of the Didache, it is evident that by the time the Constitutions were composed, the concept of the Way of Life as a "yoke" and its relationship to being "perfect" no longer had resonance.

In summary, the Didache figures prominently in canonical lists and also became the basis for an extensive tractate and expansion upon it in Apost. Con. 7. Both attest to its continuing usefulness and the regard in which it was held. For such a document it is curious that the Didache has very few verifiable citations in ante-Nicene literature. However, it is suggestive that just as epistles such as James, Jude, 2 Peter, and 2 and 3 John were considered disputed books well into the fourth century, in contrast to the Pauline epistles,[86] so too the Didache's emphasis on the Torah received short shrift.

83. *Did. apost.* 8; Connolly, *Didascalia Apostolorum: Syriac*, 86, 218–19.

84. Sandt and Flusser, *The Didache*, 27.

85. Roberts and Donaldson, *ANF*, vol. 7.

86. Eusebius *Hist. eccl.* 25.3.

The Didache's Gentile Recipients

Various features of the Didache substantiate the *incipit*'s claim that it was written with gentile recipients (τοῖς ἔθνεσιν) in mind, a supposition that forms the basis for this study's argument that the Didache applies the Torah to gentile Christians. This is in fact the growing consensus, as John Kloppenborg documented in a survey of the matter.[87] More recently, Stephen Finlan has argued for this conclusion, employing Social Identity Theory, an approach pioneered by Henri Tajfel in 1978 in which (in short) "an individual's self-concept . . . derives from his knowledge of his membership of a social group."[88] Using this framework, Finlan points out the context of the Didache's role in constructing its community's self-definition in relation to Israel, with an eye to its composition as predominantly (or completely) for gentiles.[89] Internal clues such as the prohibition of idolatry point to the recipients' non-Jewish identity. Idolatry, prohibited in the Pauline epistles and Acts, which generally had a gentile readership in view, is only twice mentioned in the catholic epistles (1 John 5:21; 1 Pet 4:2–3), which at least *prima facie* address Jews. On the other hand, in the Pauline epistles, primarily addressed to predominantly gentile churches, idolatry is repeatedly censured as in the Two Ways portion of the Didache (3.4; 5.1; 6.3).

The first explicit designation of the Didache's recipients is in its *incipit*, which some scholars suggest is not necessarily the work of the Didachist. Nevertheless, as chapters 5 and 6 will show, the *incipit* is indeed a reliable source. Its identification of the work's recipients as gentiles is an ancient witness to what was presumably a common view. It is not necessary to argue that there were no Jews in any Didachean communities; simply that the Didache does indeed have gentile recipients in view.

The term ἔθνος occurs not only in the *incipit*, but also Did. 1.3, and 14.3, both of which show an affinity to Matthew's use of the term. In Did. 1.3 the phrase οὐχι καὶ τὰ ἔθνη τοῦτο ποιοῦσιν is a close parallel to Matt 5:47 οὐχὶ καὶ οἱ ἐθνικοί τὸ αὐτὸ ποιοῦσιν. In using this saying, the Didachist has taken a saying where Jesus is chronicled as chiding Jewish listeners to practice a higher standard of behavior than "the gentiles" on the presumption that gentile behavior was lacking. The particularly Matthean affinity to the Didache is seen in that when Luke 6:32 cites the same saying, the term "sinners" is used in place of "gentiles."[90]

87. Kloppenborg, *The Transformation of Moral Exhortation*, 110.

88. Tajfel, *Social categorization*, 6363.

89. Finlan, *Identity in the Didache Community*, 24–32.

90. It must be noted that Did 1.3 is part of the *sectio*, considered by consensus to be a later insertion in the original Two Ways material, but as Niederwimmer points

In his survey of the uses of the term in Matthew, John Meier notes the "pejorative" nature of ἐθνικοί in that text as indicative of its reference to gentiles rather than Jesus' "Jewish crowd" of listeners.[91] The Didache has taken this saying and applied it to gentiles who should behave better than those gentiles outside their community, without the regard to their sensitivities as gentiles that Luke showed by using the term "sinners" instead.[92] Richard Glover terms this "the *Didache's* unique and tactless reading."[93] This is an application of contemporary sensibilities to the first century, however, and cannot discount the Didache's evident sympathy for its recipients.[94] It is thus that while the text of Did. 1.3 does not prove the gentile audience of the Didache one way or another, its use of ἔθνος signifies its affinity with Matthew's use of the term.

The second occurrence of ἔθνος is in the body of the Didache (14.3): ἐν παντὶ τόπῳ καὶ χρόνῳ προσφέρειν μοι θυσίαν καθαράν· ὅτι βασιλεὺς μέγας εἰμί, λέγει κύριος, καὶ τὸ ὄνομά μου θαυμαστὸν ἐν τοῖς ἔθνεσι. That the nations spoken of in this free quotation of Mal 1:11, 14 are the nations of the world is supported by its locative "every time and place." The Didache could have omitted this aspect and still made its point in support of the assertion in 14.2 that "your sacrifice may not be desecrated." Its inclusion of the mention of "every time and place" and the "gentiles" therefore indicates another agenda of the Didachist. This corroborates the sense evident in a number of texts that demonstrate the Didache's concern with the cosmic reach of God's kingdom. Thus, Did. 8.2 echoes Matthew's words in the prayer "your kingdom come." Didache 9.4 petitions "may your church be gathered from the ends of the earth into your kingdom." Didache 10.3 addresses the all-powerful παντοκράτορ and prays in 10.4 that he might gather the church "from the four winds into your kingdom." In the Didache's eschatological finale, 16.4 speaks of a κοσμοπλανής in the context of cosmic events of eternal and universal significance. The phrase

---

out, the *sectio* is well attested, particularly in *P.Oxy.* 1782, some 650 years before H. *The Didache*, 21–22.

91. Meier, "Nations or Gentiles?" 95.

92. In this sense, gentiles are used as a "foil" as in Pauline rhetoric. Hodge, *The Question of Identity*, 156.

93. Glover, "The Didache's Quotations," 14.

94. The *Testaments of the Twelve Patriarchs* preserve a comparable to the Didache's ambivalence. T. Levi 9 speaks of "the race of the Philistines or Gentiles" but continues in 14 with "What shall all the Gentiles do if ye be darkened in ungodliness?" (*ANF*). T. Jud. 22 predicts that "all the Gentiles may rest in peace" when the "salvation of Israel" comes, yet goes on to refer to "the pollutions of the Gentiles" (*ANF*) in 23.2. T. Dan 5.8 refers to the "abominations of the Gentiles" but in 6.7 looks forward to the day when the Lord's "name shall be in every place of Israel, and among the Gentiles—Saviour" (*ANF*).

ἐν τοῖς ἔθνεσι is thus used in the context of the Didachist's eschatological vision that includes all the nations of the world in its scope.

This cosmic scope of the Didachist, linked to his use of ἔθνος, is again characteristic of the Gospel of Matthew. Matthew's use of ἔθνος is notably epitomized in the "Great Commission" of Matt 28:18–20.[95] A number of commentators argue that its use of ἔθνη is to be read in terms of a contrast with Israel, as was common in the Hebrew Bible. Thus Douglas Hare and Daniel Harrington argue that Matthew uses the term to designate the nations other than Israel.[96] They are representative of the position that the use of ἔθνη in Matt 28:19 means gentiles in contradistinction to the Jews and appeal to Origen, Eusebius, and Chrysostom to buttress this claim.[97]

On the other hand, Meier's contrasting argument is that Matthew's use of ἔθνη is inclusive of Jews.[98] However, he does not contest the patristic evidence and allows that it supports Hare and Harrington's position.[99] David Turner seemingly concurs with Meier's position (though he does not cite him) and suggests in his commentary that the ἔθνη of Matt 28:19 includes the Jews, while the priority of the mission remains on the gentiles.[100] Ulrich Luz's conclusion is that "while it does not exclude a continuing mission to Israel, Matthew probably no longer has great hopes for it."[101] The positions of various commentators are comprehensively listed by Matthias Konradt.[102]

It is in terms of the Didache's eschatological orientation that the use of this word must be determined. Craig Evans perceptively points out the connection between Matt 28:19 and Dan 7:14 where the son of man is given a kingdom where "all peoples [עם], nations [אמה], and languages [לשן] should serve him."[103] It is this relationship that provides a way out of the impasse, as the commission extends to all nations as the fulfilment of the expectation that Israel should take the leading role in bringing all the nations under the reign of Israel's God.[104] Such an interpretation can be corroborated with texts such as 4Q521 (frags. 2 + 4) that begins with "[. . . For the hea]vens and the

95. Harrington, *The Gospel of Matthew*, 416.

96. Hare and Harrington, "Make Disciples of all the Gentiles," 368.

97. Hare and Harrington, "Make Disciples of all the Gentiles," 367–69.

98. Meier, "Nations or Gentiles?" 94–102.

99. Meier, "Nations or Gentiles?" 95.

100. Turner, *Matthew*, 689.

101. Luz, *Matthew: A Commentary*, 631.

102. Konradt, *Israel, Church, and the Gentiles*, 311 n. 252.

103. Evans, *Matthew*, 484.

104. Bruner, *Matthew: A Commentary*, 2, 817; Evans, *Matthew*, 484.

earth shall listen to His Messiah"[105] and 1 Enoch with its anticipation of the day when "the generations of truth [arise], and evil and wickedness will come to an end, and crime will cease from the earth."[106] The ἔθνη of the world may thus be seen as the nations other than Israel, but not explicitly exclusive of any Jews that may reside among them. It is these nations that the Didache is addressing. Such a position fits with the social situation of Christians in Antioch and its region, with significant Jewish-gentile intercourse, a matter that will be addressed in more detail in chapter 3.

The relationship between Matthew's Great Commission and its emphasis on the nations of the world is yet more closely related to Didache 7.1 on account of its shared triadic baptismal formula. It is not that formula that is the focus, however, but the fact that Did. 7.1 functions as a baptismal command for a disciple who has been taught the foregoing Two Ways. Matthew's phrase "teaching them to observe all that I have commanded you" in 28:20 finds here a ready example of the implementation of the Lord's command. This is part of what led Oskar Skarsaune to comment that "in many ways the *Didache* can be seen as a natural 'sequel' to Matthew."[107] In Matthew the disciples were commanded to make disciples of the nations and teach them the Lord's command, the teaching preceding the baptism in the text. In the Didache the teaching of the Lord is presented as a prerequisite to baptism, inviting the equation of the recipients to those of Matthew's Gospel. The intertextuality in this instance seems far from coincidental.

In summary, while hints such as the Didache's censure of idolatry point to the gentile identity of its recipients, its very use of the term ἔθνος in keeping with Matthew's usage and indeed Matthew's eschatological framework, points to that very same identity. This identification of the Didache's recipients is crucial to the understanding of its presentation of the Torah, especially as argued in chapter 9.

Conclusion

This chapter has opened up the possibility for further study of the Didache's reception of the Torah. The quality of the text that we have gives us a reasonable basis for determining the inclinations of its redactor. The Two Ways material is, as per the scholarly consensus, of Jewish origin, and therefore its very employment suggestive of an employment of Torah within the norms of Second Temple Judaism. The Didache is a compilation of diverse but closely

105. Wise and Abegg, *The Dead Sea Scrolls*, 531.

106. (4Q204 Frag. 5 Col. 2), Wise and Abegg, *The Dead Sea Scrolls*, 290.

107. Skarsaune, *In the Shadow of the Temple*, 213.

related sources, assembled into the form in which we now have it sometime shortly after the first Jewish war ending in 70 CE. Widely accepted in the early church, its emphasis on the Torah was nonetheless muted in later uses of its material, which could be considered characteristic of a church establishing its new identity outside of Judaism. Finally, it has been confirmed that its readers were indeed gentiles, if not exclusively, in the main.

Part Two: A Comprehensible and Authoritative Teaching

Part One of this study assessed the current state of Didache scholarship, particularly in regard to its reception of the Torah. It also established the general reliability of the text and confirmed the view that it is a written compendium of oral teachings composed for the blossoming gentile mission. With some reservation due to its emphasis on the Torah, the Didache was widely received in the early church.

Part Two will put the Didache and its teachings in their historical and religious context, chapter 3 demonstrating the often under-emphasized turmoil in Antiochian society and its influence upon the formation of Christianity in the region. Given that the Didache begins with a Two Ways teaching, the origins and significance of that topos in regards to the Torah will be developed in chapter 4. Chapter 5 will both demonstrate the authority accorded teachers in both Judaism and the early church, and prove that the Didache intentionally used that authority to mandate its teaching.

3

Crisis and Community

Introduction

From the moment the text of the Didache found in *Codex Hierosolymitanus* (H) was published, scholars sought to determine its Jewish sources and its place and role within both nascent Christianity and Judaism. The degree of success has been varied. Much attention has been paid both to redactional and textual issues, but with a scarcity of data, not much attention has been paid to the reconstruction of the social situation of the Didachean community. Kurt Niederwimmer is representative of this in just very briefly asserting in his excellent commentary that the occasion for the Didache is unknown and that it was written "in a time of transition."[1] Exactly what this transition entailed is not spelled out.

Once a first-century date was confirmed as feasible, the Didache's Jewish origin began to receive further attention and it became increasingly significant as a Christian Jewish document composed prior to the so-called "parting of the ways." This is enhanced by the fact that while it was complete by 85 CE, the Didache evidences both earlier and later strata, from different points in the history of the rapidly developing church. Further, whilst the earlier materials in Did. 1–6, and 16 are more individual in nature, the later materials in Did. 7–15 address matters of communal concern. While this study does not emphasize the redaction of the Didache, the evident developments in its social situation provide informative data and a basis upon which to examine its reception of the Torah.

In terms of methodology, this chapter will survey the literary evidence regarding the challenges the Didachean community faced. Abundant information is available not only from the New Testament but also early Jewish and Christian writings, not to mention the Didache itself.

1. Niederwimmer, *The Didache*, 3.

These historical accounts provide much data regarding the situation of the Didachean community.

A point of comparison is Richard Horsley's examination of the historical context of Q, upon which the exploration of Q "depends."[2] Horsley's engagement with the context in which documents were composed is further relevant in terms of their oral composition and delivery, a compelling parallel as there is strong evidence that at least large portions of the Didache originated as orally presented teachings. Elsewhere in that respect Horsley also notes, "Performance of Q discourses before a community involved in a conflictual life situation meant that the text always had an immediate historical social context."[3] As this chapter will show, the milieu the Didache addressed was characterized by various crises and difficulties, from without and within. As with the natural parallel in the sphere of New Testament interpretation, Horsley's approach is taken as instructive in his attempt to reconstruct, in his own words, "insofar as possible, the fundamental social structure and the corresponding social conflicts as a context for [the] actions and ideas evident in [the] literature."[4] Furthermore, in the view of Stephen Barton in regard to the Gospels, it is still legitimate to search for their social location, for "it is an important act of the historical and social-scientific imagination."[5]

This chapter is divided into three parts. The first part, "Socio-Political Conflict," describes the social and political situation in the eastern Mediterranean with a particular focus on how it affected Jewish-gentile relations in Antioch and the relationship between Christian Judaism and the wider Jewish community. The second part, "Divergent Agendas and the Didachean Community" will appraise the resultant stresses within the Didachean community itself, paying particular attention to the roles of the Didachist, the community, and the disciple, and their relationship to the rapidly growing Christian world and the gentile mission. Finally, "Transforming Crisis," will propose that against this background the Torah was a natural (if not the inevitable) paradigm for the Didache to address the problems raised by that mission in order to secure unity within the community.

2. Horsley, *The Historical Context of Q*, 46.

3. Horsley, *Introduction*, 8.

4. Horsley, *Sociology and the Jesus Movement*, 8.

5. Barton, *Can We Identify*, 194.

Socio-Political Conflict

Three related conditions during the time of the Didache's composition coalesced to bring social pressure on the Didachean community. These were 1. the troubled times in the Roman Empire at large; 2. the specific troubles in the city of Antioch and Syria as a whole due to Jewish unrest and revolt; and 3. the social troubles the community was experiencing in its relationship to the wider nascent Jewish and Christian communities.

A Troubled Empire

As the following paragraphs show, the years preceding the destruction of the Temple in 70 CE were difficult ones in the Roman Empire. Troubles for Christians and Jews both in Rome and Jerusalem were cause for concern, which had personal repercussions for Antioch, as it had connections both to Jerusalem's James and its own missionary, Paul, both of whom were killed during this time. Following this period, its aftermath was characterized by tension in western Syria.

In the preface to *Jewish War* Josephus states regarding the first Jewish revolt that "at the time when this great concussion of affairs happened, the affairs of the Romans themselves were in great disorder."[6] These years were marred by at least two events that affected Christians.

The first of these was in 49 CE,[7] when the Emperor Claudius (41–54 CE) drove the Jews out of Rome by edict, the event being reported in Acts 18:2 (=*Hist. eccl.* 2.18). The event was attributed to one "Chrestus" by Suetonius in the statement *Iudaeos impulsore Chresto assidu tumultuiantis Roma expulit.*[8] From this cryptic comment, it is generally surmised that Suetonius was referring to conflicts over Christ among the Jews that aggravated the emperor to the point of expelling at least some of the community (this expulsion followed a previous expulsion under Tiberius in 19 CE).[9] If that were so, one should not be surprised that just twelve years later (c. 61 CE) the Jewish community leaders in Rome desired "to hear from you [Paul] what your views are, for with regard to this sect we know that everywhere it

6. Josephus *War* 1.1.2 (Goold [LCL])

7. Following the accounting of Riesner, *Pauline Chronlogy*, 13–14.

8. Suetonius *Claud.* 25.4.

9. Suetonius *Tib.* 36.1; Josephus *Ant* 18.83–84. An extended treatment of Claudius' edict is provided by Jewett and Kotansky, *Romans*, 18–20. An additional article argues that Claudius expelled the Jewish people from Rome on more than one occasion. See Slingerland, "Suetonius "Claudius" 25.4."

is spoken against."[10] The last thing they would have wanted is more trouble ignited by the prisoner in Roman custody. This bolsters our interpretation of Suetonius' comment and suggests that the event was likely a source of difficulty for Roman Jews, including Christian Jews.

The second event of note occurred during the same intervening period during Nero's rule (54–68 CE). Tacitus relates that Christians were charged with the burning of Rome in 64 CE, Nero punishing them "with the utmost refinements of cruelty."[11] Even centuries later, the effect of this injustice upon the Christian mindset is reflected in Eusebius' comment regarding this event, based on a quotation from Tertullian, where he states that Nero was "the first of the emperors to be declared the enemy of the Deity."[12] Eusebius makes this statement as if it is an established understanding. Certainly, he has Tertullian and Tacitus on his side as critics of Nero, but this is a specifically Christian accusation reflecting the effects of Nero's actions upon the Christian consciousness.

Other events at a distance quite possibly also had a ripple effect upon the Didachean community. In 57 CE[13] Paul had been arrested in Jerusalem[14] and possibly after a period of freedom was executed in Rome, most likely in 67 or 68 CE.[15] Further, as recorded in *Ant.* 20.200, another prominent Christian Jewish figure, James the brother of the Lord, was killed at the instigation of the high priest in the same year.[16] While there is no record of James visiting Antioch, Paul states that James' emissaries did visit the city.[17] The high esteem in which James was held in Jerusalem, maybe even exaggerated in Eusebius' quotation of Hegesippus,[18] is arguably reflected in the influence his emissaries had in Antioch. As Paul was initially an emissary from Antioch, his death cannot have passed unnoticed, and as one who influenced the church there, James' death must have been grievous for at least some.

A few years after this, and in an era for which Josephus claimed the affairs of the Romans were in "great disorder," so much so that they created

10. Acts 28:17–22.

11. Tacitus, *Ann.* 15.44.

12. Eusebius, *Hist. eccl.* 2.25

13. Jewett, *A Chronology of Paul*, 102.

14. Acts 21:33.

15. Murphy-O'Connor, *Paul: A Critical Life*, 370–71.

16. Brandon, *The Fall of Jerusalem*, 152.

17. Gal 2:12.

18. Eusebius, *Hist. eccl.* 2.1.6; 2.23.

conditions conducive to "invention,"[19] the first Jewish Revolt began. Roman oppression in Jerusalem and Galilee combined with Jewish apocalyptic speculation to embolden such a rebellion. It has to be noted however, as Martin Goodman points out, that the motivations for revolt were more complex than simply a search for "religious tolerance in Jerusalem."[20] As Josephus noted in a reflective passage, "what did most elevate them in undertaking this war, was an ambiguous oracle that was also found in their sacred writings, how, 'at that time, one from their country would become ruler of the world.'"[21]

The 66–70 CE revolt itself was disastrous, not only for the Jews of Jerusalem and Galilee, but also throughout the region of western Syria, which from the towns Josephus lists included trans-Jordan as well as the areas north and east of the Galilee. Eusebius (heavily dependent upon Josephus and Hegesippus) passed on his understanding that during the revolt the Jerusalem Christian community fled to Pella,[22] to the east of the Dead Sea. Whether this is correct or not, a sequence of events was in place such that, as S. T. Katz observes, leadership of the early church began to move from Jerusalem to "non-Palestinian centers, for example, Antioch and the cities of Asia Minor."[23] This may well be the context behind Did. 3.10, "Welcome the things that happen to you as good, knowing that apart from God nothing happens," for gentiles were liable to be lumped in with the Jews they had joined as Christians.

The effect of the revolt upon Christian Jews in Jerusalem and its environs was of concern to Christians elsewhere. Even prior to the revolt, Paul's own collection for the Jerusalem community[24] speaks of such concern for the community during a time of hardship. When the war came to its conclusion, Vespasian made a search for royal pretenders and descendants of David who might claim the loyalty of his Jewish subjects.[25] It would be remarkable if Christians had so disassociated themselves from the family of Jesus that the emperor's inquisition caused them no consternation. In fact, quoting Hegesippus, Eusebius records both this event and a further search for descendants of David by Vespasian's son Domitian decades later. Hegesippus' record of their trial and release[26] demonstrates that their fate was

19. Josephus, *War* 1.1.1.

20. Goodman, *The Roman World*, 174.

21. Josephus, *War* 6.312.

22. Eusebius, *Hist. eccl.* 3–5.

23. Katz, "Judaism and Christianity after 70," 44.

24. 1 Cor 16:1–4; 2 Cor 8–9; Rom 15:26–31.

25. Eusebius, *Hist. eccl.* 3.13.

26. Eusebius, *Hist. eccl.* 3.20.

indeed a matter of concern to Christians across a wide geographical area. It is thus evident that the nascent church was not isolated from the changes taking place in the Levant.

Following these events, despite the restoration of order in the Empire, unrest continued among the Jewish population. 2 Esdras 10 deals at length with the grief of the Jewish people after the destruction of the Temple whereby in 10.23 "the seal of Zion—for she has now lost the seal of her glory, . . . has been given over into the hands of those that hate us." Gedaliah Alon has therefore argued that in this transitionary period the destruction of the Temple neither eradicated resistance nor necessarily broke the spirit of the Jewish people.[27] Thus it was that only six decades later a yet greater Jewish revolt broke out. This second Jewish revolt, long after the Didache was complete, ultimately resulted in the leadership of the Jerusalem church being assigned to gentile bishops.[28]

In summary, this review has shown that the years during which the Two Ways portion of the Didache was first taught were years in which Christians in the Roman Empire suffered a number of troubling injustices. Closer to Antioch, they were not only affected by the general political disorder but by concern for the fortunes of Jerusalem's Christian community.

A Troubled City

A number of observations made by early historians confirm that while the city of Antioch did not suffer directly from the regional problems and those of the Empire in general it was yet deeply affected. Information regarding the political and social situation in Antioch comes largely from the writings of Josephus, Tacitus, and Cassius Dio. Josephus' account is the most important and needs to be read in light of a few caveats. As Pauline Allen observes, "on one level Josephus' *Jewish War* needed to concur with the Flavian commemoration of the war, reflecting the glory of the Roman victory by the new ruling family. At the same time, the text was also constructed to provide a counter narrative."[29] In that narrative, Josephus demonstrated guarded sympathy for the Jewish people and their religion, as seen in his martyrology of Jews willing to suffer for their laws, and his exaltation of the Torah.[30] Perhaps, as Allen says, this is because in the face of an overwhelming Roman victory, personally and keenly felt by Josephus himself, he

27. Alon, *The Halacha in the Teaching*, 41.

28. Eusebius, *Hist. eccl.* 4.6.4.

29. Allen, *The Jewish War*, 27.

30. e.g. Josephus, *Ag. Ap.* 2.232–35; *War* 2.152–53.

needed to vindicate the God of the Jews. For "how does a person continue to honour and worship a deity that allegedly is now under the power of the Roman deities?"[31] Viewed in contrast with his record of events elsewhere during the Jewish war however, there is no reason to doubt his basic perception of the situation of Jews in the region of Antioch.

According to Josephus, in Antioch itself the Jewish population was large and had dwelt in "undisturbed tranquility" since the days of Antiochus Epiphanes (c. 175–164 BCE). Jews were not only "particularly numerous" but were very much intermingled with the general population.[32] In an indication of their general integration with the social fabric of the region, Josephus claimed that the Jews were "perpetually" active in proselytizing, thereby "in some measure" incorporating the general populace with themselves.[33] The overall picture he gives then is one of generally favorable relationships between the Jews in the region and their neighbors. Consequently, according to Josephus, Sidon and Apamea (thus the particular region for which the Didache was composed) and the city of Antioch, along with the Jewish population, remained relatively safe and secure as the Jewish revolt took hold.[34]

There is reason to suppose that relations could not have remained as harmonious as Josephus made out. Syria was far from being isolated from events in the Empire and region at large. Shortly after the Jewish revolt began in 66 CE. Cestius Gallus had taken his entire twelfth legion out of Antioch itself, with thousands from other legions, to confront the rebellion.[35] The disastrous outcome of this campaign was recorded by Josephus himself, who as a retired soldier derisorily claimed that Cestius' siege of Jerusalem was lifted "contrary to all calculation" and recorded that his enemies seizing their chance, inflicted heavy losses on his fleeing forces.[36] It therefore follows that upon the decimated forces' return to Antioch the population would have been most aware of the legion's humiliating defeat. Yet whereas the city of Antioch was therefore affected by this episode, it was elsewhere—Damascus—that an enraged population turned on the Jewish people.[37]

The rapid succession of emperors that followed Nero's death in 68 CE ended with a particular contribution from Antioch. In the midst of the war

31. Allen, *The Jewish War*, 17.
32. Josephus, *War* 7.43.
33. Josephus, *War* 7.45.
34. Josephus, *War* 2.479.
35. Josephus, *War* 2.500.
36. Josephus, *War* 2.540.
37. Josephus, *War* 2.559–61.

to suppress the first Jewish revolt at Jerusalem, Vespasian left the Roman legions under his son Titus' direction and successfully acquired power in Rome, being elected Emperor at the end of 69 CE. This was in part due to the support of Mucianus the governor of Syria. This was a major event for Antioch, which welcomed its governor's support of Vespasian.[38]

Rather than improving matters, Vespasian's accession to power and the end of the revolt exposed the underlying tensions between Antioch's Jews and the rest of the city's population. Josephus records that after the war "the Jews who remained at Antioch were under accusations, and in danger of perishing, from the disturbances that were raised against them by the Antiochians."[39] In a subsequent series of events, Antiochene Jews were betrayed and falsely accused by one Antiochus, a Jew who had turned against them. As a result many were slaughtered by other Antiochenes, but ultimately public order was restored.[40] Nevertheless, "the Jews were under great disorder and terror."[41] This was an inevitable consequence of Titus' policies following the war, as he did not shy from "making his Jewish captives serve to display their own destruction" in "costly spectacles" throughout Syria.[42] Thus, while the region surrounding Antioch may well have been more stable than elsewhere, persecutions of the Jewish people were nevertheless endemic and the relationship between the Jews and the rest of the populace fraught with danger.

Nevertheless, despite the Antiochian appeal to do so following his successful suppression of the Jewish revolt, Titus, now general of the victorious Roman army, refused to diminish the status of the Jews of Antioch.[43] Wayne Meeks and Robert Wilken have argued that "there is no evidence that the war and its aftermath produced any substantial change in the status of the Antiochene Jews."[44] In the long term, this was largely the case. However, as has been seen, highly disturbing events did occur within the Jewish community there and it would be highly remarkable if Jews were not put in a prejudicial situation.

In summary, the record left by early historians demonstrates the underlying tensions present within Antiochian society. Furthermore, with a church comprising both Jews and gentiles, the Christians of Antioch were inevitably

38. Tacitus, Hist. 2.76–80.

39. Josephus, *War* 7.41.

40. Josephus, *War* 7.47–60.

41. Josephus, *War* 7.62.

42. Josephus, *War* 7.96.

43. Josephus, *War* 7.110–11.

44. Meeks and Wilken, *Jews and Christians in Antioch*, 13, 5.

affected by these events. While the city of Antioch was a somewhat amenable environment for Jews who lived in peace with their gentile neighbors, the situation was tense and disrupted by events in the region as a whole, and in the city it resulted in occasional anti-Jewish disturbances.

A Troubled Society

Evidence that the Didachean community experienced difficulty in its relationships with both nascent Jewish society and wider nascent Christianity becomes apparent in its use of two terms: "hypocrite" and "Christian." In terms of Jewish society, Luke's account substantiates the view that a strident, assertive Jewish community[45] occasionally made things difficult for the early church. The ability of the Jewish community to do so was precisely because the early Christian community was still within its own orbit. At the same time, the Didachean account is one of differentiation. This is largely what gives rise to Jürgen Zangenberg's characterization of the Didache as a document of "alienation."[46] Certainly, the Didache evidences a conflictual relationship with parties close to it. That conflict is reflected in the use of the designation "hypocrite" in the Didache.

If it is right, as many scholars suppose, that the Didachean milieu had much in common with that of Matthew, David Sim's view that conflict with formative Judaism was the "most serious crisis facing the Matthean community" is instructive. Matthew prominently warns his readers of the "hypocrites," especially in Matthew 6 and 23. As Daniel Harrington says, in the Matthean movement the term "hypocrites" for the scribes and Pharisees is "one of Matthew's favorite designations for the opponents of Jesus and (by extension) of the Matthean community."[47] Throughout the Didache, hypocrisy is also decried and denounced.[48] In the Two Ways section, it is identified with a kind of behavior, but in Did. 8.1–2 it is identified with a particular party who "fast on Mondays and Thursdays," which were (and are) the traditional days of fasting in the Jewish world. To identify the "hypocrites" of the Didache with the scribes and Pharisees of Matthew has been difficult to confirm with certainty however.

In the early days of Didache studies, George Allen took the Didache's designation of hypocrites as "obviously" borrowed from Matthew 6.[49] More

45. Acts 9:1–2; 13:45; 15:1,5; 17:5, 13; 21:27–28.

46. Zangenberg, *Social and Religious Milieu of the Didache*, 65.

47. Harrington, *Matthew's Christian-Jewish Community*, 166.

48. Did. 2:5; 4.12; 5.1; 8.1, 2.

49. Allen, *The Didache*, 15.

recently, Draper reviewed the evidence and concurred with "most scholars" that as in Matthew, the Didache does indeed have the Pharisees in view. In this, he acknowledged that he differs from Harnack, Audet, and Niederwimmer, but does so in view of the likelihood that the Didache refers to "the Pharisees in particular."[50] Nevertheless, the consensus remains that it is not simply the Pharisees who are called hypocrites. Willy Rordorf revisited the issue shortly after, concluding that the hypocrites were certain Judaeo-Christians who remained attached to Jewish ritual practices, but not the Pharisees.[51] Aaron Milavec, adding among other points the observation that the Pharisees were not distinguished by fasting, therefore confirmed the view that the hypocrites of the Didache were not specifically Matthew's Pharisees.[52] The discussion confirms the view that whether or not it is the Pharisees or some other group or party within the Jewish world, in both Matthew and the Didache there is an attempt to disparage a party with similar ideals but with less-than-ideal execution of them.

After 70 CE, the difficulties of the Didachean community with the Jewish world did not improve along with the relative restoration of peace to the Empire and region. Jewish sectarianism had indeed in some ways abated in the wake of the Temple's destruction, yet while "after 70 the rabbis tolerated and preserved different opinions"[53] the tolerance did not extend to "heretics" who refused to accept the majority opinion.[54] Christian Jews were no exception to this intolerance, thus the use of an isolating term such as "hypocrites" for others in Jewish society should be no surprise.

In addition to a difficult relationship to Jewish society, the churches addressed by the Didache also had problems related to the Jesus movement as a whole. Here too we are alerted to the situation by terminology, in particular their apparent adoption of the word Χριστιανός. It is in Did. 12.4 that the word first appears in the non-canonical record after its initial occurrence in Acts 11:26. In the Acts context it is with reference to Barnabas and Saul teaching "a great many people" in Antioch with the result that, according to Luke, their new "disciples" were first called Χριστιανούς. The Didache's usage points to similar acceptance of the term. In this they were to be identified with the Jesus movement.

Χριστιανός is used in Did. 12:4 without explanation, suggesting that by that time the term was well known. Its use in the Didache thus parallels

50. Draper, *Christian Self-Definition*, 233.

51. Rordorf and Tuilier, *La Doctrine Des Douze Apôtres*, 224. "Il est donc clair que les hypocrites évoqués par le didachiste au ch. 8 désignent principalement certains judéo-chrétiens qui restaient attachés aux pratiques rituelles du judaïsme."

52. Milavec, *The Didache: Faith*, 302–3.

53. Magness, *Sectarianism*, 71.

54. Magness, *Sectarianism*, 71–72.

that of Acts 11:26 in respect to there being no suggestion of the opprobrium evident in the later texts and 1 Peter. The origin of the term is a matter of some discussion. David Horrell indicates that "there is a good deal to be said for the thesis that it was first coined in Latin, in the sphere of Roman administration, arising from the encounter between Christianity and the imperial regime (in the provinces?)."[55] In this case, the term would have borne a somewhat negative connotation, as the new Jesus movement was hardly likely to have come to Roman attention as a commendable development.

The use of the term "Christian" in a deprecatory sense is seen in 1 Pet. 4:14, 16 which attests to a Christian attempt to transform the insult into a badge of honor. Certainly this was Ignatius of Antioch's approach to the term in the early second century[56] and by the late second century Theophilus of Antioch expresses the very same sentiment. Theophilus writes "you call me a Christian, as if this were a damning name to bear, I, for my part, avow that I am a Christian."[57] None of this is demonstrable from the Didache however. If the term did have negative connotations, those connotations were not so severe in Antioch to warrant comment.

A difficulty with the term was that there were those who used it for their own advantage. The Christian in Did. 12.4 is an outsider, someone who comes to join the community and needs employment. A picture emerges of a community accustomed to absorbing others, quite possibly others in difficulty and need.[58] A further adaptation, χριστέμπορος (Christ-monger), in Did. 12.5 implies that among the genuine, there were those who would abuse the hospitality of the well-meaning Christians. The term was possibly a "neologism"[59] yet relied upon the assumption that this derivation from Χριστός was comprehensible, which evidently it was. Its use in the Didache suggests an internal threat in terms of the need to defend the community from those who would seek benefit from it without contributing. As part of the Christian world, the Didachean community was subject to those who would scurrilously use their Christian identity to their advantage.

55. Horrell, "The Label Χριστιανός," 364.

56. Ign. *Eph.* 11.2; Ign. *Magn.* 4.1; Ign. *Rom.* 3.2.

57. Theophilus, *Ad Autolycum* 1.1.

58. Stephen Patterson suggests that these were refugees from the Jewish war, in *The Legacy of Radical Itineracy*. Milavec argues strongly against this on the basis that the time frame of a war would indicate only a short-term problem *The Didache: Faith*, 450–52. Since the war lasted from 66–70, and had precursors and after-effects as well, Patterson's thesis can not be so easily dismissed. In addition, other circumstances such as the famine in Jerusalem and possible periodic persecution of Christians in the city might could also have resulted in Christians seeking shelter in other communities such as in Antioch.

59. Niederwimmer, *The Didache*, 187.

In summary, the two terms "hypocrite" and "Christian" show two types of difficulties the churches addressed by the Didache faced. With the Jewish community, they found themselves at odds with a party with whom they also had something in common, and in certain respects needed to be differentiated from. With the wider Christian community, they found themselves burdened with transients who were sometimes less than willing to pull their own weight. In having surveyed the community's place in the Empire, in Antioch, and in the Christian and Jewish worlds, a rationale for the Didache as a document written in response to that situation can be countenanced. As set out in the next pages, these external challenges were matched by challenges internal to the community. The chart below accentuates major political upheavals during the time of the Didache's composition.

Timeline of Events During the Didache's Composition

Local Events		Foreign Events
	49	Jews expelled from Rome
Jerusalem Council	50	
Paul arrested	57	
James killed	62	
	64	Great Fire of Rome
Jewish Revolt begins	66	12th Legion defeated
	66	Paul, Peter killed
	67	Nero Dies
	68–69	Year of the Four Emperors
	69	Vespasian becomes Emperor
Temple destroyed	70	Titus affirms Jewish status in Antioch
Didache redacted	70–85	
Jewish Revolt ends	73	

Divergent Agendas and the Churches of the Didache

The external circumstances for the churches of the Didache are reflected in the divergent agendas of its parties: the Didachist, the churches "he" addressed, and the Christian world. A clearer depiction of these makes it possible to construct a framework for the Didache's reception of the *Torah*, which is a key to understanding how the Didachist intended it to be implemented in the Didachean community.

The Disciple

The background of the disciple and the disciple's affinity to "Judaism" is not stated, but he or she is reasonably presumed to be of pagan origins. There are various indicators of this, the most prominent being the Didache's title. Arguably authentic, as discussed in chapter 2, the title explicitly addresses the Didache to the "gentiles." Van de Sandt and Flusser propose that "the ethical catechesis incorporated in the Didache (the Two Ways *plus* Did. 6:2–3) and the Didache itself envisage converts to Christianity from paganism."[60] The task and agenda of the Didachist's disciple was thus to renounce the Way of Death, associated with his or her pagan background, and conform to the Way of Life.

The Two Ways section of the Didache addresses the inductee regarding what seem to have been Jewish notions of "gentile" vices. Such notions can be seen in the Pauline epistles,[61] although in the broader context of all those "outside Christ."[62] 1 Peter 4:3 epitomizes this, contrasting living "for the will of God" with living as the "gentiles want to do, living in sensuality, passions, drunkenness, orgies, drinking parties, and lawless idolatry." Matthew also reveals such conceptions, 5:47 and 6:32 betraying the assumption that Jews should live by a higher moral code than others. That such attitudes were not peculiar to Christianity, or Christian Jews, is plain from the Qumran literature. Thus, Peter's concern with idolatry, similar to Did. 3:3, 5:1, and 6:3, is echoed in 4Q395, which likens it to fornication. Without belaboring the point, gentile attitudes towards Judaism were sometimes also characterized by "not so much hatred as aversion."[63] Suffice to say that despite the inductee's attraction to Judaism, in this case Christian Judaism, the two parties came from different worlds.

60. Sandt and Flusser, *The Didache*, 32.

61. E.g. Rom 1:18–32; 1 Thess 4:5.

62. López, "Pauline Passages with Vice Lists," 302.

63. Schürer, *The History of the Jewish People*, 3.1, v. 3.1, p. 153.

The disciple was being brought into a community of believers by different criteria and procedures than converts to Judaism. While the Didache was written for the very purpose of inducting non-Jews into the Christian community, circumcision is not even alluded to in its pages. As one of its goals is to encourage the inductee to bear as much of the "yoke" of the Lord as possible (Did. 6.2) this is all the more remarkable. In common with the early church in general, the Didachist demonstrates a motivation to induct non-Jewish converts despite cultural disparities and Jewish opposition. In his survey of evidence regarding Jewish-Christian relations before 70 CE, Jack Sanders demonstrates that the Christian Jewish readiness to accept gentiles into their community without the need for circumcision or conversion to Judaism was a key cause of friction between Christian Jews and those of the mainstream. "What seems certain is that Paul, himself, and others contemporary with him and perhaps prior to him were flogged in synagogues for allowing Gentiles to become Christians without at the same time becoming converts to Judaism (by being circumcised)."[64]

The disciple was highly motivated. The Didache makes it clear that she or he was seeking a costly way of life that would divorce him from his presumably pagan background. The disciple sought to avoid such practices as περικαθαίρων, or ritual cleansings (Did. 3:4) which were pagan "rites intended to remove the contagion of sin or ritual impurity.[65] The disciple's motivation is indicated in his willingness to risk being hated (Did. 1.3). Further, without having to speculate as to the social situation as does Milavec,[66] the disciple is indisputably motivated enough to accept an ethos that accepts abuse from others and "turns the other cheek" (Did. 1.4). From the milieu from which he may have come as a God-fearer, he is required to separate from "hypocrites" as in Did. 8.1–2.

While it will be argued later that the Two Ways comprised a Torah for gentiles, regardless of the outcome of that discussion the disciple was willing to undertake a radical and demanding discipleship program and at the very least assent to it as an ideal and not deviate from the teaching given (Did. 6.1; 11.2); to seek to bear the "whole yoke" of the Lord (Did. 6.2); avoid idolatry (Did. 6.3); and upon baptism adopt a life integrated with that of the community (Did. 7–15). The disciple was making a substantial change in life that would allow full participation in a community that prayed together, ate together, celebrated the Eucharist together, and had a rudimentary welfare system to which all members contributed and all

64. Sanders, *Schismatics, Sectarians*, 9.

65. Knox, "περικαθαίρων (*Didache* iii 4)," 146–47.

66. Milavec, *The Didache: Faith*, 743–68.

could potentially benefit. Lastly, in view of the eschaton, the inductee had the potential to be found "perfect" in the Eschaton (Did. 16.2). Whereas the Didachist's agenda was to regulate the community, the disciple's agenda ultimately involved personal benefit even at great personal cost. While the two agendas coincided, in this they also potentially diverged.

In summary, the disciple had taken a daunting choice to adopt a new and costly way of life that would divorce him from his past, requiring significant motivation. This would, at least on a temporary basis, require that his agenda was a personal one as he sought acceptance in his new community.

The Community

As much as the Didachist had an agenda, so did the Didachean community. Following the Two Ways material of the Didache there is a notable switch from singular to plural in Did. 7.1 which signifies that the Didachist is now addressing the community in general. As a major literary feature of the Didache, it is to this change of voice that we now turn.

As seen in chapter 2, the Didachean community was more than a sole congregation and not limited to the city of Antioch. Thus, the Didachist's instructions regarding liturgical form, appointment of leaders, and rules regarding migrants all lend themselves to adoption by multiple groups. In this regard, the community addressed in the Didache fits well with the New Testament picture, which portrays the early Jesus movement as a network commonly meeting in houses. This is seen in Luke's account in Acts 5:42; 8:3; 12:12; 16:40; 18:7; 20:20; as well as in Rom 16:3–5; Col 4:15; and Phlm 1–2. Various writers have come to this conclusion. As Bradley Blue writes, this "was the period of the 'house church': a domestic residence used by the Christian community *before* any physical alterations were made to the building itself in order to better facilitate the communities (sic) specific needs."[67] Shaye Cohen also finds little evidence that synagogues were very common in this time.[68] It is therefore reasonable to doubt that the Didacheans would have had many, if any of their own facilities. More likely, in addition to homes as Edward Adams' research bears out on the basis of "literary references and/or ecclesiastical archaeology" they used places such as "shops and workshops, barns and warehouse cells."[69]

67. Blue, *Acts and the House Church*, 2, 188.

68. Cohen, *Evidence on the Ancient Synagogue*, 161.

69. Adams, *The Earliest Christian Meeting Places*, 156. Representing the traditional view, Roger Gehring in his recent study on house churches suggests that "we can assume a plurality of house churches in Antioch" *House Church and Mission*, 112–13.

It is also likely that the groups addressed extended beyond the confines of the city. This mixed urban/rural picture seems possible from a reading of the rules for tithing in Did. 13.3–7. In those rules there is a repetition of the command which begins with a more agricultural tithe at the "wine-press and threshing floor" which possibly points to an accommodation for agricultural workers. Didache 13.5–6 then includes tithes from bread, and jars of wine or oil. As Milavec points out, the latter is much more suited to "artisans and merchants" rather than "farmers and herders."[70] The suggestion of diversity is also bolstered by the various modes of baptism proposed in Did. 7.1–3. Evidently various groups did not have plentiful access to water, whereas within Antioch, the river Orontes supplied the needs of the city's population. Thus Niederwimmer can speak of "the region from which the tradition of the Didache comes.[71] Such diversity brings its own problems with it. This gives support to Richard Bauckham's point as he connects the diversity of early Christianity with its lack of order, writing, "the evidence for conflict and diversity in early Christianity supports my picture of the early Christian movement as a network of communities in constant communication."[72]

Within this environment Magnus Zetterholm suggests a yet further possible complication: that the Didache was written directly to counter the "troublesome apostle" Paul, whose "model for interaction between Jews and non-Jews had to be completely rejected."[73] If that was so, it suggests that the community also had to deal with internal dissension. Whether or not Zetterholm is correct, the writer of the Didache wrote in such a manner as to present his teaching so as not to cause offense outside of the community. For a community that was seeking to define itself in relation to both the Jewish and Christian worlds, the form of the Didachist's writing is conciliatory rather than inflammatory.

The Didachean community was a minority in both the Christian and Jewish worlds, and thus a minority of a minority. Didache 4.3 "Do not cause division, but reconcile those who fight" and 14.2 "Don't allow any who has a dispute with his neighbor to come together with you until they reconcile"

Libanius interestingly writes in the fourth century about his search for teaching venues and the options of museums, temples, and the public square (ἀγορά) (*Or.* 1.102). In the Pseudo-Clementine recognitions, on the other hand, Peter is depicted as teaching in "a certain apartment, arranged after the manner of a theatre, and beautifully built" (*Clem. Recogn.* 8:38 [ANF]).

70. Milavec, *The Didache: Faith*, 522.

71. Niederwimmer, *The Didache*, 200.

72. Bauckham, *For Whom Were the Gospels Written?* 43.

73. Zetterholm, *The Didache, Matthew, James-and Paul*, 90.

express a real concern for harmony within various group. Against a background of instruction on how to behave towards one another and those traveling by, it would seem that a high priority was placed on keeping the peace. The potential for disruption and the need for guiding principles in the community are exemplified in the controversy of Gal 2:1–16, and the fact that according to that account it arose due to an action of Peter's, in Antioch, which was motivated by political considerations.

In summary, given the somewhat marginal status of the community, its somewhat scattered locales, and its seeming divergence from Pauline attitudes regarding the Torah, the Didache's emphasis on unity and cohesion within the community is a natural consequence. The concern of the Didache and its teachers was thus distinct from that of the disciple, as the survival of the community was at stake.[74]

The Christian World

In addition to the divergent agendas and stresses in the community, the Didachean assemblies had to contend with the Christian world at large, and there is substantial evidence that the Antiochian controversy put lasting stress upon the community. Regardless of the chronological sequence, the controversy in Antioch centered around two events. The first was a debate concerning circumcision for gentile converts in Antioch and elsewhere (Acts 14:26—15:29). The controversy erupted on a different occasion when Paul challenged Peter regarding his separation from gentiles at meals in Antioch (Gal 2:11–14).

Both conflicts arose out of the difficulties associated with incorporating gentiles in the new movement and point to a climate in which the practicalities of Jewish association with gentiles were difficult to work out. Significantly, these events both occurred *circa* 48 CE and thus before the Didache was committed to writing.

Ostensibly the conflicts were resolved in the Jerusalem Council of Acts 15, and in that vein Shailer Matthews argued that the Council "had completely won its case," by which he meant "Judaism was no longer regarded as necessary to salvation."[75] However, although Luke reported the congregation in Antioch "rejoiced because of its encouragement" (Acts 15:31),

74. In somewhat of a corroboration of this *Sitz im Leben*, Georg Schöllgen in his survey of Did. 7–15 calls the Didache a "selective church order" that is "concerned to correct abuses and to address new rules to changed circumstances." *The Didache as a Church Order*, 63.

75. Matthews, "The Council at Jerusalem," 342.

there is reason to think that the difficulties were not fully settled, on the basis of Paul's ongoing encounters with the Law party in Jerusalem alone (e.g., Acts 21:17–24). Indeed, James continued to see it as an issue in Acts 21:21 and required Paul to demonstrate in deed that he did not teach Jews to forsake the Law of Moses. Further, as Pierson Parker notes in a separate discussion, in his controversy with Peter, Paul did not cite the Decree of Acts 15 in Gal 2, suggesting that this was "no victory for Paul."[76] Paul's later arrest in Jerusalem no doubt made it even harder for him to argue his case regarding gentile obligations to the Law.

Nevertheless, as time went on, Paul's position on the Law prevailed in the church. The failure of the first Jewish Revolt had a pivotal role in this. If, as S. G. F. Brandon argues, Paul's influence in arguing for his interpretation of the Jerusalem Decree was muted by his arrest, the voice of Jerusalem was all the more silenced as the revolt took hold, paving the way for the eventual reception of the Pauline interpretation.[77] Even before the revolt had been suppressed, the Didachist took up the task of instructing new members of the community. The challenge the Didachist faced was to present his Torah-based teaching in a way that would bring unity to the Didachean community rather than cause further disruption. As Brown and Meier state, "No doubt it was not always easy to keep peace between the two groups with their conflicting viewpoints and programs."[78]

The conflict appears to have persisted for some time. While certainty as to this is impossible, as Raymond Brown suggests, "the portraits of the church we get decades later, first at the time of Matthew's gospel and then at the time of Ignatius, may offer some clues."[79] Following this methodology, it can be confirmed that these early church writings substantiate the impression of an enduring conflict. Preeminent among them in this regard is Ignatius, bishop of Antioch, from whose letters insight into the situation of the Didachist and his community can be inferentially gleaned.

Ignatius' antipathy to "Judaism" is apparent from his epistles. The identity and doctrines of those who taught the "Judaism" he opposed is of interest to Didache studies. He wrote between 98–117 CE, well after the Didachist and shortly before his martyrdom under Trajan,[80] and repeatedly referred to various opponents in strong terms. To the Magnesians he wrote "do not be deceived by false opinions or old fables that are of no

76. Parker, "Once More," 176.

77. Brandon, *The Fall of Jerusalem*, 153.

78. Brown and Meier, *Antioch and Rome*, 41.

79. Brown and Meier, *Antioch and Rome*, 40.

80. Eusebius, *Hist. eccl.* 3.36.

use. For if we have lived according to Judaism until now, we admit that we have not received God's gracious gift."[81] Later in the same letter he pointedly argued that "Christianity did not believe in Judaism, but Judaism in Christianity."[82] To the Smyrneans he warned further about "those who spout false opinions."[83] While Ignatius did not clearly identify who these false teachers might be, William Schoedel does not appear to be far off the mark in connecting Ign. *Smyrn.* 6.2 to Ign. *Magn.* 8.1 "where grace stands opposed to Jewish practices."[84]

There is good reason to see a connection between Ignatius' antipathy to Judaism and his antipathy to certain Christians whom he deemed as Jewish. To the Philadelphians he instructed "if anyone should interpret Judaism to you, do not hear him" (μὴ ἀκούετε αὐτοῦ).[85] This is quite likely a pointed repudiation of Did. 11.1–2, "if the one teaching turns to teach another teaching leading to destruction, do not hear him" (μὴ αὐτοῦ ἀκούσητε). As will be seen later, this was the Didachist's attempt to ensure that only teachers who uphold his view of the Law could teach in the Didachean community. Ignatius, seemingly contradicting this instruction continued in the same verse to say "For it is better to hear Christianity from a man who is circumcised than Judaism from one who is uncircumcised."

Various theories about the identity of Ignatius' "uncircumcised" teachers of Judaism have been proposed. On the basis that they were physically uncircumcised C. K. Barrett sees them not as "orthodox Jews" but "Christian Jews."[86] This does not sit well either with the tenor of the New Testament, where Paul had Timothy circumcised because he had a Jewish mother,[87] or with Epiphanius' fourth-century description of the "Nazoraeans." There, these "followers of the apostles" (which one could conjecture implies a link to the Didache, entitled in part 'διὰ τῶν δώδεκα ἀποστόλων') are described as "They were Jewish, were attached to the Law, and had circumcision."[88] It is probable, rather, that they were not Jews at all. Shaye Cohen argues this point thoroughly, pointing to the implausibility that there were any Jews who were not circumcised. From this he infers that Ignatius' use of the terms "circumcised" and "uncircumcised" demonstrated the "divide between different

81. Ignatius, *Magn.* 8.1.

82. Ignatius, *Magn.* 10.3.

83. Ignatius, *Smryn.* 6.2.

84. Schoedel, *Ignatius of Antioch*, 239.

85. Ignatius, *Phil* 6.1 (Ehrman [LCL])

86. Barrett, *Jews and Judaizers in the Epistles of Igantius*, 226–27.

87. Acts 16:3.

88. Epiphanius, *Panarion*, 29

groups or currents within the church."[89] In other words, the "uncircumcised Jew" who taught Judaism seems to have been a gentile adherent to a Jewish form of Christian faith opposed by Ignatius.

Ignatius' assertion that there were "uncircumcised" people preaching "Judaism" to Christians fits well with the Didache on three counts. First, as Thomas Robinson's description of Ignatius' opponents shows, there is no hint in this reference of the docetism that Ignatius is also battling.[90] As Paul Donahue wrote, "In the two letters in which Ignatius addresses the problems posed by Jewish Christianity, he never accuses his opponents of denying the reality of Christ's incarnation."[91] Second, the "place of the Law is the fundamental issue."[92] As Ign. *Magn.* shows, Ignatius argued that "those who lived according to the old ways came to a new hope, no longer keeping the Sabbath but living according to the Lord's day."[93] In fact, Ign. *Magn.* 8–10 is actually one sustained dialogue against the practices of Judaism. Thirdly, the Didache did not require circumcision of gentile converts, but rather baptism, in order to be fully accepted in the community.[94] Thus, it is entirely possible that gentile members of the Didachean community were both uncircumcised and taught what Ignatius saw as "Judaism" as seen above. Their "Judaism" may well have been marked by the twice weekly fasting and thrice daily prayer, practices the Didachist held in common with other Jews. Although they were gentiles, those who practiced such things were "Jews" in Ignatius' mind. Thus, from the perspective of this study, it is reasonable to proceed on the basis that Ignatius' opponents held enough in common with the Didachean community that it must have formed at least part of their history.

If Ignatius' opponents can indeed be identified with groups related to the Didache's initial recipients a few decades earlier, his hostility suggests long-running differences in the region of Antioch. Virginia Corwin, in enumerating the various parties evident in Ignatius' epistles describes him as holding a centrist position between the docetists on the left and those on the right, "deeply influenced by the Old Testament, who wished to see the Christian pattern become more strongly Jewish."[95] This is entirely within reason, but does not obviate the fact that even if he was not specifically

89. Cohen, "Judaism without Circumcision," 406.

90. Robinson, *Ignatius of Antioch*, 113–14.

91. Donahue, "Jewish Christianity," 87.

92. Donahue, "Jewish Christianity," 89.

93. Ignatius, *Magn.* 9:1.

94. Did. 7.1–4; 9.5.

95. Corwin, *Ignatius and Christianity in Antioch*, 52.

criticizing the Didachean community, Ignatius certainly criticized those who would have had strong resemblance to them. Thus the "Law" controversy proves to have remained a sticking point between the Didacheans and the wider Christian world.

Beyond Ignatius, one might draw a line to the rhetoric against Judaism in the fourth century by Antioch's John Chrysostom. While such a connection might be tenuous, confirmation of the ongoing dispute can be seen in the Pseudo-Clementine writings, in particular, that part of it called the *Epistle of Peter to James*. As early as the second century, and most probably written in Syria, the Epistle reflects a decidedly Christian-Jewish perspective. The writer's position is Law-affirming, as he has Peter assert that "the law of God . . . was spoken by Moses, and was borne witness to by our Lord in respect of its eternal continuance; for thus he spoke: 'The heavens and the earth shall pass away, but one jot or one tittle shall in no wise pass from the law.'"[96] The epistle has Peter complain that "some from among the gentiles have rejected my legal preaching, attaching themselves to certain lawless and trifling preaching of the man who is my enemy."[97] The language is strong, and naturally brings to mind the conflict between Peter and Paul in Gal 2. In a further allusion to ongoing conflict, the writer has James instruct that the epistle's teachings only be imparted to "one who is good and religious, and who wishes to teach, and who is circumcised, and faithful".[98] In this there is an apparent attempt to avoid conflict with those who would oppose the teaching of the Law to gentiles. Thus one can agree with Louis Martyn that like the "teachers" in Galatians, there are indeed later evangelists in the region who "pursue their own Law-observant mission among Gentiles."[99]

Further stressors on the Christian community in Antioch are found elsewhere in the book of Acts, where Luke records a number of significant events in the life of the Antiochian church.[100] Perhaps, if Eusebius' understanding was correct, this is because Luke was himself an "Antiochene by birth,"[101] accounting for his interest in the city. Luke portrays a church that was dynamic, multi-faceted, and growing and had much to do with the missionary enterprise in Asia Minor as well as having relational ties to Jerusalem.

96. Ps.-Clement, *Ep. Pet. to Jas.* 3.

97. Ps.-Clement, *Ep. Pet. to Jas.* 2.

98. Ps.-Clement, *Ep. Pet. to Jas.* 4.1.

99. Martyn, "A Law-Observant Mission," 323.

100. *I.e.* Acts 11:19–30; 13:1–3; 14:24—15:35.

101. Eusebius, *Hist. eccl.* 3–4.

In the account of Acts, links between Antioch and Jerusalem are first noted during the early days of the church when the proselyte Nicolaus of Antioch was appointed as one of seven men to look after the daily distribution of food to widows.[102] Luke's account later depicts the church in Antioch as composed of dispersed Jews from Jerusalem,[103] who along with their converts and converts from among the Ἑλληνισταί[104] eventually became known as "Christians." The Antioch community therefore had a strong relationship with the Jerusalem church[105] that was facilitated by ongoing travel between the two cities.[106] The strength of the relationship is demonstrated in that while Jerusalem naturally provided spiritual direction, when a famine caused distress in the Jerusalem community Antioch reciprocated by providing fiscal relief.[107] The church in Antioch was thus initially a Jewish community.

In light of the underlying tensions in the city, it is not surprising that as far as the record goes, Antioch was "the place where controversy between Jews and Gentiles first erupted within the church."[108] According to Paul, this controversy arose on account of the behavior of Jerusalemites and their influence upon the Antioch congregation's behavior.[109] It seems that there is more to it than just that, however, due to the intensity with which Paul prosecutes his case. Atsuhiro Asano rightly suggests the possibility that a territorial issue was at stake—and in light of Jewish conceptions regarding the extended boundaries of *Eretz Israel* there was an attempt by James to "claim his jurisdiction over the church in Antioch."[110] Certainly, "inter-ethnic" dining was an issue for the church there.[111] What does seem clear is that Peter and Paul found themselves in a difficult situation. Evidently the relationship between Antioch and Jerusalem was not always comfortable. The controversy even divided Paul and Barnabas (Gal 2:13). This puts teeth

102. Acts 6:5.

103. Acts 11:19.

104. Acts 11:20.

105. Acts 11:22, 27.

106. Acts 11:19–27; 13:1; 14:19; 15:1–30.

107. Acts 11:27–30.

108. Meeks and Wilken, *Jews and Christians in Antioch*, 13, 13.

109. Gal 2:11–14.

110. Asano, *Community-Identity in Galatians*, 134.

111. Asano, *Community-Identity in Galatians*, 140. Philip Esler describes various other conflicts that would have been present. He argues that underlying the break in table fellowship were Jewish concerns regarding food purity, ritual purity, and the possibility of food tainted by idolatry in *Galatians*, 98. These issues would have been common wherever the possibility existed for Jews and gentiles to eat in proximity or together.

into J. H. Schütz's observation that "the inclusion of Barnabas [in Antioch's delegation to Jerusalem] suggests that, especially in light of events narrated in vv. 11ff., the Jerusalem meeting was not merely a personal accommodation to Paul. It was a formal negotiation between Antioch and Jerusalem, two independent centers of Christianity."[112]

In summary, the Christian world of Antioch was a difficult environment for the Didache's recipients, where the evidence suggests that the controversy over circumcision never fully died down. Later records from Ignatius and Pseudo-Clement demonstrate an opposition to "Judaism" suggesting the possibility that the Didache's teachings endured for at least some decades, despite efforts of some to suppress them. What emerges is that there was a latent conflict between the agendas of Jerusalem and Antiochene Christianity that has to be considered if the Didache is to be interpreted as an Antiochene document. This is particularly true as the issues at stake all had something to do with the Didache's reception of the Torah.

Transforming Crisis

The pressures exerted upon the Didachean community from within and without provided a distinct context for the composition of the Didache. The final part of this chapter sets forth two emerging concerns of the Didache: The gentile mission and community unity. The crises the community faced thus contributed to a transformational approach to the Torah that minimized opposition and preserved the community.

The Gentile Mission

Just as the community of the Didache was diverse and had a minority status, it was also faced with the challenge of incorporating gentile adherents in a hostile environment. The birth of the mission to the gentiles had been precipitated by controversy, later reflected in Luke's retrospective account of Acts 10, with Peter's decision to visit the Roman centurion Cornelius. Whereas Acts 10 provides an apologetic for Peter's decision to do so, Acts 11:1–18 shows the disfavor that his actions drew, particularly in regard to the inevitable compromise of Jewish sensitivities that association with gentiles entailed. The issue was a live one in the early church, coming to the forefront when Paul faced the report that he had taught Jews to forsake not only Moses, but "our customs" in Acts 21:21. The gentile mission was fraught with peril.

112. Schütz, *Paul and the Anatomy*, 138.

James Dunn puts it well: "For to preach a Jewish Messiah to non-Jews was a striking enough development. But to accept gentiles as themselves believers, and thus full members of the new sect (Acts 11:21–24), without demanding that they become proselytes, was quite exceptional."[113]

Christian Jewish conversion of gentiles was not so strange to the Jewish world as sometimes supposed. The accusation of Matthew 23:15 "Woe to you, scribes and Pharisees, hypocrites! For you travel across sea and land to make a single proselyte, and when he becomes a proselyte, you make him twice as much a child of hell as yourselves" underscores what the Jewish expectation was of presumably gentile converts. This account is of special importance in light of the supposed general absence of evidence of Jewish proselytism in the first century (one can also bring to mind the conversion of the royal house of Adiabene as in Josephus *Ant.* 20.2).

In a discussion of the Matthean record and the Adiabene conversions, James Carleton Paget argues forcibly that such activity did occur.[114] In addition, the *Serek Hayaḥad* expressly regulates gentile converts, something that would not be so likely if conversions were rare. *Serek* 5.6–8 provides that the *Yahad* are to "are to atone . . . for those who belong to truth, and for Gentile proselytes who join them in the community . . . . Every initiate into the party of the *Yahad* is to enter the covenant in full view of all the volunteers. He shall take upon himself a binding oath to return to the Law of Moses."[115] Whereas the general scholarly debate is whether or not such activity was common, at least in the Qumran record, conversion to Judaism was known, although there is no record of proselytism as an activity. Furthermore, both Matthew and the *Serek* signify that conversion and observance of Torah were closely linked, a fact that points forward to the Didache's use of the Torah in its teaching of gentile disciples, as will be seen.

The Didachean groups were a product of the gentile mission having taken on a life of its own. The Didache itself is evidence of the ongoing Jewish attempt to manage this development. They were indeed accepting members without requiring conversion. Nowhere does the Didache advocate or even mention circumcision. Nevertheless, it was written to "the gentiles" and, as Thomas O'Loughlin describes it, this was a community that viewed "itself as having chosen the Way of Life and rejected the Way of Death."[116] It might be too much to hope for, however, that the gentiles addressed in the Didache were in every respect happy with the teachings of the Didachist.

113. Dunn, *The Rise and Expansion*, 191.

114. Paget, *Jews, Christians and Jewish Christians*, 173–77.

115. Wise, Abegg, and Cook, eds., *The Dead Sea Scrolls*, 122.

116. O'Loughlin, "The Missionary Strategy of the Didache," 79.

The Didacheans were gathering adherents during a time that saw a "growing confrontation between Jews, Judaeo-Christians, and Gentile Christians."[117] Navigating the theological waters whilst at the same time pursuing a mission to the gentiles was perilous.

A point of comparison is found in the related Matthean community, which was in some ways positioning itself, in Anthony Saldarini's words, as a "reformist movement or sect within Judaism."[118] Matthew's position in regards to gentiles and whether they needed to convert to Judaism is ambiguous in Saldarini's view.[119] This serves to highlight the possibility that this was still an unresolved issue in at least some respects, and while an argument from silence, lends weight to the idea that there was no clear consensus on the issue. Fortunately for the Didachist, as Simon Mimouni observes, there is no evidence in the Didache that conflict between "Judaeo-Christian circles" and "Pagano-Christian circles" had "broken out" or "assumed a decisive ultimate turning-point."[120] Yet this very observation acknowledges that there was indeed a growing tension, a brewing crisis implicit in the gentile mission.

To summarize, therefore, the Didachist's position as transmitter of the Lord's teaching through the apostles put him at the crux of the "gentile mission" controversy. The community could not remain apart from the fray, and the role of the Torah in the gentile mission could not remain unaddressed.

Communal Cohesion

The concern of the Didache was clearly not merely to adjudicate a position on gentile membership in the church, primarily its own community, but also to ensure the community's well-being. It is no surprise in this regard that Henderson picks up on a particularly "eirenic" argumentative goal, more than "polemic or even didactic."[121] In regard to its concern for the community's well-being, the Didache bears further comparison to the *Serek*.

The community's diversity within a region suffering from ongoing tensions and crises did not lend itself to consistent harmony. This accords with the picture frequently found in the New Testament where conflict resolution has to be addressed and harmony enjoined.[122] Similarly in Did. 4.2

117. Tomson, *Transformations of Post-70 Judaism*, 115.

118. Saldarini, *Matthew's Christian-Jewish Community*, 114.

119. Saldarini, *Matthew's Christian-Jewish Community*, 157.

120. Mimouni, *Early Judaeo-Christianity: Historical Essays.*

121. Henderson, "Didache and Orality," 292.

122. E.g. Matt 18:18; 15–17; Rom 15:5; Jas 4:1.

there is the admonition to "seek out the presence of the saints every day" and in 4.3 to "not create a schism." That such a concern runs through the work is seen in 4.3 "Do not cause division"; 9.5 "Do not let anyone eat or drink . . . but those who have been baptized"; the extended discourse on itinerants in 11–13; and the election of leaders in Did. 15. This ongoing concern of the Didachist is the decisive reason for taking his admonition along these lines in Did. 16.2a as an appeal for unity in the church. Didache 16.2a instructs the community to "be closely assembled seeking what is appropriate for your souls." Niederwimmer takes this verse as similar to "Heb 10:25 and Barn. 19.10, where similar admonitions are placed in an eschatological context."[123] However, while that element of the exhortation cannot be dismissed, to limit it to this divorces the admonition from the thrust of the book as a whole. Taras Khomych is in agreement with this, having argued that the phrase πυκνῶς δὲ συναχθήσεσθε denotes an appeal to unity in the church, in part on the basis that πυκνῶς may not only imply frequency of meeting, but intensity of purpose in doing so.[124]

In this respect, the Didachean community bears comparison to that of the *Serek* in the fact that both communities were comprised of groups with a distinctive halakah and teaching. The community of the *Serek* appears to have gathered in communities that might not even have had a quorum of ten men.[125] The *Serek*, somewhat comparably to the Didache contains "the regulations that govern when they are gathered together as a community."[126] Another point of comparison is that in both communities the teacher had a key role, and was subject to specific statutes.[127] He also functioned somewhat as a gatekeeper to the community.[128] This too is a characteristic of the Didache. Demonstrating a similar concern for unity, the *Serek* advises that "the men of the '*Yahad*,' each will walk blamelessly with his fellow, guided by what has been revealed to them."[129]

Both the Didache and the *Serek* fulfilled a necessary role in their communities. Their extensive acceptance and distribution should therefore be no surprise. John J. Collins surmises that the "view that the *Yaḥad* was an association dispersed in multiple settlements may . . . explain why different editions of the *Serek* continued to be copied" and why there were so many

123. Niederwimmer, *The Didache*, 215.

124. Khomych further provides much helpful data, and ultimately demonstrates well the "common concern" in the Didache for the "integrity of the community." Khomych, "The Admonition to Assemble," 141.

125. *Serek* 6.3.

126. *Serek* 5.7. Wise, Abegg, and Cook, eds., *The Dead Sea Scrolls*, 122.

127. *Serek* 9.12, 21.

128. *Serek* 9.15.

129. *Serek* 9.19. Wise, Abegg, and Cook, eds., *The Dead Sea Scrolls*, 122.

copies of the *Serek* found in Qumran.[130] As seen in chapter 2, the Didache also had a wide geographic distribution and was positively mentioned by the church fathers, suggesting that it found a positive reception not only in its target community but in the church at large. Like the *Serek*, the Didache addressed the need for unity among its adherents.

In summary, the Didache is comparable in a number of respects to the *Serek* in its concern for communal cohesion. Both were distinctive in their commitment to the Torah, and minorities within religious society as a whole. In a religious world riven by fault lines, the Didache was affected by tensions arising from the "gentile mission" and, comparable to the *Serek*, both doubled down on its distinctives vis-à-vis the Torah and combined its commitment to its Torah with commitment to the unity of the community.[131] This the Didache did in a transformational way that stayed within the bounds of acceptability in the church at large.

Conclusion

The Didache was composed during a time of crisis and distress. Empire-wide instability played a part and contributed to regional social disorders that had a profound effect upon the city of Antioch and its inhabitants, even though the city maintained a degree of stability during those chaotic times. The Jewish people and the Christian community were affected in different ways as persistent troubles brought increasing alienation between Jews and gentiles in Antiochene society. Within the Didachean community, we have shown that the Didachist addressed a disparate and diverse community in which various parties had their own inherent agendas. In the midst of this context, new converts being inducted into the community were introduced to a set of teachings that would bind them to that same community via its code of conduct. That community had its own concerns for self-preservation of itself and its distinctives in the context of opposition within the Christian world. Finally, the flux of the gentile mission transformed the way in which the Didache presented Torah, neither betraying its commitment to it, nor arousing the opposition of a wary church.

130. Collins, "Beyond the Qumran Community," 360.

131. Francois Viljoen comes to a similar conclusion in his essay on Jesus' teaching on the "Torah" in the Sermon on the Mount, stating: "The crisis of 70 C.E. led to reconsidering the correct interpretation of the *Torah*. Matthew claims that Jesus brought the correct teaching of the *Torah*." See Viljoen, "Jesus' Teaching," 152.

4

Two Ways and the One Way of Torah

Introduction

THIS CHAPTER ESTABLISHES THE relationship between the Two Ways metaphor and its suitability as a vehicle to establish a Way of Life based on the Torah. As has just been argued, the church of the Didache was a church inducting new converts during a socially and politically fraught time. Chapter 3 has included examples of how teaching, and in particular teaching of community standards and the Torah was an implicit part of such induction in the Jewish world. In this context, the Didache's use of the Two Ways topos will now be shown to be eminently suited to its teaching of new disciples.

Wilhite has commented that "The ways of life and of death are contrastibly extensive lists of virtues and vices that mark the ethical moorings of the community." He continues to note that "In Did. 2, the ethical material uniquely corresponds with the material in the second half of the Decalogue. The Didachist most likely reflects upon the Decalogue to provide a positive reception of the Torah for the community."[1] While agreeing with this, I would take this further, and in part would base my argument on greater weight being placed upon the use of the Two Ways metaphor in the Hebrew scriptures and in Second Temple Judaism.

The Two Ways teaching of the Didache is both in primary place, in contrast to Barnabas, where it is almost an appendix as James Rhodes notes,[2] and just over 50 percent of the Didache's word count. The Two Ways is also the most prominent feature of the Didache's earlier material, comprising the first six and the last (sixteenth) chapters. The general structure of the Didache's Two Ways section is readily discernible and is set out below:

1. Wilhite, *The Didache*, 74.
2. Rhodes, "The Two Ways Tradition," 799.

1.1–6.2	The Two Ways
1.2–6	Teachings of the Lord
2.1–4.14	Teachings on Lawfulness—Torah
2.1–6	Torah and Explanatory Teachings
3.1–6	Torah and Halakhic Teachings
3.7—4.14	Torah and Relational Teachings
5.1–2	Teachings on Lawlessness—Torah
5.1	The Curses
5.2	The Cursed
6.1–2	The Yoke of the Lord

The following pages will survey the use of the Two Ways metaphor in pagan traditions, the Hebrew Bible, and the Second Temple Judaism of the first century. Particular attention will be paid to the suitability and utilization of the metaphor in relationship to the Didache's Torah mandate. It will be seen that as an accepted topos, the Two Ways concept was well known to its readers whatever their knowledge of Judaism, which contributed to its adaptability for the instruction of gentiles. Part Three of this study will follow the Didache's employment of this inherent relationship between the Two Ways and Torah in Second Temple Judaism to authoritatively apply it; make it incumbent upon the disciple to choose the Way of Life; validate it as mediated by the Lord Jesus; and equate it with the Torah. The disciple who takes on the "yoke of the Lord" can expect salvation ἐν τῷ ἐσχάτῳ καιρῷ.[3]

Pagan Traditions and the Two Ways

Given that the Didache was redacted with gentile recipients in view, the question should be asked whether the Two Ways topos was familiar to disciples not necessarily schooled in Jewish tradition. Was the Two Ways topos comprehensible to the gentile disciple who may not have been familiar with its Jewish frame of reference, and how would the implications of the format have been perceived?

The Didache does not presume a familiarity with the Hebrew scriptures, and therefore presumably with the Two Ways choice of Deut 30:11–20. The Epistle of Barnabas provides a helpful point of comparison. Generally dated between 80 and 130 CE,[4] Barnabas is almost certainly later than the

3. Did. 16.2.

4. Paget, *Barnabas*, 9.

Didache and requires a much greater familiarity with the Hebrew scriptures, suggesting that it was written to those who had some knowledge of the scriptures. Other than David,[5] however, the Didache never mentions a figure from the Hebrew scriptures by name. In contrast, Barnabas speaks not only in general terms of the prophets[6] and Moses,[7] but also of Daniel,[8] Adam,[9] Abraham, Isaac, and Jacob,[10] Abraham individually,[11] Isaac individually,[12] Jacob individually,[13] Joshua,[14] Amalek,[15] King David,[16] Isaiah,[17] Isaac and Rebecca,[18] Joseph,[19] and Ephraim and Manasseh.[20] In addition, the pseudepigraphal Enoch[21] is cited, although it is likely the tradition of 4QpsEzekiel that Barnabas attributes to him.[22] Furthermore, the book is replete with references to places, stories, quotations, allusions, and even seemingly midrashic Jewish traditions unattested elsewhere, as in Barn. 12.2 Moses stacks shields to stand on in the war against Amalek, as in Exod 17:8–15. After his teaching from the scriptures with their presumption of the recipient's knowledge, the Barnabist introduces the Two Ways with the phrase "But let us turn to another area of knowledge and teaching,"[23] as if to differentiate it somewhat from what he has already written. The Two Ways material he now uses,

5. Did. 9.2; 10.6,

6. Barn. 1.7; 4.1; 5.6; 14.8–9.

7. Barn. 4.7–9; 6.8; 10.1, 11; 12.2; 14.2–4; 15.1.

8. Barn. 4.5.

9. Barn. 6.9.

10. Barn. 6.8; 8.4.

11. Barn. 9.7–8; 13.7.

12. Barn. 7.3.

13. Barn. 11.9; 13.4–5.

14. Barn. 12.8–9.

15. Barn. 12.9.

16. Barn. 12.10–11.

17. Barn. 12.11.

18. Barn. 13.2–3.

19. Barn. 13.4–5.

20. Barn. 13.5.

21. Enoch 4.3.

22. Barn. 4.3: "the Master shortened the seasons and the days, that his beloved may hurry and arrive at his inheritance." (Ehrman, [LCL]) is paralleled most closely by 4QpsEzekiel (4Q386) in which the Lord says, "are not the days hastening on so that the children of Israel can inherit [their land?" Martínez and Tigchelaar, *Dead Sea Scrolls Study Edition*, 769. Paget adequately discusses the textual issues in a note *Barnabas*, 10 n. 38.

23. Barn. 18.

unlike what has gone before, does not presume prior scriptural knowledge. In support of this view, Nancy Pardee observes that there is no assumption in the Didache of a "familiarity with the Scriptures on the part of its audience."[24] The exception is Did. 14.3, where the prophet Malachi is quoted with the introductory formula "For this is the word of the Lord."

It is thus notable that the Two Ways concept is present in various non-Jewish literature to such an extent that the metaphor was all but certainly accessible to gentiles unacquainted with the teachings of the Hebrew scriptures. The juxtaposition of good and evil themselves are a natural contrast and so it is not surprising to see the same theme in ancient non-Jewish sources. Thus in §125.7 of the Theban recension of the Egyptian "Book of the Dead," dated by Wallis Budge as between 1600 and 900 BCE, is what should be said "when the overseer of the house of the overseer of the seal, Nu, triumphant, cometh forth into the Hall of double Maāti so that he may be separated from every sin which he hath done." He is to say "I have come to thee, and I have brought Maāt (*i.e.*, right and truth) to thee, and I have destroyed wickedness for thee."[25] Michael Fox refers to a Ramesside Egyptian tomb autobiography where a tomb owner says his "god instructed him . . . who set him on the way of life"[26] and asserts that the "WAY OF LIFE [*sic*] is important in Egyptian literature of all periods."[27] Here we do not necessarily have two ways, or paths, but the contrast and opposition between right and truth versus wickedness is readily apparent.

The contrast between good and evil, not surprising in itself, is a prerequisite to the metaphor found in the fifth century BCE with Prodicus' account of "The Choice of Heracles," recounted by Xenophon's Socrates. In Xen. *Mem.* 2.1.21–33 the story recounts that when "Heracles was passing from boyhood to young manhood, where the young, now becoming their own masters, show whether they will approach life by the path of virtue or the path of vice, he went out into a quiet place." The story's popularity is shown in the number of ancient authors writing in the first century who recounted it including Philo, Ovid, Lucian and Silius Italicus.[28] Heracles was a model for both the Spartans and the Romans, his myth being "pervasive and fundamental."[29] The story of the choice that he had between two ways was well-known as well. In particular, G. Karl Galinsky states that the "impact

24. Pardee, *Genre and Development*, 27.
25. Budge, *The Book of the Dead*, 360.
26. ÄHG #173, cited by Fox, *Proverbs 1–9*, 114.
27. *Proverbs 1–9*, 130.
28. Sansone, "Heracles at the Y," 125.
29. Granitz, *Heracles and the Founding*, BA, 76.

of Prodicus' parable was immediate and left its mark even on the fourth century, when the vogue which Herakles had enjoyed during the entire fifth century [BCE] . . . did not continue."[30]

Similar paradigms abounded. In the Greek Corpus Hermeticum, the discourse of Hermes Trismegistus with Poimandres chapter 1 is a tale of how Hermes is shown how he might exist as "light and life." In Corp. Herm. 1.1.29 , Hermes describes how those not open to the given teachings are those who have "surrendered themselves to the way of death."[31] While the term way of life is not specifically used, in the context it is the implicit corollary. It is thus that Niederwimmer[32] provides further examples of the "two ways" in ancient literature, and Sandt and Flusser come to the conclusion that the "Two Ways device was widespread in the early Mediterranean world."[33] Margaret McKenna has catalogued parallels in not only Greek literature, but also Iranian, Taoist, Buddhist, and Hindu.[34]

In Hesiod's *Works and Days* 11–14, the writer proclaims "truths to Perses," speaking of two "strifes" (νοήσας), one worthy of praise, the other blameworthy. Later, the theme is expressed differently in 286–92 "To you, Perses, you great fool, I will speak my fine thoughts: Misery is there to be grabbed in abundance, easily, for smooth is the road, and she lives very nearby; but in front of Excellence the immortal gods have set sweat, and the path to her is long and steep, and rough at first—yet when one arrives at the top, then it becomes easy, difficult though it still is."[35]

It is therefore evident, by comparison with Barnabas, written to a slightly later audience, and by a brief survey of literature extant in the first century, that Jewish teachers such as the Didachist could presume upon the comprehensibility of the (Hebrew) Two Ways topos among gentiles who did not have direct knowledge of the Hebrew scriptures from which it was drawn.

The Hebrew Scriptures and the Two Ways

Audet saw the Two Ways motif as having a very early place, linking it with "l'espérance de la bénédiction et la menace du châtiment" of Deut 30:15–20 and finding it analogous with the even earlier "arbre de vie et . . . menace

30. Galinsky, *The Herakles Theme*, 103.

31. Copenhaver, *The Greek Corpus Hermeticum*, 6.

32. Niederwimmer, *The Didache*, 83–84.

33. Sandt and Flusser, *The Didache*, 58.

34. McKenna, *The "Two Ways" in Jewish and Christian Writings*, PhD, 272–73.

35. *Hesiod*, 1, Most (LCL).

de la mort" of Gen 2:9; 3:2–3.[36] In that vein, Philip Schaff, among the earliest commentators on the Didache,[37] also saw a parallel to the Lord's pronouncement "Behold, I set before you the way of life and the way of death" in Jer 21:8, as did Charles Taylor.[38] The parallel is apparent not only in the dualistic contrast of good and evil, but also in the use of ὁδός in both Deut 30:16 (LXX ἐν πάσαις ταῖς ὁδοῖς αὐτοῦ) and Jer 21:8 for the way one chooses. In both cases, either communal or individual existence is determined by the choice made. Willy Rordorf and André Tuilier, in their search for scriptural antecedents to the Two Ways topos also cite Ps 1; Jer 21:8; Prov 2:10–22, 4:18; and Sir 2:12, 33:14.[39]

Further amplification of the Two Ways' biblical antecedents is found in the prophetic literature. Isaiah 30:20–21 connects a Teacher (מורה MT) and the way: "your eyes shall see your Teacher. And your ears shall hear a word behind you, saying, 'This is the way, walk in it.'" Thomas O'Loughlin cites Jer 6:16, which reads "Thus says the Lord: 'Stand by the roads, and look, and ask for the ancient paths, where the good way is; and walk in it, and find rest for your souls.' But they said, 'We will not walk in it'" and affirms that by the time of the Didache "this notion had been in use in Judaism for centuries."[40]

In the wisdom literature, the Two Ways appears metaphorically. In its place of primacy, heading the first of five books of Psalms, Psalm 1 sets the tone for the entire corpus with its contrast of the "way of the righteous" and the "way of the wicked." Thus, a context is created where the mere mention of a right or wrong "way" often evokes the choice between the two. Similarly Prov 2:12–13 instructs the reader that wisdom will deliver you "from the way of evil" and from those who "walk in the ways of darkness." The concept is not developed—as a well-known metaphor it was used to construct an aphorism that did not require explanation. Niederwimmer, one not given to speculation, presents various occurrences of the Two Ways in the wisdom literature (notably Pss 1; 139:24; Prov 2:13) and suggests that the Two Ways topos "may also lie behind expressions such as those in Deut 11:26–28; 30:15–20; and Jer 21:8."[41]

This comment of Niederwimmer highlights a point of contention among scholars as to definitions and which passages are actually occurrences

36. Audet, *La Didachè*, 256.

37. Schaff, *The Oldest Church Manual*, 18.

38. Taylor, *The Teaching*, 7.

39. Rordorf and Tuilier, *La Doctrine Des Douze Apôtres*, 26 n. 1.

40. O'Loughlin, *The Didache: A Window*, 29.

41. Niederwimmer, *The Didache*, 60.

of the Two Ways topos. A number of scholars have taken a cautious view in defining the "Two Ways" topos in relation to the Hebrew scriptures. This is helpful in that careful delineation helps to define exactly what the Two Ways topos is; to precisely locate its antecedents in the Hebrew scriptures; and to avoid potential confusion with other topoi. Jack Suggs championed this approach with the appropriate caveat that "the temptation is always present to read Two Ways ideology into every use of the two ways metaphor."[42] Suggs' criteria were: a) a sharply dualistic introduction; b) lists of virtues and vices; and c) an eschatological conclusion.[43] However, while helpful, over-dependence upon such restrictive parameters results in the minimization of a significant topos in the Hebrew Bible.

In contrast, Huub van de Sandt and David Flusser differentiated between the topos of the Two Ways and its form in their extensive study of the topos. They thus posited that while the "topos of the Two Ways occurs frequently in such passages as Deut 11:26–28; 30:15–19; Jer 21:8; Pss 1:1–6; 119 (118):29–30; 139 (138):24; Prov 2:13; 4:18–19; 11:20; 12:28 (LXX), and so forth . . . they do not evidence a Two Ways tradition in that they contain separate lists of virtues and vices, such as is found in the present Two Ways form of the Didache."[44] This more nuanced approach, allowing for variation, is also followed by Margaret McKenna, who makes "the explicit employment of the phrase 'Two Ways' in a textual unit, the criterion for selecting texts for initial analysis."[45] It is on the basis of McKenna's further delineation of the typical Two Ways structure[46] that Darian Lockett determines the same motif to be present in James, demonstrating its pervasiveness in the early Jesus Movement.[47]

Within a less restrictive definition of the Two Ways topos, or tradition, evidence can be presented showing that it is a device specifically linked to Torah observance. Whether it is the two ways metaphor, or the covenant context that has overshadowed it, this has not been adequately addressed in the context of Didache studies, but can be seen in various examples from the Hebrew Bible as follows.

In Deut 30:15, Moses spoke to Israel saying "See, I have set before you today life and good, death and evil, which I command you today to love the Lord your God, to walk in his ways, and to keep his commandments

42. Suggs, *The Christian Two Ways*, 63.

43. Suggs, *The Christian Two Ways*, 64.

44. Sandt and Flusser, *The Didache*, 58–59.

45. McKenna, "The "Two Ways" in Jewish and Christian Writings," 32.

46. McKenna, "The "Two Ways" in Jewish and Christian Writings," 257.

47. Lockett, "Structure or Communicative Strategy?" 285.

and his statutes and his judgements" (lit.).[48] In this archetypical passage, Moses presents the choice, but then commands Israel which way to go. The way they are to go is a path (דרך), and that path is characterized by the LORD's commandments, statutes, and judgements (מצוה, חקה, משפט). Moses, as Israel's leader and teacher of the Torah offers a choice but exhorts that the right choice be taken. Furthermore, it is the Torah, not the choice between ways, that Moses mandates to be read before Israel every seven years.[49] The reader is left in little doubt that obedience to the precepts of the Torah is the way of life.

In Jer 21:8, the prophet uses the same imagery of the way of life and the way of death as he declares "Thus says the LORD: behold I set before you the way of life and the way of death."[50] The reference to the Torah is implicit, although he does not refer to its commands. Rather, the "way of life" is to accept Jeremiah's special revelation from the Lord and surrender to the Chaldeans in order to survive. As William Holladay comments, it is "a grotesque adaptation."[51] Here the way to life is not obedience to commandments, statutes, and judgements, but obedience to the prophet's voice.

Just as the prophet uses irony to offer the surrenderer's life as a form of booty,[52] so his reference to the way of life is ironic, for it is his message that Judah has not walked in the way of life at all and the time for repentance is over. This is in the context of the book's previous references to the two ways. In Jer 7:23–24, Jeremiah reminded his hearers of the Lord's command to walk in the Way of Life, with an explicit connection between the topos and the Torah. The text holds the implicit expectation that Jeremiah expected his hearers to know of Moses' ultimatum and understand the metaphor, as he spoke for the Lord and warned his hearers to "walk in all the way that I command you, that it may be well with you. . . . Yet they did not listen to me or incline their ear, but stiffened their neck." The promise for compliance is reiterated, two ways are spoken of, and the Lord's commands are invoked in this prophecy. In 18:11, Jeremiah again exhorted his hearers to turn each one from his "evil way" and "walk rightly in your ways

48. רְאֵה נָתַתִּי לְפָנֶיךָ הַיּוֹם אֶת־הַחַיִּים וְאֶת־הַטּוֹב וְאֶת־הַמָּוֶת וְאֶת־הָרָע אֲשֶׁר אָנֹכִי מְצַוְּךָ הַיּוֹם לְאַהֲבָה אֶת־יְהוָה אֱלֹהֶיךָ לָלֶכֶת בִּדְרָכָיו וְלִשְׁמֹר מִצְוֹתָיו וְחֻקֹּתָיו וּמִשְׁפָּטָיו . . . .

(My translation follows the LXX, which translates אֲשֶׁר as ἅς).

49. Deut. 31:9–13.

50. כֹּה אָמַר יְהוָה הִנְנִי נֹתֵן לִפְנֵיכֶם אֶת־דֶּרֶךְ הַחַיִּים וְאֶת־דֶּרֶךְ הַמָּוֶת

51. Holladay, *A Commentary on Jeremiah*, 1, 573.

52. Carroll, *Jeremiah: A Commentary*, 411; Holladay, *A Commentary on Jeremiah*, 1, 574.

and your deeds" and with their refusal to do so, the prophet stated that the Lord was resolved to punish them.[53]

The clear reference to the topos in 21:8 is therefore in the context of Jeremiah's previous appeals to it and its role as a criterion for blessing or punishment. In Jer 21:8, the prophet is therefore presuming his audience's familiarity with the way of life topos, and affirming the fulfilment of its negative provisions in his day. The topos as a whole is not expounded, but it is essential to his audience's ability to comprehend the full import of his remarks.

In the wisdom literature, the two ways topos remains intrinsically linked to its Torah identity and the commands, statutes, and judgements thereof. As previously mentioned, Psalm 1 stands in pride of place, and contrasts the way of sinners with the way of the righteous. The key characteristic of the righteous is that "his delight is in the law [תורה] of the LORD, and in his law [תורה] he meditates day and night."[54] The opening verse of Ps 119, a form of *magnum opus* in the collection, begins with the proposition "Blessed are those whose way is blameless, who walk in the law [תורה] of the LORD." This Torah is described using the very same three terms as in Deut 30:15. Psalm 119:4 refers to the Lord's statutes (חקה), 119:5 to his commandments (מצוה) and 119:6 to his judgements (משפט). Psalm 119:29–30 contrasts the way of "falsehood" (דֶּרֶךְ שֶׁקֶר) with the way of "truth" (דֶּרֶךְ־אֱמוּנָה), concluding that he has chosen the way of faithfulness, using the same verb (בחר) as in Deut 30:19's "choose life that you . . . may live." Finally, it must be noted that the metaphor of a way of life and death does appear in the book of Proverbs, but it remains merely that. There is no sustained argument, but as Fox writes "Any behavior that leads to life is a WAY OF LIFE [*sic*], and conversely for those that go to death."[55]

In summary, it can be seen that key two ways texts in the Hebrew Bible either explicitly or implicitly connect the two ways to its initial proclamation and the requirement to keep the Torah. The topos is a compelling metaphor that does not need to be explained in full in every instance.

Second Temple Judaism and the Two Ways

This intrinsic connection between the Two Ways and Torah is further evident in the Second Temple period, as the Two Ways topos remained in use. From the time the remarkable manuscript of the Didache found in H was published by Bryennios in 1883, scholars have suspected an underlying Jewish *Vorlage*

53. Jer 19:15.

54. Ps 1:2.

55. Fox, *Proverbs 1–9*, 130.

to the Two Ways in the Didache. Taylor wrote in his 1885 lectures that "We are thus led to postulate the existence of an earlier form of manual of the Two Ways, of Jewish character and possibly pre-Christian in date."[56] More modestly, Rendel Harris reckoned that any discussion of its origins would "have to take account of Hebraisms in style and in thought which colour the book almost from beginning to end" and suggested its title could be rendered תלמוד השליכים.[57] George Salmon believed that "the real original had been a purely Jewish document" on the basis of "the almost complete absence of Christian references in all that we can certainly ascribe to the earliest form of the document."[58] Adolph von Harnack basically concurred with this proposition, noting a minimum of twenty-three allusions and "längeren oder kürzeren Zitaten" from the Evangelist's source material.[59] Proceeding to compare Barnabas to the Didache, and noting a common, early source, Harnack concluded that it was obvious that the Two Ways were a Jewish product "auf dem Dekalog und einer Verfeinerung seiner Gebote beruhend."[60] The following paragraphs demonstrate from occurrences of the metaphor and more specifically the topos that the connection to their Jewish origin in the Torah was maintained in Second Temple Judaism, in particular the emphasis on the Way of Life as keeping the commandments.

As has been seen in chapter 1, suspicions regarding the Jewish source of the Two Ways material were substantiated by Audet, who was the first to take advantage of the then-recent Dead Sea Scrolls discoveries and compare the Two Ways of the *Doctrina apostolorum* to the *Serek Hayaḥad* 3.13—4.26. In the course of this investigation he observed that "les deux textes ont un cadre littéraire étroitement apparenté, et donc aussi, une ligne générale de développement presque identique."[61] Despite the difference in metaphor (light/darkness in the *Serek* versus life/death in the Didache) the parallels were undeniable and sharp enough that a fundamental reassessment of the Didache occurred. Audet's discovery ensured that the Two Ways could no longer be viewed as simply a Christian invention as some had done despite the arguments of Harnack and others. Rather it was an "image très simple, classique en Israël."[62] As Audet argued, the *Serek* and the Didache's Two Ways follow similar lines of development.

56. Taylor, *The Teaching*, 22.

57. Harris, *The Teaching of the Apostles: Newly Edited*, 78.

58. Salmon, *A Historical Introduction*, 563.

59. Harnack, *Die Apostellehre*, 9–10.

60. Harnack, *Die Apostellehre*, 14.

61. Audet, "Affinités littéraire et doctrinales," 232.

62. Audet, "Affinités littéraire et doctrinales," 255.

The undeniable relationship yet the verbal dissimilarity suggest either an underlying common tradition, or that the Didachist relied upon the *Serek*, adapting its form to suit its own purposes. It is thus that Niederwimmer's view becomes representative of the modern consensus. As he put it: "In the beginning was a Jewish 'primitive form.'"[63]

Audet's comparison of the Didache's Two Ways was with "la deuxième section du *Manuel*" *Serek* 3.13—4.26. No doubt purposefully due to the scope of his research, Audet did not take note of the substantial connections between the *Serek* as a whole and the Two Ways of the Didache, but these connections point to a literary relationship between them. The language of the *Serek* is that of light versus darkness:[64] Light is associated with truth, and darkness with deceit.[65] There are paths of light[66] and paths of darkness.[67] This is borne out by use of the same metaphor in 1Q Genesis Apocryphon (=1QapGen ar) 6.2–3 in which Noah states "all my life I behaved in truth, and walked in the paths of eternal verity" versus "the path of falsehood which lead (sic) to darkness."[68]

Both the *Serek* and the Didache function as community rules. Just as the *Serek* says "This is the rule for the men of the Community who freely volunteer to convert from all evil and to keep themselves steadfast in all he commanded in compliance with his will,"[69] so the Didache presumes a voluntary conversion to the Way of Life. Just as the *Serek* turns from matters of the Law and commitment to it to "the Rule for the session of the Many"[70] and matters of community order, so the Didache turns from its rules and counsel regarding the Way of Life to matters of community administration—baptism, meals, and hospitality. Just as the *Serek* subsequently instructs regarding the appointment of leaders,[71] so does the Didache in 15:1. The *Serek* fits the pattern suggested by Niederwimmer in saying that the Two Ways of the Didache "probably belonged within the broader context of the community rules of Jewish religious communities."[72]

63. Niederwimmer, *The Didache*, 40.

64. *Serek* 1.9; 3.3, 13; 3.25.

65. *Serek* 3.19.

66. *Serek* 3.20

67. *Serek* 4.11.

68. Martinez and Tigchelaar, *Dead Sea Scrolls Study Edition*, 31.

69. *Serek* 5.1.

70. *Serek* 6.8.

71. *Serek* 8.1.

72. Niederwimmer, *Die Didache*, 37.

The *Serek* sets the context for its Two Ways teaching early on, self-consciously instructing its teachers in *Serek* 1.1–3 "to do what is good and just in his presence, as he commanded by the hand of Moses and by the hand of all his servants the Prophets."[73] In this, its stress on the importance of Torah is established, although it is not only the Torah of Moses, but the prophets as well which are in view. However, this stress of the *Serek* on Torah is reiterated shortly thereafter without reference to the prophets in 1.11–13. There the metaphor is presented in terms of a "path" or "way," with the *Serek* requiring that all "those who submit freely to his truth will . . . refine their knowledge in the truth of God's decrees [חוקי] and marshal their energies in accordance with his perfect paths [דרכיו]."[74] Again, just before the Two Ways of the *Serek* is introduced, it commands in 3.9–11 that the inductee "steady his steps in order to walk with perfection on all the paths [דרכי] of God, as he has decreed concerning the appointed times of his assemblies and not turn aside, either right or left, nor infringe even one of all his words."[75]

The *Serek*'s presentation of its Two Ways material is supported by its ongoing emphasis on keeping the Torah in its ensuing instructions which speak about the conditions upon which one must enter the community. Whereas the Didache conditions baptism upon the acceptance of "all the preceding having been said,"[76] the *Serek* declares in 5.7–9: "Whoever enters the council of the Community enters the covenant of God in the presence of all who freely volunteer. He shall swear with a binding oath to revert to the Law of Moses according to all that he commanded, with whole heart and whole soul."[77] These statements of the *Serek* underscore that its Two Ways material is in the context of a mandate that the Law of Moses be observed wholeheartedly. The Two Ways topos is thus a integral part of a document making this point.

A second text in the Dead Sea Scrolls also bears upon the Two Ways of the Didache. 4QThe Two Ways (=4Q473) is referred to by Jörg Frey as a "fragmentary sapiential document" that attests to the "idea" of the Two Ways.[78] This puts it in the wider context of dualistic thought, but does not divorce it from its roots in the Torah. It has been reconstructed to read in part "[. . .] while he gives [. . .] [two] ways, one good [and one evil. If you walk on the good way . . .] and he will bless you; but if you walk

73. Martinez and Tigchelaar, *Dead Sea Scrolls Study Edition*, 71.

74. Martinez and Tigchelaar, *Dead Sea Scrolls Study Edition*, 71.

75. Martinez and Tigchelaar, *Dead Sea Scrolls Study Edition*, 75.

76. Did. 7.1.

77. Martinez and Tigchelaar, *Dead Sea Scrolls Study Edition*, 81.

78. Frey, *Flesh and Spirit*, 401.

on [the evil] way [. . .] he will br[ing up]on you, and he will destroy you [. . .]."[79] While the document stands alone, and its context is unknown, its particular emphasis on the consequences of the two ways, namely blessedness versus cursedness, echoes the topos' deuteronomistic origin and is comparable to the Didache in that respect.

Michael Wise connects 4QThe Two Ways directly to the Didache, finding it "immediately reminiscent of our scroll."[80] Whereas the *Serek* contrasts light and darkness and the Didache contrasts life and death, 4QThe Two Ways simply contrasts a way which is "good" and a way which Martínez and Tigchelaar reconstruct as "evil." This accords well with Audet's early assertion that the Two Ways is an "image très simple, classique en Israël" as noted above.[81] It brings out the important point that what is significant is not the imagery of light, life, or goodness versus darkness, death, or evil, but that there are two ways. The Two Ways material of the Didache contrasts life and death.[82] While the terminology is not identical to that of other documents, comparable texts show that the same parallel is intended.

Testament of Asher 1.3 paints the whole metaphor, if not the topos, in broad terms saying "God has granted two ways to the sons of men, two mindsets, two lines of action, two models, and two goals. Accordingly, everything is in pairs, the one over against the other."[83] This model of righteousness is put in the context of Torah, as T. Ash. 6.1 states "give attention to the Lord's command, pursuing truth with singleness of mind."[84] Here the "Lord's command" is τὰς ἐντολὰς Κυρίου, similar to the admonition of Did. 4.13 "Do not forsake the commands of the Lord." While the "recovery of a Jewish original" to this Testament is "highly problematic,"[85] even M. de Jonge, who views the Testaments as of "Christian origin," acknowledges that "tradition material used in the Testaments had also been transmitted earlier in Jewish circles."[86] In addition, while it is a less developed exemplar, 1 En. 91.19 gives the advice "Now listen to me, my children, and walk in the way of righteousness, and do not walk in the way of wickedness, for all those who walk in the ways of injustice shall perish.[87] Thus, in these examples, there is a degree of likeli-

79. Martinez and Tigchelaar, *Dead Sea Scrolls Study Edition*, 955.

80. Wise, Abegg, and Cook, *The Dead Sea Scrolls*, 516.

81. Audet, "Affinités littéraire et doctrinales," 255.

82. Did. 1.1.

83. Charlesworth, *The Old Testament Pseudepigrapha*, 1.819.

84. Charlesworth, *The Old Testament Pseudepigrapha*, 1.819.

85. DeSilva, "The *Testaments of the Twelve Patriarchs* as Witnesses," 64.

86. Jonge, "The Transmission of the Testaments," 12, 15.

87. Charlesworth, *The Old Testament Pseudepigrapha*, 1.73.

hood that here too is an example of the Two Ways topos being presented in conjunction with reference to the Torah.

A further comparable is found in Barnabas, which while a later Christian text cannot be entirely separated from the context of Second Temple Judaism, the "parting of the ways" not yet being a *fait accompli*. Barnabas uses various terms for each of the Two Ways. Thus what the Didache terms the Way of Life, and at the beginning of Barnabas' Two Ways section is the way of "light"[88] is also termed the way of "righteousness"[89] or of the "righteous."[90] Likewise, what the Didache terms the Way of Death is the way of "darkness" at the beginning of Barnabas' Two Ways section,[91] as well as the "evil" way,[92] the "way of the ungodly,"[93] the way of death,[94] and the way of the black one and eternal death.[95] Most startling is that after Barnabas' formal introduction of the Two Ways material in Barn. 18.1, just a few lines later in 18.2 it correlates the way of darkness to the 'ὁδῷ θανάτου, the very term used by the Didache.

This combination of various images was not novel and can be seen in other earlier Jewish texts as well. Thus, Sir 15:11 reads "Do not say, 'Because of the Lord I left the right way'" and continues in 15:16–17 "He has placed before you fire and water, stretch out your hand for whichever you wish. Before a man are life and death, and whichever he chooses will be given to him" (RSV). The language of fire versus water, and life and death, both serve as descriptors for the reference to the Torah as is evident in the verse preceding,[96] which states, "If you will, you can keep the commandments [ἐντολὰς], and to act faithfully is a matter of your own choice." In this case the Two Ways reference describes the choice to keep the commandments.

The Targumim provide yet further insight into the teaching of the Two Ways as it endured past Second Temple Judaism. Targum Neophiti, commonly dated to the late second century, interprets the way of life as "*the instruction of the law of* the Lord *your* God [sic]" in Deut 30:20. The much later Targum Jonathan likewise clarifies the command to choose the way

88. Barn. 18.1
89. Barn. 1.4, 5.4.
90. Barn. 11.7, quoting Ps 1:6.
91. Barn. 18.1.
92. Barn. 4.10.
93. Barn. 11.7, quoting Ps 1:6.
94. Barn. 19.2
95. Barn. 20.1.
96. Sir 15:15.

of life in Deut 30:19: "Choose then the way of life, *which is the law*."[97] This connection between the Way of Life and Torah will be addressed in detail later. In the famous Talmudic account of b. *Ber.* 28b also, R. Yochanan on his deathbed says to his disciples אלא שיש לפני שני דרכים, אחת של גן עדן ואחת של גיהנם, ואיני יודע באיזו מוליכים אותי (there are two ways before me, one of the Garden of Eden and the other leading to Gehinnom, and I do not know which way I shall be brought). This does not necessarily point specifically to the Two Ways as in the Didache—those of lawfulness and lawlessness—but does suggest his doubt as to whether he had properly kept to the Way of Life. Further, it corresponds with the Didache's assertion that the end of each path is either life or death. We would concur with Sebastian Brock who compares this saying to Targum *Neofiti* to ascertain that R. Yochanan is alluding to the Two Ways of Deut 30:15.[98]

In summary, a number of significant documents from the age of Second Temple Judaism substantiate the claim that the Two Ways topos had a specific conceptual place in terms of the observance of commands of the Lord given in the Torah. This has been seen in the Serek, 4QThe Two Ways, and other contemporary witnesses. In addition, some later Jewish Texts have been adduced to show that the metaphor continued to be used in Jewish literature and maintained its connection to Torah observance.

Conclusion

A brief survey of literature extant in the first century has demonstrated that regardless of their knowledge of the Hebrew scriptures, on the basis of pervasive "two choice" mythology in the ancient world, the Didache could presume that its gentile recipients would understand the topos and build upon that. In a general sense, the Two Ways topos of the Hebrew scriptures bore a resemblance to this ancient mythology, yet not merely in an ethical or philosophical sense, but also in implicit and explicit connections to the initial proclamation of the Two Ways in Deut 30 and its requirement to keep the Torah. This connection between the Two Ways topos and the

97. Sebastian Brock has demonstrated that the reason the Targumim have not been highlighted earlier in studies of the Two Ways is due to two factors: the lack of attention to the Targums by Hermann Strack and Paul Billerbeck in their *Kommentar zum Neuen Testament aus Talmud und Midrasch*; and the fact that "By the time that the Deuteronomy volume of the dramatic new Palestinian Targum witness in MS Neofiti 1 came to be published (1978), the standard modern critical editions and commentaries for the *Didache* and *Barnabas* had already appeared (1978 and 1971 respectively)." Brock, *The Two Ways and the Palestinian Targum*, 146.

98. Brock, *The Two Ways and the Palestinian Targum*, 144.

Torah is borne out in the Second Temple period with numerous indications in the extant literature that the Way of Life was identified with Torah observance. We have thus established the relationship between the Two Ways metaphor and its implicit connection to the Torah.

5

An Authoritative Torah and Teacher

Introduction

THE PREVIOUS CHAPTER HAS established that within Second Temple Judaism the Two Ways topos, and to some degree the metaphor itself, were directly associated with the Torah. This chapter builds on that observation to demonstrate that in Second Temple Judaism, both Christian Judaism and the Didache were heirs to the tradition that imparted the authority inherent in the Torah to its interpreters. As a Christian Jewish document, the Didache both assumes this authority for itself and endows it upon its teachers. The authority of the Didache's teachings is both corroborated and augmented by the authority of the Lord Jesus himself. Consequentially, this chapter will argue that the Didache viewed its Two Ways teaching as Torah within the framework of Jesus' authority.

The relationship between the Didache's teachings and its assumption of authority has been touched on by various scholars. Edwin Broadhead in his *Jewish Ways of Following Jesus* suggested that the Didachist drew on "two streams of authority: the Old Testament (1.6; 14.3; 16.7) and the gospel of the Lord (8.2; 11.3; 15.3; 15.4)."[1] He therefore proposed that the authority the Didachist ascribed to his teaching is not simply found in the earlier material of the Didache, but is borne out in the later material as well. While Broadhead does not belabor the point nor expand upon it, the point is substantiated by the markers affirming authority found in text of the Didache's Two Ways.

In the context of discussion regarding the authority presumed by the Didachist throughout the Teaching, Clayton Jefford builds on William Varner's observations,[2] which incorporate the elements of the "essential

1. Broadhead, *Jewish Ways of Following Jesus*, 132.
2. See Varner, "The Didache's Use of the Old and New Testaments."

nature" of the Didache as "evolved literature," and insights from canonical criticism.[3] Jefford's study proceeds to assert that a "similar tradition of interpretation" between the Didachist and a secondary editor (designated as Did2) postulates a "single trajectory of vision, but with a clear evolution of perspectives and development of literary authority."[4] It is thus that various scholars have observed that the assertion of authority by the Didache is particularly evident in the earlier material of Did. 1–6, subsequently being borne out in the later material of Did. 7–16.

The purpose of this chapter is to proceed from this observation and argue that the Torah's authority forms the basis for the Didache's presumption of authority to present its teaching as Torah as it pertains to gentiles. This authority was employed by the teachers and interpreters of the Torah, and the Didache in particular employs this authority not only as a valid record of the teaching of the apostles, but the Lord Jesus himself.

Torah Teachers and Their Authority

Those who taught the Torah were granted significant interpretive authority in Second Temple Judaism, including Christian Judaism. This is evident throughout the Didache, a product of Christian Judaism at the end of the Second Temple era.

Second Temple Judaism and Its Teachers

The Dead Sea Scrolls, with their strong emphasis on the Torah are particularly helpful. As Wise, Abegg, and Cook propose,[5] somewhat along the lines of Norman Golb's challenge to the prevalent hypothesis that they are primarily the library of the Dead Sea Essenes,[6] they do not simply represent one homogeneous community. If these authors are correct, as I believe they are, the DSS are particularly relevant to our enquiry as they therefore represent a variety of streams of Jewish thought, with some ideological commonalities. All the more so as the DSS share "certain broad views" with the New Testament, one of which is "a pervasive dualism expressed as Light versus Darkness."[7] This affinity, not only to the New Testament, but also to the Didache, suggests

3. Jefford, *Authority and Perspective*, 35–36.
4. Jefford, *Authority and Perspective*, 58.
5. Wise, Abegg, and Cook, *The Dead Sea Scrolls*, 27–35.
6. Golb, *Who Wrote the Dead Sea Scrolls?*
7. Wise, Abegg, and Cook, *The Dead Sea Scrolls*, 35.

that the views found in the Dead Sea Scrolls regarding teachers are worthy of more than just a passing glance.

Various terms are used for teachers in the Dead Sea Scrolls, indicating that not all teachers had the same status or function. The preeminent teacher in the DSS record is the Teacher of Righteousness, "to whom God made known all the mysteries of the words of his servants, the prophet," as seen in Pesher Habakkuk (1QpHab.) 7.4–5.[8] This Teacher is introduced in 1QpHab. 1.4bc, where the evildoer, or Wicked Priest, is apposed to "the righteous" man. In commenting, 1QpHab. 1.4c picks up the third person singular of צדק (righteous), amplifies the contrast, and identifies the prophet's "righteous" as the community's very own Teacher of Righteousness. Thereafter, 1QpHab. 2.2f claims that the words of the Teacher of Righteousness are from the "mouth of God." In contrast, the Wicked Priest is once again identified in 1QpHab. 9.9 and 11.4–8 as the one standing in direct opposition to the Teacher of Righteousness, where he is described as the one "who pursued the Teacher of Righteousness to consume him with the heat of his anger in the place of his banishment."[9]

While the identities of these two apparently historical figures are not known, it is clear that due to the Teacher of Righteousness' roles as priest and teacher, he is a person of some influence. In terms of his followers, throughout 1QpHab., whomever the righteous (plural) may be, they are those who are faithful to the Torah[10] and who are loyal to the Teacher of Righteousness.[11] Contrastingly, 1QpHab. leaves no doubt that the wickedness of the Priest is his lawlessness[12] and betrayal and persecution of the Teacher of Righteousness.[13] A triad comprising righteousness, Torah, and the Teacher of Righteousness stands in opposition to the triad of wickedness, lawlessness, and the Wicked Priest. In this way, loyalty to the Teacher is directly associated with loyalty to the teachings of the Torah presented by him.

The same need for attentiveness to the Teacher is propounded by various hymns of the Hodayot in which, possibly drawing upon and intensifying the admonition of 4QInstruction, the Teacher is somewhat more prominent. In 1QH[a] 12.24, the Teacher declares וישומעוני ההולכים בדרך לבכה ויערוכו לכה ("Those who walk on the path of your heart have listened to me") as the writer passionately expresses himself in the first person.

8. Wise, Abegg, and Cook, *Dead Sea Scrolls Study Edition*, 17.

9. Wise, Abegg, and Cook, *Dead Sea Scrolls Study Edition*, 19.

10. 1QpHab. 5.5; 7.11; 8.1; 12.4–5.

11. 1QpHab. 2.2; 8.2.

12. 1QpHab. 8.8–10.

13. 1QpHab. 8.8–9; 9.9–10; 11.4–5.

Magnifying his importance, in 4Q427 (=4QH[a]) 7.8 he expansively boasts [. . . דעת הכינ[ו]תה מתכמי וכבד[תני ("you have established knowledge in my vitals and [you] have glori[fied me . . .]"). In these examples from the Hodayot, to reject the Teacher's instruction is to refuse to walk in the "path" of God's "heart" and to turn away from the one he has "glorified." The very transmission and retention of these sayings demonstrates the community's acceptance of them. Their Teacher thereby occupied a place of honor and authority in the community.

Not only the Teacher of Righteousness, but also other teachers were to be carefully heeded by virtue of their relationship to the Torah, as other terms for teachers in the Scrolls demonstrate. However, the relationship between the Teacher of Righteousness and other teachers is not always clear. For example, 4QPsalms Pesher[a] (=4Q171) 1.25–27 warns that failure to listen to the מליץ דעת (Interpreter of Knowledge) resulted in many being misdirected by deceptive words uttered by the איש הכזב (Man of Lies). Contextual considerations suggest that this Interpreter is the same as the Teacher, but the connection is not explicit.

In one response to the multiplicity of terms for teachers in the Scrolls, Steven Fraade suggested a differentiation between the commonly recognized Teacher of Righteousness and the איש דורש בתורה (man who studies the Torah) of *Serek* 6.6 and 8.11–12.[14] This secondary figure, who arguably interprets the teaching of the Teacher of Righteousness, was (according to CD 13.6.2) a priest learned in the Torah whom the community was charged to obey. Following up on Fraade, Charlotte Hempel further distinguished between the activities of practicing and leading in interpretation.[15] Focusing particularly on CD as found in Caves 1 and 4, she surveyed key texts that led her to the conclusion that they restrict "access to the interpretation of the law by referring to individuals and groups with privileged access and special revelations."[16] It follows that not only the Teacher of Righteousness, but also other teachers wielded a measure of authority in the community.

Other teachers are referenced in the DSS corpus. 1Q Words of Moses (=1Q22) advises its readers 2.7–9 "When I [have finish]ed to [. . .] the covenant and to decree the pa[th] on [whi]ch you must] (sic) walk, [choose for yourselves wise men who will] have the task to explain [to you and to] your [sons] all these words of the L[aw.]."[17] In 4QInstruction (=4Q415–18), an instruction in righteousness in a sapiential form, an illuminating reference

14. Fraade, "Interpretative Authority," 62.

15. Hempel, "Interpretative Authority," 61–62.

16. Hempel, "Interpretative Authority," 79.

17. Martinez and Tigchelaar, *Dead Sea Scrolls Study Edition*, 61.

to teachers arises. 4Q418, 81.17 contains the reminder ומיד כול משכילכה הוסף לקח [. . .] ("And from all your teachers get more understanding [. . .]"). For the reader, this is an aspect of the faithful life that will result in an "abundance of good things."[18] Here the teacher is a Maskil (משכיל), presumably not a member of the priesthood which supplied the pre-eminent leaders of the Qumran communities. This teacher is not necessarily a leader, but his teachings are to be heeded in order to gain understanding.

It was the Maskil in *Serek* 9.12–19 who stipulated that the Instructor should "lead them with knowledge and in this way teach them the mysteries of wonder and of truth in the midst of the men of the Community, so that they walk perfectly (תמים) . . . ."[19] Thus in executing the task of transmitting knowledge to the community, the teacher had a powerful influence over the practical conduct of his pupils. The Maskil also features prominently in 4QShirShabb (=4Q400–407), which contains further references to an instructor, or teacher, who occupies a key role in the worshipping life of the community. Within these Sabbath songs, 4Q400, 4Q401, 4Q403.30, and 4Q405.18 are all addressed למשכיל ("to the Maskil"). The attribution is also the probable incipit of the *Serek*. Similar to the Didache, it is a "For [the Instructor . . .] . . . for his life, [book of the Ru]le of the Community: in order to seek God with [all (one's) heart and] with a[ll (one's) soul]."[20] In a teaching comparable to the Didache and the Two Ways, the *Serek* juxtaposes light with darkness (1.9–10 cp. Did. 16.1–3), and the teacher's significance is seen in *Serek* 3.13, as the one "who is to enlighten and teach all the Sons of Light about the character and fate of humankind."[21]

This reverence for teachers endured past the Second Temple period. In this period, particularly after the Jewish Wars, sayings exalting teachers and ultimately the rabbinate multiplied. In part, the rabbinic claim to authority was in connection with the transmission of the Torah. In this regard m. Pirke 'Avot begins with the *Mishnah* "Moses received the Law from Sinai and handed it down to Joshua, and Joshua to the elders, and the elders to the prophets, and the prophets committed it to the men of the Great Assembly."[22]

18. Martinez and Tigchelaar, *Dead Sea Scrolls Study Edition*, 872–73.

19. Martinez and Tigchelaar, *Dead Sea Scrolls Study Edition*, 92–93.

20. Martinez and Tigchelaar, *Dead Sea Scrolls Study Edition*, 71. Vermes translates the incipit as "[the Master shall teach the sai]nts to live(?) [[according to the Book]] (4Q255, 257) of the Community [Rul]e, that they may seek God with a whole heart and soul . . ." *The Complete Dead Sea Scrolls*, 98. Here is the same introduction of the teacher and the invocation of the Shema (Deut 6:4) found in the Didache's incipit and Did. 1.2.

21. Draper provides a helpful survey of such texts in the Qumran literature in his commentary on Did. 4.1 "A Commentary on the Didache," 83–86.

22. Blackman, *Mishnah*, 4.489.

On the basis that the Men of the Great Assembly were entrusted with the Law from Sinai, it is entirely appropriate that the student should respect the interpretive authority of the person through whom that Law is passed on. In this regard, m. 'Abot 4.12 attributes the following saying to R. Akiba's disciple R. Elazar ben Shammua, "Let . . . the reverence for your master be like the fear (כבוד) of Heaven."[23]

The proximity of Christian Judaism to its Jewish world of thought is possibly preserved in an acknowledgement of the Oral Law is preserved in Ps.-Clem. 3.47, where Peter is said to argue that Moses did not write down the Law, but others did out of ignorance.[24] The reverence for teachers, those who orally transmit their teachings, is likewise preserved in the Didache's command to honor one's teacher "as the Lord," as will be discussed below. Here it is enough to see the connection between the authority of the Torah and its teachers.

In summary, the DSS record has provided a broad picture of Torah teachers in the Second Temple period. Theirs was not specifically a role of authority over individuals or the community, but their teaching was authoritative and the basis of individual and community life. Such authority was commensurate with the fact that their teachings had practical ramifications for day-to-day life. To disregard their teachings was a grave error, and as will be seen this is reflective of the role of the teacher in the Didache.

Christian Judaism and Its Teachers

The role and authority of teachers within Christian Judaism is evident in the New Testament and certain apostolic texts. To the extent that the New Testament reflects contemporary Jewish religious expectations (and this varies with the document in question), readings of the Gospel accounts of Matthew and John both testify to the role of teachers and religious authorities.

It is Matthew that provides the first record of religious teachers in relation to their role in interpretation and application of Torah within their sphere of influence. In the words of Jesus to his disciples in Matt 23:2–4, ("The scribes and the Pharisees sit on Moses' seat, so do and observe whatever they tell you, but not the works they do. For they preach, but do not practice. They tie up heavy burdens, hard to bear, and lay them on people's shoulders, but they themselves are not willing to move them with their finger") Matthew laid bare the willingness in his milieu to criticize the Torah observance of the Pharisees as a class. The passage holds interest, for it does

23. Blackman, *Mishnah*, 4.520.

24. *ANF*, 8.247.

not represent a bald denigration of all scribes and Pharisees, but is consistent with Matthew's multifaceted characterization of them.

Matthew's account, which includes criticism of the scribes and Pharisees, also includes scribes among Jesus' disciples,[25] suggesting that this was not intended as a blanket condemnation. In particular, several of the disputes that Matthew records between the Pharisees and Jesus have a decidedly *intra muros* aspect.[26] Thus, while writers such as Ulrich Luz might decry Matthew's "wholesale judgments about scribes and Pharisees,"[27] Matthew's characterization only serves to heighten the sense of internecine discord between parties that have much in common. This *intra muros* aspect has been argued on the basis of an exegetical analysis of Matt 23:2–3. W. D. Davies and Dale Allison, for example, see both Matt 6 and 23 as having "originated in the same Jewish-Christian community, one with close ties to the synagogue."[28] Much of the discussion surrounds Jesus' declaration that the scribes and Pharisees sit on "Moses seat" and Jesus' followers are presumably to respect their resultant authority. This *intra muros* aspect is corroborated by Kenneth Newport's detailed source critical analysis of Matthew 23.[29] The point was not that the yoke of the Torah was "an intolerable burden" as Newport explains, noting that while it was not the easy option it was nevertheless one that may would willingly take, but the criticism of those who "neglect fully the observance of the Torah which they themselves preach."[30] In fact, as Newport writes earlier and in line with the argument we are making, "These Jewish leaders are accepted as authoritative teachers who should be obeyed."[31]

Matthew's conflict with the scribes and Pharisees then, particularly as those who taught regarding what is to be observed from "Moses seat," was specifically within the context of their sphere of influence, which included the Matthean community. It should properly be viewed in the context of Second Temple Judaism, of which Christian Judaism was a part. In this regard, it was common for various parties to criticize others, particularly in regard to their interpretation of Torah and its observance. In a broad sense, there is the condemnation of those who "rebel" against the Torah as in the Damascus Document (CD) which in CD 5.20–21 looks back at the

25. Matt 23:2, and 8:19–20; 13:52.

26. Matt 9:11, 14; 12:2.

27. Luz, *Matthew: A Commentary*, 94.

28. Davies and Allison, *The Gospel according to Saint Matthew*, 3, 266.

29. Newport, *The Sources and Sitz im Leben of Matthew 23*, 80–85, 118–24.

30. Newport, *The Sources and Sitz im Leben of Matthew 23*, 126.

31. Newport, *The Sources and Sitz im Leben of Matthew 23*, 120.

"age of devastation of the land" and in describing the unfaithful of that day condemns "those who shifted the boundary and made Israel stray . . . for they spoke of rebellion against God's precepts (given) through the hand of Moses."[32] This is a critique against those who do not keep Torah, but also those who reinterpret it (shifting the boundary) and cause people to stray. Psalms of Solomon 4.1 likewise specifically criticizes the "profane man" who sits "in the council of the devout." Therefore, both the precepts of teachers of the Law and the teachers themselves were open to criticism if they did not uphold the Law in their personal conduct.

This is the type of criticism of teachings and teachers seen in Matthew 23:2–4. While not a bald denigration of the scribes and Pharisees, the pericope underscores Matthew's perception of what their role and function should in fact be. The "burden" they tied on others is expressed with the same noun (φορτίον) used in Matt 11:30 with its reference to Jesus' yoke (ζυγός), "For my yoke is easy, and my burden is light." The metaphor of the yoke and the burden a yoke entails provides a conceptual bridge to Did. 6.1–2 (see chapter 4), connecting Jesus' yoke and the authority of the scribes and Pharisees to the type of instruction embedded in the Two Ways material of the Didache. It is not their role, authority to teach, or position that is challenged by Jesus in Matt 23:2–3, but their faithfulness in adhering to the precepts they teach. While this raises the potential criticism that their burden is too onerous for even them, and Mark Powell does raise the question as to how this endorsement of their authority fits with Jesus' criticism of it,[33] in this text Matthew supports the *position* these teachers hold as arbiters of the Torah even while he criticizes the way in which they implement it.

It is this disconnect between teaching and practice that gave rise to Jesus' subsequent designation of the Pharisees as hypocrites in 23:13ff. In agreement with Draper,[34] there is little doubt that "hypocrites" in the Didache should also be identified as Pharisees. As does the Matthean account, the Didachist proscribes their behavior; teaching the value of humility in saying "do not exalt yourself,"[35] and admonishing his readers that "your fasts shall not be kept with the hypocrites."[36] This suggests that if the Didachean community was indeed related to that of Matthew's, this is not the type of self-serving leadership the community permitted teachers to exert.

32. CD 5.21, Martinez and Tigchelaar, *Dead Sea Scrolls Study Edition*, 559.

33. Powell, "Do and Keep What Moses Says (Matthew 23:2–7)," 421.

34. Draper, *Christian Self-Definition*, 233.

35. Did. 3.9.

36. Did. 8.1.

Powell argues that the authority of the scribes and Pharisees is not one that they "ought" to have, but is one that they have in practice. In other words, Matthew "acknowledges the reality of the situation in which the disciples must live and conduct their ministry."[37] Rather, it seems that is a question the text doesn't raise. It simply points to a better way and a higher standard. Thus the very criticism of hypocrisy on the Pharisees' part elevates Jesus' teaching (and similarly the Didachist's) to a position superior even to theirs. This is why Matthew acknowledges their position, and then in criticizing them in the Sermon on the Mount, asserts Jesus' superior authority, as Anthony Saldarini describes in detail.[38] All this substantiates the teaching of the Lord, or Matthew—or, later, the Didachist. Thus, Matthew affirms the authority of the Pharisaic teachers even while criticizing them, but also makes Jesus' teachings the ultimate guide.

The Gospel of John provides an additional vantage point from which to observe the role of teachers and their authority in a Christian Jewish milieu, although issues surrounding its provenance remain uncertain. J. Louis Martyn's position was that John reflects a community of "*Christian Jews*" that was in the process of becoming separated from the Synagogue and becoming "a separated *community of Jewish Christians*."[39] However, while the Gospel corresponds with a milieu of Jews who are of "Christian" faith (the term "Christian" doesn't occur anywhere in John's Gospel, of course) and addresses issues peculiar to people or a community in such a situation, the identity or existence of this "Johannine Community" is far from settled, a point that Andreas Köstenberger is at pains to make.[40] Given such caveats that caution against any connection between the Johannine community and that of the Didache, it should be noted that the Gospel is generally dated in the years shortly after the Didache's final redaction, which this study takes as no later than 85 CE.[41] As seen in chapter 3, the Didachean community itself was affected by the first Jewish revolt and in light of the widespread impact of the revolt and the date of both documents it is reasonable to view this as a point of contact between them. Köstenberger thus presents an intriguing argument for the Gospel as

37. Powell, "Do and Keep What Moses Says (Matthew 23:2–7)," 435.

38. Saldarini, *Matthew's Christian-Jewish Community*, 46–55.

39. Martyn, *History and Theology*, 66.

40. Köstenberger, *Response: Progress and Regress*, 106; *A Theology of John's Gospel and Letters*, 55–57.

41. The discovery of Rylands Greek Papyrus 3.457 has led various writers to affirm a much earlier date, but Brent Nongbri has demonstrated that on the basis of paleography the papyrus cannot be proven to be as early as first thought "The Use and Abuse of P52.".

a response to the destruction of the Temple,[42] thereby putting it in the same period of social and political turmoil.

Not only does the political context bear comparison, but John and the Didache resonate with various common themes. The *crux interpretum* for John is often taken to be the conflict between the blind man and the Pharisees in John 9 in which a man whom Jesus healed of his blindness on the Sabbath was brought before the Pharisees and threatened with expulsion from the synagogue. This pericope led to the conclusion that the *birkat ha-minim* (the prayer against heretics in the *amidah*) lies behind the conflict. This view, championed by Martyn himself,[43] is increasingly contested,[44] particularly in light of the lack of early credible references to the prayer; exemplars found in the Cairo Genizah and *b. Ber. 28b–29a* being far later than the period in question. Rather than reflecting an established decree, the focus of the passage is more on the teaching and authoritative role of the Pharisaic teachers themselves, both in this instance and elsewhere in the Gospel. When there was a question regarding the man born blind, the neighbors brought the man to the Pharisees.[45] The Pharisees deliberated among themselves to determine the facts about Jesus, and notably while in their view Jesus had broken Sabbath law, this was not decisive against him.[46] After this, the Pharisees are simply termed "the Jews" in typical Johannine fashion.[47] In this way John's Pharisees emerge as another exemplar of the connection between temporal and religious authority on the part of teachers.

While appearing throughout the Gospel, John's Pharisees are not finely nuanced, in some ways acting as a literary foil, unlike their characterization in the Synoptics. This led to Ellis Rivkin's sharp criticism, later repeated by Raimo Hakola and Adele Reinhartz,[48] that they are "featureless," a device used in order to serve John's literary aims.[49] Those literary aims were not only to portray their growing opposition to Jesus[50] but also to show the abuse of their authority and ultimate collusion with the Sadducees and

42. Köstenberger, *A Theology of John's Gospel and Letters*, 53–67.

43. Martyn, *History and Theology*.

44. Broadhead, *Jewish Ways of Following Jesus*, 291; Langer, *Cursing the Christians? A History of the Birkat HaMinim*, 26–29.

45. John 9:8–13.

46. John 9:15–16.

47. John 9:13–16.

48. Hakola and Reinhartz, *John's Pharisees*, 136–37.

49. Rivkin, *A Hidden Revolution*, 98.

50. John 7:47–48; 8:13; 9:16.

culpability in his death.[51] In this pericope, however, the Pharisees are described as adjudicators,[52] and disciples of Moses.[53] Further, they viewed themselves as above being taught by one born in "sin"[54] as can be deduced from their response to the newly sighted man: σὺ διδάσκεις ἡμᾶς; and ruled on the basis of their position as teachers. This served John to point to their blindness,[55] making the same point found in 3:10, where Jesus chided Nicodemus by asking: σὺ εἶ ὁ διδάσκαλος τοῦ Ἰσραὴλ καὶ ταῦτα οὐ γινώσκεις; John's implication is that teachers are expected to be enlightened and fair judges. The assumption is that certain teachers have significant authority and influence within the community, even if they should abuse it. This corroborates the Matthean picture of teachers as arbiters of the Torah, even while their implementation of it is open to criticism.

A further stream of literary evidence regarding the position of teachers in Christian Jewish milieus can be brought to bear from the portrayal of Peter in early Christian literature, particularly as Markus Bockmuehl has recently argued for greater acknowledgment of the "remembered Peter."[56] While it is still difficult to separate his memory from his person, the Pseudo-Clementine Epistle of Peter to James represents an early view of the apostle's estimation of the importance of teachers. In the Epistle, Peter commits the books of his preachings to teachers whom he likens to the seventy elders who succeeded Moses, saying, "give the books of my preachings to our brethren, with the like mystery of initiation, that they may indoctrinate those who wish to take part in teaching."[57] This is the central theme of both the Epistle and James' response which follows it, in which teachers have a sacred trust and are charged with passing on Peter's preachings. Peter holds his sermons as of paramount importance "For some from among the Gentiles have rejected my legal preaching." He further appeals to the Lord's continuing to say "The heavens and the earth shall pass away, but one jot or one tittle shall in no wise pass from the law."[58] Equating his "legal preaching" to the immutability of the Torah, Peter is portrayed here as a teacher wielding the authority of the Torah.

51. John 11:47; 12:42; 18:3.
52. John 9:13.
53. John 9:28.
54. John 9:34.
55. John 9:35–41.
56. Bockmuehl, *The Remembered Peter*, 12–14.
57. *ANF*, 8.215.
58. *ANF*, 8.215.

In summary, the two Gospels surveyed show the authority of teachers in their milieus. Matthew stresses the commandments and shows that the scribes and Pharisees were accorded authority in conjunction with their role as teachers. The Gospel of John underscores the case that in the Jewish society that he knows, teachers wielded significant social and religious authority that could extend to expelling members from the synagogue. Notably, the Didache reflects both concerns, stressing the importance of fidelity to the Lord's commandments,[59] and socially, showing concern for community loyalty and unity.[60] In addition, the Epistle of Peter to James represents an early church memory of an apostle who took the authority of teachers and their relationship to the Torah with utmost seriousness. Torah, its interpreters, and the authority of the teacher were bound up with one another.

The Didachean Community and Its Teachers

The Didache contains ample internal evidence of its underlying assumptions concerning teachers and their authority. References to teachers in the Didache substantiate how teachers were to be regarded, the conditions under which this was to be granted, and the extent of the influence accorded them.

The Didache accorded teachers extensive influence over their disciples, bordering on the authoritative, providing that they were accepted and legitimate. The first suggestion of this is found in Did. 4.1, where the pupil is exhorted to honor (τιμάω) the teacher "as the Lord." Niederwimmer casts this teacher-to-pupil relationship in terms of piety, claiming "Es ist durch das Grundgebot der Pietät bestimmt" on the basis of the connection between the Lord's presence and the place where his lordship is spoken of.[61] The thought is continued in the following verse, which enjoins the disciple to seek teachers (τῶν ἁγίων) out daily "in order that you may find comfort in their words."

More than just an issue of finding comfort, however, the Didache's instruction has much to do with the teacher's authority. This meaning is apparent on the basis that the instructions of Did. 4.1–2 serve as the conclusion to the prophylactic τέκνον teachings of Did. 3.1—4.2. They thus bear comparison with the admonition of Did. 6.1–2, which concludes the Two Ways section, for in addition to their concluding positions, both passages address the teacher/disciple relationship and in both the teaching

59. John 14:21; 15:10–17, cp. Did. 1.2; 2.1; 4.13; 6.2–3; 16.2, 4.

60. E.g. John 13:35; 15:9–17; 17:20–23, cp. Did. 1.2; 2.7; 4.2–14; 12.1; 13.1–7.

61. Niederwimmer, *Die Didache*, 136.

itself is the subject of the passage. Whereas 4.1 makes the connection between the teaching and the presence of the Lord (κύριος), 6.1 elaborates and warns that false teaching separates the individual from God (θεός). Something similar is found in 1QpHab 2.2–3, which describes the words of the Teacher of Righteousness as "from the mouth of God" (מפיא אל).[62] Thus the peculiar phrase ὅθεν γὰρ ἡ κυριότης λαλεῖται, ἐκεῖ κύριός ἐστιν,[63] which Niederwimmer considers "sprachlich merkwürdig,"[64] is not as strange as might be supposed, for it does not have to do with mere reverential awe, or "der Pietät," but with the Didache's appropriation of the Lord's authority for its Teaching.

Didache 4.1 also elevates the authority of the teacher with the instruction to honor teachers ὡς κύριον. Contra Clayton Jefford's assertion that the command "as the Lord" is common "throughout early Christian literature,"[65] apart from Ign. *Eph.* 6.1, it is not to be found in any of the writings of Ignatius, Barn., 1–2 Clem., Ps.Clement, or Polycarp or Mart. Pol. It is also not present in the New Testament, where only two texts come close (if one omits Col 3:18–22 on the basis of it being a disputed epistle). Ephesians 6:5 instructs servants to honor their masters, which demonstrates the possibility of reverencing a person as Christ: Οἱ δοῦλοι, ὑπακούετε τοῖς κατὰ σάρκα κυρίοις μετὰ φόβου καὶ τρόμου ἐν ἁπλότητι τῆς καρδίας ὑμῶν ὡς τῷ Χριστῷ. Hebrews 13:7 instructs its readers to imitate leaders, who are portrayed as teachers also: Μνημονεύετε τῶν ἡγουμένων ὑμῶν, οἵτινες ἐλάλησαν ὑμῖν τὸν λόγον τοῦ θεοῦ, ὧν ἀναθεωροῦντες τὴν ἔκβασιν τῆς ἀναστροφῆς μιμεῖσθε τὴν πίστιν. The Didache's use of this term is therefore *remarkable*, particularly as the Didache uses it a second time in Did. 11.2, in which case this teaching is repeated not just for the pupil but the community as a whole in the saying that if a teacher's teaching "leads to righteousness and the knowledge of the Lord, receive him as the Lord."

The esteem granted teachers in the Didache is naturally tied to the importance of their teaching and is conditional upon its rectitude. As Wilhite comments, in Did. 4.13 "the Didachist sees his teaching as an extension of the 'Lord's commandments (ἐντολὰς κυρίου).'"[66] This connection between teacher and teaching becomes further evident in 6.1: Ὅρα, μή τις σε πλανήσῃ ἀπὸ ταύτης τῆς ὁδοῦ τῆς διδαχῆς, ἐπεὶ παρεκτὸς θεοῦ σε διδάσκει (Watch, lest one deceive you from the way of the Teaching, for he

62. Martinez and Tigchelaar, *Dead Sea Scrolls Study Edition*, 10–11.

63. Did. 4.1. "For where his Lordship is spoken of, the Lord is there."

64. Niederwimmer, *Die Didache*, 136.

65. Jefford, *Did Ignatius of Antioch Know the Didache?* 344.

66. Wilhite, *The Didache*, 147.

teaches you away from God). The phrase τῆς ὁδοῦ τῆς διδαχῆς is a clear reference to the Way of Life, which has been taught in Did. 1–5. However, the Didache does not define who the teacher is who might "deceive you from the way of the Teaching" and teach you "away from God," and Milavec suggests that he could even be the one orally training the disciple.[67] What is apparent is that such a teacher had considerable influence in the disciple's life, should the disciple accept his teaching.

A further direct reference to the conditions under which a teacher is to be heeded is found in Did. 11.1–2, which instructs that if a teacher should come "teaching all these preceding things" he is to be received as the Lord. What a teacher should teach is that which leads "to righteousness and the knowledge of the Lord."[68] Rather than taking this instruction in the didactic sense that is most natural to the document, Niederwimmer views the instruction in a theological manner, stating that "both 'righteousness' and 'knowledge' are, for the Didachist, the descriptive terms for the 'essence' of the new faith" leading to the conclusion that "such a teacher should be received 'as the Lord.'"[69] In contrast, Draper points to the technical nature of the term καταλῦσαι in Did. 11.2, as a "reference to undermining Torah."[70] Yet the Didache has nothing to say about "faith." While articles of faith do occur, such as the triadic baptismal formula of 7.1, 3, nowhere does the term πίστις appear. Rather, the whole tenor of the work is instructive. The term "as the Lord" in each of its uses carries practical ramifications in terms of the respect to be afforded worthy teachers, those who speak the word of God, apostles, and those who come in the name of the Lord.[71]

The extent of a teacher's influence is illustrated by the Didache's references, within its earlier material, to the effect of false teachers on individuals and even the world. In Did. 6.1, the false teacher deceives (πλανάω), in a context marked with direct reference to the Teaching and a concern that the disciple might be taught away from the Teaching and thereby from God. Immediately after this, Did. 6.2 follows the warning against false teachers by enjoining the "whole yoke of the Lord" upon the disciple. Full adoption of this "yoke" is the Didache's ideal (as will be discussed in detail in chapter 10).

In Did. 16.4, the archetypical false teacher is described as the world-deceiver with a term derived from the same root as the term for the false

67. Milavec, *The Didache: Faith.*

68. Did. 11.2.

69. Niederwimmer, *The Didache*, 172.

70. Draper, "Torah and Troublesome Apostles," 357.

71. The three are addressed in this regard in Did. 4.1; 11.4; 12.1.

teacher (κοσμοπλανής). In Did. 16.4, the world-deceiver emerges in an apocalyptic passage decrying a lack of Law observance, specifically into a world characterized by ἀνομία. This "world deceiver" is suggestive of the πλανήσῃ ἔτι τὰ ἔθνη (the one who would deceive the nations, or Satan himself) in Rev 20:3. The relationship does not appear to be accidental; Alan Garrow has satisfactorily demonstrated significant commonalities between the Didache and Revelation, which suggest that "the Didache's eucharistic and eschatological traditions were the fountainhead from which Revelation was born."[72] This lawlessness is diametrically opposed to the Way of Life taught by the Didache and pre-empts judgement in 16.5 and the ultimate vindication of truth in 16.6.

In both passages the antagonists practice deception, and both do so with similar disregard for the teaching of the Didache. Whereas there is no indication in Did. 6.1 that the one who teaches "away from God" is of cosmic significance, such false teaching stands in continuity with the travesty of lawlessness, which Did. 16.4 reveals will indeed have a worldwide reach. Here the deceptive teacher, the one who teaches, is at the crux and is paradigmatic of the one who will deceive the nations at the end.

After the Didache, the phrase ὡς . . . κύριον occurs in Ign. *Eph.* 6.1 as Ignatius counsels the Ephesians to "look upon the bishop as the Lord himself."[73] This, in the context of his well-known bid to shore up the influence of the bishopric, does not remove the term far from the inference of inherent authority for the approved teacher. In contradistinction, Barn. 19.10 replaces the instruction of Did. 4.1 to "remember night and day the one who speaks the word of God to you" with "remember the day of judgment day and night," omitting the phrase "as the Lord."[74] It is therefore possible that Draper is correct in suggesting that the writer of Barnabas "naturally" omitted this instruction "as a dangerous exaltation of the teacher."[75] Both texts, one positively and the other backhandedly, suggest an ongoing understanding that teachers were to be highly esteemed and honored.

In summary, it has been shown that teachers in the milieu of the Didache were viewed as crucial figures in the community. Those who would teach differently than the Didache were to be shunned and not heard, whereas those who advocated taking on the yoke of the Lord were to be honored. Honor due to the teacher went hand in glove with respect for the Didache's teaching.

72. Garrow, *The Didache and Revelation*, 505–7, 513.

73. Ehrman, (LCL)

74. Ehrman, (LCL)

75. Draper, "A Commentary on the Didache," 84.

The Didachist thus stood in the mainstream of Jewish tradition in terms of his position of authority and influence as a teacher. This has been argued from the literary record of Second Temple Judaism, Christian Judaism, as well as from the Didache itself. Dependent as it was on its teachings, Judaism in the Second Temple period entrusted a significant amount of influence to those who interpreted them, demonstrating the natural authority that would have been accorded those who interpreted the Torah. Likewise, the Didache's stress on the importance of its teachers underscores and supports the view that it took its teachings as equivalent to the Torah that gave other teachers their authority.

The Authority of the Lord

The second part of this chapter will examine the authority of the Lord as it is employed by the Didache in the imposition of Torah. On the basis of his own authority as a teacher, the Didachist employed his advantageous position in order to mandate his Torah for the Didachean community. References to the Lord in the earlier material[76] further enhanced his authority and the authority of his teaching. That the Didache employs the authority of the Lord is initially signaled in the work's *incipit*, which will be examined in the light of recent research into the Didache's title and genre. It is borne out by the use of the Lord's authority in the *sectio evangelica*. It is further confirmed by the depiction of the Lord in the Didache's eschatological material, Did. 16.

The Authority of the Lord in the Incipit

This study takes the majority position that the *incipit* is the Didache's original title, in accordance with the arguments and evidence presented by Nancy Pardee,[77] but contra those of Niederwimmer.[78] In contrast to the *inscriptio*, which is almost certainly a later addition, as noted above the Didache's *incipit* uses qualifiers to assert that its teaching is both of the Lord (κύριος) and to the gentiles (ἔθνη). The recipients doubtless knew the contextual meaning of ἔθνη, but in the words διδαχὴ κυρίου the

76. Did. 1–6, 16.

77. Pardee, *Genre and Development*, 118–23.

78. Niederwimmer, *The Didache*, 56–57. Milavec proposes that both titles were the work of scribes as the orally communicated Didache transitioned to being a written text *The Didache: Faith*, 57–58.

Didachist left some ambiguity regarding the Lord's identity, presumably also viewing it as self-evident.

The Didache makes a strident and assertive claim to authority, yet as Gerd Luedemann noted, while claims to apostolic authority were not unknown in early church writings, the Didache is not in this category.[79] The Didache's claim for authority is based on the person of the Lord himself, so ambiguity regarding the identity of the Lord needs to be addressed. I argue here against the majority of scholars who have identified κύριος in the *incipit* as referring to the Lord God. Rather, it is the Lord Jesus, and it is Jesus' authority that is adduced. This is a case that I have previously argued, demonstrating that the weight of evidence leads to the conclusion that where the Lord is referred to in the Didache, it almost without exception refers to Jesus.[80]

It almost goes without saying that the juxtaposition of "Lord" to the "Twelve Apostles" in the *incipit* gives the initial impression that this must refer to the Lord Jesus and his disciples, the number twelve being indicative, even though the twelfth, Judas, had been replaced. In addition, as Willy Rordorf and André Tuilier suggested, the *incipit* echoes Christ's command in Matt 28:19, πορευθέντες οὖν μαθητεύσατε πάντα τὰ ἔθνη.[81] This should be taken to indicate that κύριος in the *incipit* refers to Jesus, a view corroborated by the Didache's use of an identical baptismal formula to that of the same Matthean text.

Wilhelm Bousset's comment on the Didache was that it, too, conformed to this paradigm, even though he excluded Did. 1–5 on the basis of it being "einer jüdischen Schrift."[82] This was the approach of his influential *Kyrios Christos*, where he argued that κύριος was "'der' neue Titel für die Person Jesu in den paulinischen Briefen."[83] While Bousset might be expected to argue this in order to support his thesis, it is nevertheless an unsurprising likelihood that the Didache would use κύριος in a similar manner to other early Christian documents, *viz.*, to most frequently use it to refer to Christ.

In contrast to Bousset's view, Audet asserted regarding the *incipit* that "Le κύριος n'est donc pas ici Jésus mais Yahvé."[84] Likewise, Aaron Milavec's survey of the Didache's use of the term begins with the assertion that "In each instance the context can be explored in order to discern whether the

79. Luedemann, *Opposition to Paul in Jewish Christianity*, 315 n. 70.

80. Nessim, *Didache and Trinity*, 3–8.

81. Rordorf and Tuilier, *La Doctrine Des Douze Apôtres*, 16.

82. Bousset, *Kyrios Christos*, 272 n. 2.

83. Bousset, *Kyrios Christos*, 95.

84. Audet, *La Didachè*, 253.

'Lord God' of the 'Lord Jesus' is meant" and concludes that all occurrences refer to the "Lord God."[85] Neither of these opinions are in fact fully supported by the text, as has just been shown.

Draper argued yet further, based on evidence from a seventh-century Nestorian Chinese version of the Two Ways material called the "Jesus Messiah Sutra."[86] The "Jesus-Messiah Sûtra" (*Jes*) was translated from the Chinese by P. Y. Saeki and dated between 635 and 638 CE.[87] Draper quoted the Sutra's opening phrase in which it is named "the teaching of the Lord of Heaven" in support of this.[88] Nevertheless, a closer reading of this text does not support Draper's assertion that the text unambiguously refers to the Lord God. While the Sutra begins with the words "At that time, preaching the laws of Hsü-po (i.e., Jehovah) who is the Lord of Heaven" it continues without interruption to say "the Messiah spoke thus." While the Lord of Heaven is clearly God and these are his laws, it is the Lord Jesus who transmits the Teaching in this version of the Two Ways.

On this basis, we may proceed to reiterate that while the Didache's *inscriptio* introduces the Teaching as that of the Twelve Apostles, the *incipit* clarifies that it is from "the Lord" Jesus, and subsequently conveyed through the apostles. The *incipit*, "The Teaching of the Lord through the Twelve Apostles to the Gentiles" describes the content of the letter with the term διδαχή, a term which is used four more times in the work. In the first instance the preface to the *sectio* (in Did. 1.3) describes it as the "words" (λόγων) of the Teaching, and following the *sectio* the Decalogue-related list of Did. 2 is described as the "commandment" (ἐντολή) of the Teaching. Twice more in the Didache the Teaching as a whole is referred to using the noun διδαχή, in Did. 6.1 and 11.2. In both of these instances the purpose is to warn the disciple concerning those who might deceive or lead them away from it. These four occurrences of the noun διδαχή thus function in two discernible ways: to define the Teaching and to safeguard its observance. The διδαχή not only lends its name to the work, but is presented as teachings and commandments that are of indispensable importance.

Despite the ambiguity for the modern reader, the significance of the Lord as the source of the Teaching is inescapable. As Wengst writes, "Natürlich ist zu erwarten, daß 'der Herr' eine Autorität ist."[89] This signifi-

85. Milavec, *The Didache: Faith*, 663–66.

86. Draper, "A Commentary on the Didache," 14; *Christian Self-Definition*, 225.

87. Saeki, *The Nestorian Documents and Relics in China*, 117.

88. Draper, "A Commentary on the Didache," 14. See also Saeki, *The Nestorian Documents and Religious Monuments*.

89. Wengst, *Didache (Apostellehre)*, 24.

cance is seen not only in the *incipit* but in the Didache's recurrent reference to the Lord throughout. It then follows that the identity of the κύριος in the *incipit* is critical as it gives crucial information regarding the basis of the Didache's claim of authority.

In summary, as the Didache's *incipit* identifies the Lord as the source of the teaching being communicated by the twelve apostles, men distinguished by their personal relationship with the Lord Jesus as their teacher, the immediate context indicates that the Lord referred to here is Jesus rather than the Lord God. This does not imply that his teaching is not to be identified as that of the Lord God, particularly in light of the Decalogue commands of Did. 2, but that it is Jesus' imprimatur that is brought to bear. This supports the view that the Didache is using Jesus' authority—in the *sectio* and following Two Ways material—to endorse the teaching presented.

The Authority of the Lord in the *Sectio Evangelica*

The proximity of the *sectio evangelica* to the *incipit* further substantiates the thesis that the Didachist intentionally used the Lord Jesus' authority as teacher and interpreter of the Torah to authenticate the Torah of the Two Ways.

The *sectio* draws upon known sayings of Jesus, as is evident from the usage of the same material in both Matthew, Luke, and presumably Q. Among scholars there is a range of opinions regarding the literary relationship between these texts as exemplified by Garrow's argument that of the points of contact between Matthew and Did. 1.1–6, "none of these *requires* the *Didache*'s knowledge of Matthew's Gospel."[90] Nevertheless, at the least, there are three (possibly four, if one considers Q) roughly contemporaneous texts transmitting the same sayings, testifying to their wide reception. It can be said then, that the Didache's recipients would not only have clearly recognized that the *incipit* spoke of the Lord Jesus' teaching, but also the *sectio*.

In terms of its relationship with Matthew, with which the *sectio* has the greatest affinity in terms of common content, wording and the amount of material, it is noteworthy that in the precepts of Did. 1.3–5 (see Matt 5:39–44) there is no replication or hint of the formula "You have heard . . . But I say to you . . . ." While it elevates the teachings of Jesus, in no way does the *sectio* criticize the Law or other interpretations of it.

Significantly, not only is the *sectio* drawn from material closely paralleling Jesus' teaching regarding the Torah in Matt 5—7, but this material is used frequently throughout the Didache.[91] Not only does this suggest

90. Garrow, *Matthew's Dependence on the Didache*, 220.

91. In addition to the established arguments for their relationship, John Welch has recently identified seven "inversions" between the Didache and the Sermon (e.g. Matt

an undercurrent of commitment to Jesus' teachings in the Didache, but in particular those teachings that touch upon the Torah. Representative of the common assumption, Nautin argued "Celui qui l'a faite a trouvé que la source enseignait seulement à ne pas commettre le mal et qu'elle restait insuffisante au regard de la loi chrétienne de charité, qui exige qu'on aime positivement les autres. Il a christianisé cette morale juive."[92] Nautin fails here to go far enough, as he does not address the implication that any such Christianization is in fact an endorsement of the foundational material that is being Christianized. Neither does he address the Lordship of Jesus as the teacher and thereby the Teaching's imputed authority.

Finally, it is worth noting that in addition to the proximity of the *sectio* to the *incipit*, the redactional comment of Did. 1.6 may well confirm the authoritative nature of the *sectio*'s sayings. This verse could quite possibly be considered a gloss, as Audet discusses,[93] but regardless of its history was accepted into the text and evidences the Didachist's convictions. With the phrase περὶ τούτου δὲ εἴρηται it introduces a quotation, as when the Didache quotes the Lord in Did. 9.5, and as in Luke's account of the temptation of Jesus[94] where Jesus answered the devil "it is said" (εἴρηται) and proceeded to quote Deut 6:16 "You shall not put the Lord your God to the test." It is not scripture that the Didachist quotes, but a sentiment akin to that of Sirach 12.1, 4–5 which advocates careful discrimination in whom among the needy to give help to.[95] Following a midrashic format, the Didache is in effect commenting on the *sectio* as an authoritative text, and casting light upon it from another authority. It's use of εἴρηται is comparable to any number of Mishnaic introductory formulae, many of which have been catalogued by Bruce Metzger.[96]

In summary, the *sectio*, drawing as it does upon recognizable sayings of Jesus and proximate to the *incipit*, which specifically refers to Jesus as the mediator of the Teaching, employs Jesus' authority as Lord within the Two Ways material. Following the *sectio*, the Didachist comments upon it

5:40 "tunic/cloak" vs. Did. 1.4 "cloak/tunic"), forming part of his demonstration of an extensive relationship between the entirety of the Didache and the Sermon *From the Sermon to the Didache*, 337–38, 355–61.

92. Nautin, "La compositioni," 201.

93. Audet, *La Didachè*, 277.

94. Luke 4:12.

95. Investigation into the source of the Didache's quotation and its later use seems to have begun with Charles Taylor in 1888 "Tracings of a Saying," 115. and is most recently the subject of a substantial study by Niederwimmer in his commentary *The Didache*, 83–86. Rather than the source of the saying, the focus here is on what its use signifies in terms of the authority accorded the *sectio*.

96. Metzger, "The Formulas," 300–302.

as an authoritative text using a formula frequently used to refer to quotations of scripture.

The Authority of the Lord in the Eschaton

The final assertion of the authority of the Lord Jesus is made in the Didache's eschatological conclusion, in Did. 16. Here again, it is necessary to establish that κύριος of 16.1, 7, and 8 whom the Didache speaks of as returning in the clouds is Jesus. Milavec argues here, based on context, that κύριος in the Didache again means "Lord God."[97] This accords with the inter-textual context, of which the Didachist was surely aware, having prefaced his statement with the reminder to his readers that ἥξει ὁ κύριος καὶ πάντες οἱ ἅγιοι μετ' αὐτοῦ,[98] in close parallel to the prophecy of Zech 14:5 καὶ ἥξει κύριος ὁ θεός μου καὶ πάντες οἱ ἅγιοι μετ' αὐτοῦ (LXX). What is neglected is the larger context of the Jesus movement's interpretative framework reflected in Matt 16:27 and 25:31 that the "Son of Man" will come in his Father's glory; a teaching drawn upon by Paul in 1 Thess 4:16.

A further indication that the Lord Jesus is in mind is seen in Did. 16:8 τότε ὄψεται ὁ κόσμος τὸν κύριον ἐρχόμενον ἐπάνω τῶν νεφελῶν τοῦ οὐρανοῦ. Here the Didachist uses the imagery of Daniel 7:13, imagery which is specifically referenced by Jesus in Matt 24:30 (=Mark 13:26) and 26:64. Here Niederwimmer identifies κύριος as Jesus.[99] So did Wilhelm Bousset before him, representing the majority of scholars.[100] This is confirmed by the juxtaposition of Did. 16.4 and 6. Whereas 16.4 speaks of a "world deceiver" who "appears like the Son of God and makes signs and wonders," 16.6 speaks of the "sign of truth" followed by the description of the Lord's advent in 16.7–8. In this parallel structure, the σημεῖα of the κοσμοπλανής and the σημεῖα of ἀληθείας are juxtaposed, and as the text builds the contrast, the natural juxtaposition between the "world deceiver who appears like the Son of God" (υἱὸς θεοῦ) is surely the true Son of God rather than the Father. As Jens Schröter argues from Matthew, James, the Pauline epistles and 1 Clement, ascribing such traditions to "the Lord" shows that *the* "exalted Lord is the authority."[101]

The authority of the Lord Jesus is seen in Did. 16.4 in the context of him setting the cosmos to rights, particularly in regard to lawlessness (ἀνομία), which is positioned as the culmination of evil in the last days. The reference

97. Milavec, *The Didache: Faith*, 665–66.

98. Did. 16.7.

99. Niederwimmer, *The Didache*, 226.

100. Bousset, *Kyrios Christos*, 291.

101. Schröter, *Jesus Tradition in Matthew, James, and the Didache*, 239–40.

to lawlessness comes after a description of the last days in Did. 16.3, and is comparable to the one other occurrence of the noun at the end and culmination of the Torah vice list of Did. 5, where "lawless judges of the needy" is the final characteristic of those on the Way of Death. It is also after the comment that "in the last days the false prophets and the corrupters will be multiplied." The Didache has already warned against false prophets in Did. 11.8, where the community has been instructed that a false prophet can be discerned by whether or not they have the "conduct of the Lord." This concern goes back to Did. 6.1, where the inductee is warned to watch lest anyone should teach them away "from the way of the teaching," referring to this same thing—conduct according to the Way of Life. For these reasons I would agree with Draper who states "the word ἀνομία is linked, in my opinion to the problem of false teaching which destroys and refers to those who refuse to abide by the ethical provisions of Torah, as understood and interpreted by this Christian Jewish community."[102]

In summary, the eschatological conclusion of the Didache identifies the Lord Jesus as the Son of God who comes in the clouds following the culmination of evil in the last days. That evil is epitomized in lawlessness, the disregard for the precepts of Torah, particularly as interpreted and presented in the Didache's Way of Life. Overall, in the second part of this chapter, the *incipit*, *sectio*, and eschatological conclusion of the Didache have been examined to demonstrate that the authority of the Lord has been employed by the Didachist to mandate the Way of Life. If the authority of the Torah devolved to its interpreters, Jesus was the ultimate interpreter and the ultimate authority. His imprimatur on the Didache's Two Ways affirmed its status and role, and as Part Three will show, this was commensurate with its identification with the Torah.

Conclusion

In the context of Second Temple Judaism, and more specifically that of Christian Judaism and its own milieu, the Didache assumes for itself the authority that was typically accorded to religious teachers by the faithful. The Didachist's claim is grander than one of mere apostolic authority for the teaching he presented. As seen throughout the earlier material of the Didache, this was implicitly and explicitly given the additional weight of the Lord Jesus' authority to make the Torah teachings of the Didache, imparting to it the character of a mandate.

102. Draper, *Eschatology in the Didache*, 576.

Part Three: Torah for the Lord's Community

PART TWO OF THIS study has described (in chapter 3) the crises and distress that characterized the period in Antioch where the Didache was formed. This awareness forms a backdrop before which the Didache's uncompromising yet non-controversial approach to teaching the Torah can be regarded. A further survey of the Two Ways topos in the Hebrew Bible, nascent Judaism, pagan traditions, and Christian Judaism (chapter 4) has argued that the Two Ways theme was well suited for the Didachist's application of his teaching to his gentile recipients. This teaching has been cast by the Didachist as authoritative, even adducing the authority of the Lord Jesus (chapter 5).

Part Three of this study will proceed to demonstrate from key passages in the Didache that its Way of Life was a Christian-Jewish application of the Torah for its gentile constituents, evidencing a reception of the Torah distinct from the commonly held polarities typified by the opposition of "Law" to "grace." Rather, the nature and meaning of gentile obligation to the Torah as mediated by the teachings and authority of Christ made it mandatory for the Christian disciple. Further, adherence to the Way of Life was the requirement for participation in the eschatological community of all believers that would be united at the appearance of the Lord.

Chapter 6 will therefore make a case that the *inscriptio* and Did. 1.1 as we have it, presented the Christian disciple with a stark choice between two alternatives that compelled a decisive acceptance of the Way of Life. Chapter 7 tackles the *sectio evangelica* and portrays it as a carefully worded preface to the Two Ways that substantiates the authority of the following material. Chapter 8 proceeds to demonstrate that the structure of the Didache's Two Ways not only asserts it as effectually Torah, but does so in a way that is specifically suitable for the gentile convert to Christianity. This leads to chapter 9 and the Didache's placing of the "yoke of the Lord" upon the disciple. Finally, chapter 10 turns to the Didache's concluding chapter to demonstrate that observance of its Torah was the basis for the unity of all believers, Jews and gentiles indistinguishable, in a final eschatological vision.

As Part Three closely follows the text of the Didache, the following outline of the book serves as a guide:

Outline

Title(s): *inscriptio* and *incipit*

1.1—6.2	The Two Ways
1.2–6	Teachings of the Lord
2.1—4.14	Teachings on Lawfulness—Torah
2.1–6	Torah and Explanatory Teachings
3.1–6	Torah and Halakhic Teachings
3.7—4.14	Torah and Relational Teachings
5.1–2	Teachings on Lawlessness—Torah
5.1	The Curses
5.2	The Cursed
6.1–2	The Yoke of the Lord
6.3—15.4	The Way of the Community
6.3	Prefatory admonition
7.1—10.6	Community Traditions
7.1–4	Baptism into the community
8.1–3	Prayer in the community
9.1–5	Christocentric thanksgiving before meals
10.1–6	Christocentric thanksgiving after meals
10.7—13.7	Community Hospitality
14.1–3	Instructions for the Eucharist
15.1–4	Instructions for Governance
16.1–8[1]	The Judgement of Mankind and the Deliverance of the Perfect

1. Robin Aldridge "The Lost Ending of the *Didache*." has provided a plausible reconstruction of the end of the Didache, bringing it to 16.12, but as a reconstruction this will not be relied upon as primary evidence.

6

The Two Ways Choice

A STARK CHOICE BETWEEN two alternative opposites is fundamental to the Didache's Two Ways topos, and also to its agenda. This chapter will analyze the Didache's titles, its subsequent differentiation between the Ways in Did. 1.1, and the following "Double Love" command in Did. 1.2 to demonstrate their function in the book's underlying purpose of securing gentile adherence to the Torah.

The Teaching

Both the *inscriptio* (short title) which states that the Didache is "The Teaching of the Twelve Apostles" and the *incipit* (longer and subsequent title) "The Teaching of the Lord through the Twelve Apostles to the Gentiles" have received significant scholarly attention. The value of the titles in terms of their relevance to the Two Ways section and the Didache as a whole has been a matter of dispute, however. Niederwimmer's position is unambiguous in his assertion that it "would be utterly aberrant to derive an instruction for reading from the long title in H, and to see that title as an expression of the document's own self understanding."[1] Like Niederwimmer, Christopher Tuckett also expresses misgivings regarding the dual title.[2] Nevertheless, Niederwimmer's low view of the titles has been subject to criticism. Spivak argues that Niederwimmer's view is based on nothing but a "presumption" that the long title is "pseudepigraphic."[3] While this is not an accurate characterization of Niederwimmer's view—which is in fact based on other witnesses to the Didache, his own redactional

1. Niederwimmer, *The Didache*, 57.

2. Tuckett, *Synoptic Tradition*, 120.

3. Spivak, "A Christian-Jewish School," 162–63.

conclusions, and the fact that "the document itself nowhere lays explicit claim to apostolic authority"[4]—it is true that Niederwimmer's view has not found acceptance as it is indeed based on inadequate evidence and is not persuasive. The same can be said for Tuckett's view, as he does not produce any substantial argument other than to say that "it is doubtful whether we can deduce too much from the title."[5]

Without a strong argument against the usefulness of the *incipit*, it is much more reasonable to accept it at face value and to concur with Garrow,[6] Draper,[7] and Pardee,[8] who all find the *incipit* to be significant in our attempt to understand the Didache. A number of factors combine to provide additional evidence for the incipit's originality. While no final proof can be given that the *incipit* was penned by the Didachist, the fact that it is a more complex statement, and that there is the much less detailed *inscriptio*, presumably the title of the document written on the outside of its scroll to identify it, suggest that the *incipit* is from an earlier date. In other words, the writer of the *inscriptio* was no doubt simplifying and abbreviating the already extant *incipit* which he or she found too long and cumbersome for the customarily brief title on the outside of a scroll.

A further telling feature of the *incipit* that both speaks to its originality and purpose is its use of the limiting phrase τοῖς ἔθνεσιν, which Garrow rightly notes would be an uncharacteristic term for a pseudepigrapher seeking to "widen" the "applicability of the teaching."[9] Frequently, a work was limited by the audience the author had in mind. In both the NT and the Apostolic Fathers, letters are limited to the church(es), physical locales such as cities or provinces, or individuals, or left open to all Christians, as in Barn. 1.1: Χαίρετε, υἱοὶ καὶ θυγατέρες. In a few cases, letters were addressed to Christian Jews. Thus, James is addressed to ταῖς δώδεκα φυλαῖς, and 1 Pet 1:1 ἐκλεκτοῖς παρεπιδήμοις διασπορᾶς (however one might interpret Peter's recipients in light of the rest of the epistle). The Didache is in keeping with this form, but is distinct in that it addresses the gentiles, such a limitation not being found in the *Doctrina apostolorum* or the Didascalia, each of which begin with a Two Ways statement. It only finds a reprise in the address some three centuries later of Apos. Con. 1.1 "to all those who from

4. Niederwimmer, *The Didache*, 56.
5. Tuckett, *Synoptic Tradition*, 120.
6. Garrow, *Matthew's Dependence on the Didache*, 143–46.
7. Draper, *Christian Self-Definition*, 225.
8. Pardee, *Genre and Development*, 104.
9. Garrow, *Matthew's Dependence on the Didache*, 146.

among the Gentiles have believed in the Lord Jesus Christ."[10] This distinct characteristic of the *incipit* therefore speaks to the nature of the teaching given as one specifically for gentiles, thereby suggesting that the book addresses matters in a way that particularly pertains to them.

In summary, while doubt has been cast on the originality of the Didache's *incipit*, various points have been advanced in addition to those made by other scholars which demonstrate that it was quite likely original to the document. In addition, in its *incipit* title, the Didache presents itself in terms of the teaching of the Lord, which is the *Lectio difficilior*; and its limiting term τοῖς ἔθνεσιν is uncharacteristic of a later addition that would presumably seek to make the work appeal to a wide audience. In addition, the *incipit* is congruent with the work as addressed to gentiles.

The Choice

In a teaching for gentiles, the choice between Two Ways is an intriguing adaptation of the ultimatum initially presented to Israel by Moses in Deut 27—30 prior to the crossing of the Jordan. While the listed curses of Deut 27:15—26 may well have been part of the inspiration behind the curses of Did. 5,[11] it is the overall opposition between blessings and curses of Deut 28–30 that Moses drew upon to face Israel with the choice between "life and good, death and evil" of Deut 30:15, and "life and death, blessing and curse" of 30:19, famously commanding Israel to "choose life."

Having introduced its teaching in its *incipit* as that of the Lord, the Didache presents the disciple with the same stark choice: life versus death. The Apostolic Constitutions seems to have caught the intent of the Didachist in this regard, as in its later adaptation of the Didache, Apost. Con. 7.1.6–8 states that we "are obliged to say that there are two ways—the one of life, the other of death; which have no comparison one with another, for they are very different, or rather entirely separate."[12] It is thus that following the *incipit*, the very first words of the Didache place a stark choice before the reader: "There are two ways; one of life and one of death, and the difference is great between the two ways." It is what M. Jack Suggs termed

10. *ANF*, 7.391.

11. Yair Hoffman instructively refers to Deut 27:15–26 as a form of "negative confession" and notes that it "might allude, if at all, only to four commandments—the second, fifth, sixth, and possibly the tenth." He sees Jer 7:9 as a better Decalogue list, with its words "Will you steal, murder, commit adultery, swear falsely, burn incense to Ba'al, and go after other gods." *The Status of the Decalogue in the Hebrew Bible*, 39–40.

12. *ANF*, 7.391.

a "Sharply dualistic introduction," one of three characteristics of the Two Ways genre along with "Lists of 'virtues' and 'vices' and a concluding 'eschatological admonition.'"[13] While such an introduction has been identified as a characteristic of the Two Ways teaching in general, the framing of this choice in the Didache is notably abrupt.[14]

The contrast between the Two Ways in the Didache is seen in the literary construction presenting the Two Ways following the introductory statement ὁδοὶ δύο εἰσί. In this literary construction both the Way of Life and the Way of Death are introduced in a similar fashion with the introductory adjective πρῶτον.

Introductions to the Two Ways:

(1.2) πρώτον	ἀγαπήσεις τὸν θεὸν τὸν ποιήσαντά σε,
	δεύτερον τὸν πλησίον σου ὡς σεαυτόν
(5.1) πρώτον	πάντων πονηρά ἐστι
	καὶ κατάρας μεστή

As Jonathan Draper suggests, the use of πρῶτον is likely "the hand of the redactor" at work.[15] This suggests that it is intended as a device to introduce each of the Two Ways in parallel form in order to highlight the fact that they are opposite in character. Indeed, after the term πρῶτον, each Way is described by a pair of phrases that separate the Way being described into two different aspects. By this device the Way of Life is summarized with the "double love" command enjoining love of God and then one's neighbor. Respectively, the Way of Death is summarized negatively as both πονηρός (evil) and κατάρας μεστή (full of cursing).

Insofar as the content of each Way follows the outline set forth in that initial double description, the two Ways are juxtaposed against each other. In the Way of Life, the first section comprises the Christian interpolation followed by a list of Torah based commandments original to the source Two Ways tractate (as represented in the *Doctrina apostolorum*). In the Way of Death, the first section (Did. 5.1) repeats ten of the proscribed deeds already listed in the Way of Life (Did. 2.2–6). All except one (ἐπιθυμία) are in the same order, with four other vices interjected in the list. In the second part of

13. Suggs, *The Christian Two Ways*, 64.

14. Telfer, "The 'Plot' of the *Didache*," 149.

15. Draper, "A Commentary on the Didache," 115.

the Way of Death, the behaviors listed in Did. 5.2 correspond to the heading κατάρας μεστή in 5.1. These behaviors, rather than being an arbitrary vice list, bear comparison to the second part of the Way of Life (Did. 3–4). Of these twenty one abhorred characteristics, referring to "people rather than to sins,"[16] nine are reflections of admonitions already presented in the Way of Life. The list in the Way of Death then continues with nine additional vices listed. Thus we should not go so far as to call it a "doublet" of 2.2–7 as Niederwimmer suggests.[17] It is rather the opposite of the Way of Life. The Two Ways contrast is seen in its outline:

Way of Life	**Way of Death**
1.2—2.7 Lawful deeds	5.1 Lawless deeds
3.1—4.14 Characteristics of the lawful	5.2 Characteristics of the lawless

While the dualism of the choice has been commented upon, it must also be stressed that the Didache's use of the Deuteronomic "life" versus "death" terms points to its particular focus on the Torah. A brief summary of the metaphors used in the documents closest to the Didache demonstrates this:

Dualistic Metaphors

Deuteronomy 30:1	blessing and curse
Deuteronomy 30:15; 19	<u>life and death</u> (good and evil)
Jeremiah 21:8	<u>life and death</u>
Serek 1.9, 3.3	light and darkness
Serek 3.17–19	spirits of truth and deceit
Didache 1.1	<u>life and death</u>
Barnabas 18.1	light and darkness
Doctrina apostolorum 1.1	light and darkness
Test. Asher 1.6–8	good and evil
Test. Levi 19.1	light and darkness

16. Draper, "A Commentary on the Didache," 121.

17. Niederwimmer, *The Didache*, 114.

While Deuteronomy uses various metaphors to emphasize the contrast, the contrast between life and death is the most prominent, as it reoccurs in the injunction to "choose life" in 30:19 and 20. The context is different in Jeremiah, where life is the reward for capitulating to the invading Chaldeans. As already noted in chapter 3, the *Serek*, like the Didache, addresses at least in part the gentile convert (*Serek* 5.6). Both documents also have a high view of the Torah. Here, however, the Didache returns to Deuteronomy's metaphor of life and death, in contrast to its related writings. While the reason is not explicit, the usage correlates to the legal context of the following Two Ways chapters,[18] pointing the reader towards the teaching's origins in the Torah.

Put negatively, in other Two Ways texts the thrust is not so sharp, as seen in Barn. 18.1 and its introduction to the Two Ways where the choice is softened by Barnabas' limiting characterization of the Two Ways as "two paths of teaching and authority."[19] Further, rather than the Didache's ζωή and θάνατος, Barnabas uses the softer terms φωτός and σκότος. These are the same terms seen in the *Doctrina apostolorum* 1.1: *lucis et tenebrarum*. This formulation "recalls the dualist conception of the Qumran texts" where angels portray the way of life, and the angels of satan the way of shadows.[20] While "light and darkness" are somewhat less forceful and more metaphorical than "life and death" Barnabas does provide vivid contrast after the initial contrast in 18.1 by later on describing "the way of the black one" as "the way of eternal death and punishment" in 20.1.[21] The Didache, however, does not have any ameliorating language to soften the impact of the terms "life" and "death" or its relationship to Torah.

In contrast to Barnabas, the Didache's abrupt presentation of the choice between life and death is accentuated rather than ameliorated by the subsequent phrase "the difference is great between the two ways" (διαφορὰ δὲ πολλὴ μεταξὺ τῶν δύο ὁδῶν). With such words the inductee is given no room for compromise. Thus the Way of Life has almost legal force, as in Audet's words "Le «chemin de la vie» est celui de la fidélité aux commandements, et le «chemin de la mort» celui de la transgression."[22] The Didachist is mandating that his student make a choice and there is no third option presented. It is an echo of the Torah's instruction that sharply emphasizes the difference between the two ways,[23] and similarly concludes

18. Did. 2–5.
19. Ehrman, (LCL).
20. Mimouni, *Early Judaeo-Christianity: Historical Essays*, 167.
21. Butler, "The 'Two Ways,'" 28.
22. Audet, *La Didachè*, 257.
23. Deut 30:15–20

with the choice imposed on the Israelites between החיים והמות (life and death). The parallel is thus both in the initial contrast and then in the subsequent mandatory "choice." Given that the terms "life" and "death" provide an intertextual link, as well as the halakic subject matter in the wider context, it is evident that the parallel is by design, and the legal force comparable to that of the Torah in Deut 30:19.

In summary, the Didache's life and death terminology, uncharacteristic of contemporary Two Ways metaphors, corroborates the work's relationship to the Torah. The Didache adds weight to the gravity of the choice facing the disciple with an emphasis on the difference between the two ways.

The Double Love Command

The Double Love Command is based on the commandment "You shall love the LORD your God" in Deut 6:5 and the command "you shall love your neighbor as yourself" in Lev 19:18. The tradition arising from these commands is reflected, somewhat abstractly at times, in T. Sim. 5; T. Iss. 5, 7; T. Zeb. 5; T. Dan. 5; T. Jos. 11; and T. Ben. 3, which reveal it to be a readily available trope for the writer even had it not been in the Gospel tradition. Josephus similarly describes the initiation of Essenes as involving two "tremendous oaths": πρῶτον μὲν εὐσεβήσειν τὸ θεῖον, ἔπειτα τὰ πρὸς ἀνθρώπους in *Wars* 2.139. In terms of Two Ways texts, Sandt and Flusser's reconstruction of the Didache's Two Ways *Vorlage*, the archetypal "Greek Two Ways" exhibits the same Double Love Command as the Didache.

Later Christian texts carry on the tradition but with an emphasis on the first commandment. Therefore the late third-century Apostolic Constitutions amplifies that "The first way, therefore, is that of life; and is this, which the law also does appoint: 'To love the Lord God with all thy mind, and with all thy soul, who is the one and only God, besides whom there is no other'; 'and thy neighbour as thyself.'"[24] Here the first command is amplified, but the second command is not. This betrays a difference in perspective for a text dependent upon the Didache. Accordingly, while the early fourth-century ACO has the apostle "John" replicate the entire Double Love Command using both πρῶτον and δεύτερον, it repeats πρῶτον and emphasizes that love for God is the first commandment.

In its first-century setting, the "double love" command of Did. 1.2, considered by almost all scholars to be interpolated into the Two Ways tradition by the Didachist, is of key importance in order to understand the Didachist's concern to ensure the new disciple choose the Way of Life. In

24. (Apos. Con. 7.2). *ANF*, 7.465.

the Didache the Double Love Command is found immediately following the introduction to the Two Ways, and precedes the *sectio evangelica* in Did. 1.3b–6. In all three of the Synoptic Gospels it is found as Jesus' summary of the Torah,[25] and has antecedents in Deut 6:5; Lev 19:18; and later, combined, in Tob 4:15.

The Double Love Command is related to the Way of Life in terms somewhat similar to the *Serek*. In the *Serek* the Double Love Command is not a tight dyad as found in the Gospels or the Didache, but its position at the head of a community rule puts it in a similar introductory position, setting the tone and agenda for the teachings to follow. Thus the *Serek* begins with a dedication to the Instructor "in order to . . . seek God with [all (one's) heart and] with a[ll (one's) soul]."[26] While this paraphrase of Deut 6:5 does not itself command love, the source does and in addition, a few lines later the Instructor is informed that it has been given to him "in order" that he might teach his students "to love all the sons of light."[27] Here the two elements of both love for God and love for one's neighbor combine as a motivation to keep God's commands.[28]

The Way of Life is presented as twofold, reflecting the blessedness of keeping the Torah and the cursedness for neglecting it, as presented to Israel by Moses.[29] However, there is no reference to the Way of Death from this point until the start of Did. 5 which details the Way of Death in a much more summary manner. This contrasts to Barn. 19.2, which warns οὐ κολληθήσῃ μετὰ τῶν πορευομένων ἐν ὁδῷ θανάτου. The lack of attention paid to the Way of Death underscores the fact that it is not the Way the Didache is advocating, and is wholly other from the way of the community being addressed and thus does not need elaboration. This emphasis on the Way of Life in contrast to the Way of Death supports Milavec's argument that διδαχή should be translated as "'training' or 'apprenticing.'"[30]

While the Double Love Command can readily be set in the context of nascent Judaism, its more immediate context, within that, is that of nascent Christianity, which did not have an identity in contradistinction to Judaism at that time. In the first part of the Double Love Command, the wording differs from that of the Synoptics, as each of these begins with the identical phrase ἀγαπήσεις κύριον τὸν θεόν σου whereas the Didache uses the

25. Matt 22:37–39; Mark 12:30–31; Luke 10:27.

26. *Serek* 1.2, Martinez and Tigchelaar, *Dead Sea Scrolls Study Edition*, 71.

27. *Serek* 1.9, Martinez and Tigchelaar, *Dead Sea Scrolls Study Edition*, 71.

28. *Serek* 1.3–8.

29. Deut 11:29, 30:1–20.

30. Milavec, *The Didache: Text*, 47.

phrase ἀγαπήσεις τὸν θεὸν τὸν ποιήσαντά σε, omitting κύριον and adding τὸν ποιήσαντά σε. As Jefford has discussed, the Didache's turn of phrase indicates that the redactor followed a Two Ways source independent of the Gospels. The same may be said for Barnabas, as Barn. 19.2 both omits any name or title at all for God and simultaneously amplifies the saying, balancing love for God with fear of God, writing: ἀγαπήσεις τόν ποιήσαντά σε, φοβηθήσῃ τόν σε πλάσαντα.

The Double Love Command

Deut 6:5 LXX	ἀγαπήσεις κύριον τὸν θεόν σου
Mark 12:30	ἀγαπήσεις κύριον τὸν θεόν σου
Matt 22:37	ἀγαπήσεις κύριον τὸν θεόν σου
Luke 10:27	ἀγαπήσεις κύριον τὸν θεόν σου
Didache 1:2	πρῶτον ἀγαπήσεις τὸν θεὸν τὸν ποιήσαντά σε
Barn 19.5	ἀγαπήσεις τόν ποιήσαντά σε, φοβηθήσῃ τόν σε πλάσαντα

The Didache's omission of κύριον and addition τὸν ποιήσαντά σε provides a distinct emphasis on its subject as love for the Lord God. This is in line with God as the subject in both the Synoptics and Barnabas, but in the context of the Didache's Christocentric incipit serves in addition to remove any ambiguity that the Didachist means the Lord God (rather than the Lord Jesus) is the object of the Teaching here being summarized.

Niederwimmer, taking the position that the Gospels preceded the composition of the Didache, has suggested that the most immediate antecedents to the Didache's use of the Double Love Command are those of the Christian tradition.[31] Christopher Tuckett likewise asserted the Didache's dependence on the Synoptic Gospels.[32] Nevertheless, the wording of the Didache is distinct from the wording in the Gospels, suggesting that a literary dependency cannot be established so simply. In particular, while the Didache uses the words τὸν πλησίον σου ὡς σεαυτόν in concurrence with the Septuagint of Lev 19:18 and all three Gospels, the subsequent Golden Rule, πάντα δὲ ὅσα ἐὰν θελέσῃς μὴ γίνεσθαί σοι, καὶ σὺ ἄλλῳ μὴ ποίει, is reproduced in none of them. While all are recognizably similar in content, as seen in the following table, none of them is followed by the Golden Rule.

31. Niederwimmer, *The Didache*, 66.

32. Tuckett, *Synoptic Tradition*, 92.

The Double Love Command and the Golden Rule

Didache 1.2	δεύτερον τὸν πλησίον σου ὡς σεαυτόν· πάντα δὲ ὅσα ἐὰν θελέσῃς μὴ γίνεσθαί σοι, καὶ σὺ ἄλλῳ μὴ ποίει.
Lev 19:18 LXX	καὶ ἀγαπήσεις τον πλησίον σου ὡς σεαυτόν· ἐγώ εἰμι κύριος.
Mark 12:31	δευτέρα αὕτη· Ἀγαπήσεις τὸν πλησίον σου ὡς σεαυτόν. μείζων τούτων ἄλλη ἐντολὴ οὐκ ἔστιν.
Matt 22:39–40	δευτέρα δὲ ὁμοία αὐτῇ· Ἀγαπήσεις τὸν πλησίον σου ὡς σεαυτόν. ἐν ταύταις ταῖς δυσὶν ἐντολαῖς ὅλος ὁ νόμος κρέμαται καὶ οἱ προφῆται.
Luke 10:27	. . . καὶ τὸν πλησίον σου ὡς σεαυτόν. εἶπεν δὲ αὐτῷ· Ὀρθῶς ἀπεκρίθης·
Barn 19.2	ἀγαπήσεις τὸν πλησίον σου ὑπὲρ τὴν ψυχήν σου. οὐ φονεύσεις τέκνον ἐν φθορᾷ, οὐδὲ . . .

The Golden Rule, an addition to the Double Love Command, amplifies the second part of the Command, placing the emphasis on the second table of the Law. The notion of two tables of the Torah, which will be presupposed in this study finds its origin in the giving of the Torah (Exod 34:21),[33] as contemporary writers such as Josephus and Philo attest.[34] In the Didache, the focus remains on the second table throughout the Two Ways.

On the basis of other parallels, including some from the New Testament, Sandt and Flusser have argued that the direct antecedents of the Golden Rule are "frequently found throughout both Jewish, Christian, and Hellenistic sources."[35] The Didache formulates it in the negative, and as Jefford points out and is well known,[36] "the negative form of the saying . . . is a form that is predominant throughout the tradition of the Golden Rule."[37] For Milavec, the negative form corresponds with the comparable phrase in Did. 2.6b "Do not accept evil counsel against your neighbor" against the backdrop of the "linguistic preference within the Didache for the weightier negative prohibitions."[38]

33. Exod 34:21.

34. Josephus *Ant.* 3.90–92. Philo *Heir* 167–173 and *Decalogue* 50–51, 106.

35. Sandt and Flusser, *The Didache*, 159.

36. E.g. Tob 4:15; b. Šabb. 31a.

37. Jefford, *The Sayings of Jesus*, 33.

38. Milavec, "Synoptic Tradition in the Didache Revisited," 451–52.

Niederwimmer's view is that the Rule is given as the reason behind the command to love one's neighbor, and argues that the Rule modifies love for one's neighbor in the same way as "the God who made you" modifies love for God.[39] This doesn't hold true in my view, as the proper modifier for one's neighbor is not the Rule, but one's own being. Thus one loves one's neighbor as oneself. In this way the Double Love Command and the Rule can be viewed as three somewhat rhythmic lines in parallel:

Symmetry in the Didache's Double Love Command and Golden Rule

πρῶτον ἀγαπήσεις τὸν θεὸν	τὸν ποιήσαντά σε
δεύτερον τὸν πλησίον σου	ὡς σεαυτόν
πάντα δὲ ὅσα ἐὰν θελέσης μὴ γίνεσθαί σοι,	καὶ σὺ ἄλλῳ μὴ ποίει.

In fact, the Rule as a prohibition stands in contrast to the second command, which is an imperative. The commands are both positive injunctions, and the Rule is in the negative. Thus, the Rule functions not as the basis for the second command, but to define its implementation. While it is thus not surprising that Rudolph Knopf suggested the Rule is "Der dritte Teil des Hauptgebotes,"[40] Niederwimmer is correct to contradict Knopf and state that the Rule is "ein Interpretament des Gebotes der Nächstenliebe."[41] In this way, the Golden Rule confirms that the emphasis of the Double Love Command is squarely on its second injunction.

In summary, it has been shown that the Double Love Command was not foreign to nascent Judaism, and as with the *Serek*, appropriate for a manual of instruction, particularly as its form reflects the form of the two tables of the Torah. In that focus, the Didache also stresses that it is the Lord God rather than the Lord Jesus who is the subject. The Didache also stresses that the second table of the Torah is the main subject of its instruction by means of the Golden Rule, as is to be seen in chapter 8. The Double Love Command thus reinforces and fleshes out the disciple's choice.

39. Niederwimmer, *The Didache*, 66–67.

40. Knopf, *Die Lehre der Zwölf Apostel*, 5.

41. Niederwimmer, *Die Didache*, 92.

Deuteronomic Dissuasion

The Two Ways choice is underscored by the Didache's own affirmation of Law-keeping behavior via confession. It is the particularly strong literary relationship between Did. 1.2 and Did. 5.1 that confirms the Didache's presentation of its commands as imperative.

Did. 1.2: Ἡ μὲν οὖν ὁδὸς τῆς ζωῆς ἐστιν αὕτη·

πρῶτον ἀγαπήσεις τὸν θεὸν τὸν ποιήσαντά σε . . . [42]

Did. 5.1: Ἡ δὲ του θανάτου ὁδός ἐστὶν αὕτη·

πρῶτον πάντων πονηρά ἐστι καὶ κατάρας μεστή·

Did. 5.1 describes the Way of Death as κατάρας μεστή, a reference to cursing that is immediately reminiscent of Deut 30:1 καὶ ἔσται ὡς ἂν ἔλθωσιν ἐπὶ σὲ πάντα τὰ ῥήματα ταῦτα, ἡ εὐλογία καὶ ἡ κατάρα.[43] As seen in Did. 1.2, the Way of Life is characterized by love for God, and conversely in Did. 5.1 the Way of Death is characterized by evil and the curse. The descriptions of the Two Ways are parallel in their structure and in their terminology, and thus function to some degree as titles for the two sections.

Underemphasizing the importance of this parallel, Niederwimmer states that Did. 5.1 "hat die Funktion einer Überschrift."[44] He does, however, point to the importance of κατάρας μεστή, which is also found in Barn. 20.1. Interestingly, Barnabas uses κατάρας in a markedly distinct manner to that of the Didache in the phrase Ἡ δὲ τοῦ μέλανος ὁδός ἐστιν σκολιὰ καὶ κατάρας μεστή in Barn. 20.1. This has the effect of weakening any linkage to the Torah (as seen in chapter 6 of this study). As noted above, the Didache uses the term κατάρας in conjunction with the Deuteronomic metaphor of life versus death.[45]

The other key word linking the two texts in addition to κατάρα is φυλάσσω, which occurs in LXX Deut 30:10 and 16, and has already been discussed in the context of Deut 4:1–2. As the theme of guarding the teaching bears on not adding or taking away from it, it also in turn is set in the Deuteronomic context of the blessings and curses. Guarding the teaching is part and parcel of the way of life.[46]

42. As discussed, this is a direct reference to Deut 6:5 and no doubt Jesus' citation of it as reflected in Matt 22:37 and Mark 12:30.

43. Deut 30:1 LXX, also in Deut 30:19.

44. Niederwimmer, *Die Didache*, 146.

45. Deut 30:1, 19.

46. Did. 4.14.

Deut 30:10, 16 (LXX)	Did. 4.13—5.1
10—φυλάσσεσθαι καὶ ποιεῖν πάσας τὰς ἐντολὰς	4.13—φυλάξεις δὲ ἃ παρέλαβες,
16—φυλάσσεσθαι τὰ δικαιώματα αὐτοῦ καὶ τὰς	μήτε προστιθεὶς
κρίσεις αὐτοῦ, καὶ ζήσεσθε	μήτε ἀφαιρῶν . . . .
	4.14—αὕτη ἐστὶν ἡ ὁδὸς τῆς ζωῆς . . . .
30:1—Καὶ ἔσται ὡς ἂν ἔλθωσιν ἐπὶ σὲ πάντα	5.1—Ἡ δὲ του θανάτου ὁδός ἐστὶν ·
τὰ ῥήματα ταῦτα,	αὕτη
ἡ εὐλογία	πρῶτον πάντων πονηρά ἐστι
καὶ ἡ κατάρα	καὶ κατάρας μεστή·

The parallel between Deut 30:1a and Did. 4.13 is in the subject of each line, the Torah, or teaching, that has been given (τὰ ῥήματα ταῦτα / ἃ παρέλαβες). Thus in Deuteronomy, the words that are to be kept[47] are the ῥήματα τοῦ νόμου, which is the Deuteronomic Torah given to Israel. The Didache, clearly conscious of this context, has just given a similar command, οὐ μὴ ἐγκαταλίπῃς ἐντολὰς κυρίου in Did. 4.13, the subject of that command being the Torah, or teaching, that it has laid out in the Way of Life.

In summary, the "curse" contained in Did. 5.1 is far more than an "Überschrift" but actually corresponds with the character of the Two Ways material as Torah. That κατάρα is also a term related to the Torah is seen in its Deuteronomic source, which also contrasts it to the Way of Life.

Conclusion

In conclusion, the Didache begins by presenting the Christian disciple with a stark choice. By depicting its teaching as that mediated by the Lord Jesus and the apostles, the *incipit* authenticates its mandate. Directly following this introduction, the Didache links its teaching to the Torah metaphor of choice between life and death, emphasizing the contrast between the two ways. This leads to its first statement regarding the Teaching, appropriate from the perspective of nascent Judaism, reflecting the two tables of the Torah, and stressing that its subjects are the Lord God and one's neighbor.

47. Deut 29:28.

In this way the Didache doubles down on the choice the disciple has to make. The addition of the Golden Rule indicates that the main subject of the Teaching is love for one's neighbor. The imperative nature of the choice facing the disciple is further underscored by the titles of the Way of Life and Way of Death, and the cursedness of the latter.

7

The *Sectio*, Jesus and the Torah

Introduction

As a key distinctive of the Didache, the *sectio evangelica* (Did. 1.3b–6) has been shown (chapter 5) to impart the Lord Jesus' authority to the Two Ways material, material that presents a choice laden with Torah specific overtones (chapter 6).

In the first part of this chapter, I will briefly substantiate the reception of the Two Ways in Christian Judaism in general before proceeding in the second part to demonstrate how the *sectio* demonstrates a particular leaning towards Torah observance. Particular attention will be paid to the contrasting way in which the tradition behind the *sectio* was understood in the Gospels and the Didache. Subsequently, the distinct paraenetic incentives offered in the *sectio* will be highlighted. The third part of this chapter will specifically examine the *sectio* as the words of Jesus employed in such a way as to provide motivation to follow the Way of Life.

Chapter 7 deals with issues related to the *sectio*'s Jewishness, distinctiveness vis-à-vis the Gospels, and as a motivational incentive in Jesus words. This forms the groundwork for chapter 8, which will continue to demonstrate the tight integration between the *sectio* and the Two Ways material, a symptom of their common overriding purpose.

The *Sectio* and the Jewishness of the Two Ways

The *sectio* appears directly before the Didache's Two Ways section, which sits squarely within Jewish and Christian Jewish tradition, as is attested by a number of key texts that locate the Two Ways, earlier Jewish origins yet closer than Audet's argument for affinities between the Didache's Two Ways and the *Serek*.[1]

On a general rather than redactional level, Sandt and Flusser have made a concise but forceful argument that the *Doctrina apostolorum* is a "Jewish document which is particularly dependent upon 1QS."[2] The *Doctrina*, a Latin translation of a Greek original, is thought to preserve the original first-century Urtext of the Didache's Two Ways and possibly represents the "original Greek text of the composition behind the Didache and Barnabas." It is on this basis that Sandt and Flusser ventured to reconstruct the even earlier, original "Greek Two Ways" (GTW) document.[3] In this document, the Double Love Command and Golden Rule proceed directly to the Two Ways in Did. 2.1, completely omitting the *sectio*.

In addition, as Theodor Schermann proposed in 1903, the Apostolic Church Order and the Epitome of the Canons of the Holy Apostles may well share a common source, generally called the *Elfapostelmoral*.[4] While a reconstructed source such as the *Elfapostelmoral* remains somewhat conjectural, the commonalities it reflects form one part of the literary evidence for a Jewish Two Ways document used within Christian Judaism, bearing some resemblance to Two Ways texts in nascent Judaism as a whole. Nevertheless, as with the *Doctrina*, there is no evidence that the common source, or *Elfapostelmoral*, included the *sectio* of Did. 1.3b–6. As a result, the *sectio* has justifiably been viewed as an interpolation by the Didachist.[5] This begs the question as to the Didache's purpose in doing so.

The same is seen with other texts, underscoring the uniqueness of the Didache's *sectio*. Edwin Broadhead, surveying a broad selection of these texts and others characterizes their literary relationships as "complex" but then oversimplifies the relationship between Didache and Barnabas, taking the view that they are from a "common source."[6] This, however, does not detract from his conclusion that if the "foundational text is Jewish, the appropriation by Jewish Christianity is no less significant; indeed it shows the ease with which Jesus could be understood within a Jewish matrix."[7] Nevertheless, here too the *sectio* is absent. Niederwimmer considers that

1. Audet, "Affinités littéraire et doctrinales."

2. Sandt and Flusser, *The Didache*, 63.

3. Eugene Spivak has argued that this Greek Two Ways was a "Christian-Jewish text produced by early Matthean scribes." "A Christian-Jewish School," 142.

4. Schermann, *Eine Elfapostelmoral*, 10. See also Sandt and Flusser, *The Didache*, 64.

5. B. B. Warfield surveyed the matter extensively as early as 1886 "Text, Sources, and Contents," 115–26.

6. Broadhead, *Jewish Ways of Following Jesus*, 129.

7. Broadhead, *Jewish Ways of Following Jesus*, 130.

the "paired questions of the originality of the *sectio* and the source of its material are among the crucial problems of the *Didache*."[8] It is of course in harmony with the Jewish origins of the source that Jesus' words are not included, corroborating an origin outside Christian Jewish circles, but this only serves to highlight the special nature of the *sectio*'s inclusion in the Two Way text as adopted by the Didache. This chapter proposes a reason for the Didache's inclusion of these sayings of the Lord Jesus.

In summary, various similar and prototype documents for the Didache's Two Ways have been proposed, underscoring its Jewish origins and antiquity. These documents do not include the *sectio* however. As a product of its milieu, its teachings were congruent with both Judaism and what is generally known of Christian Judaism, highlighting the significance of the Didache's insertion of the *sectio*, as is to be discussed.

The *Sectio* as a Torah Mandate

The contribution of the *sectio* to the Didachist's Torah mandate is evident in a second respect, related to the "besonderer Bedeutung"[9] of the *sectio*. As will be shown, the Didachist not only sought to authenticate his presentation of the Torah by recourse to Jesus' sayings in the *sectio*, but by the very sayings he selected laid bare an affinity to Christian Jewish traditions that emphasized the authority of the Torah. The majority of Jesus' sayings in the *sectio* are parallel to his sayings in Matthew and Luke but not Mark or John. Rather than being a chance occurrence, it is preferable to view the use of this material as related to a common theme between the three documents, suggestive of a similarity between the Didachist's agenda and those of Matthew and Luke.

Particularly in terms of Matthew, the textual similarities have been viewed as indicating either a common source(s) or heavy literary dependency in one direction or the other.[10] Thus, while it has been commonly noted that Did. 1.2–5 finds parallels in Matt 5:39–41 and 46–48, not enough attention has been given to the fact that much of Did. 1.2–5

8. Niederwimmer, *The Didache*, 67.

9. Niederwimmer, *Die Didache*, 94.

10. Schröter noted that "Scholarly opinion is divided here between those who argue for literary dependence and those who plead for independence," in *Jesus Tradition*, 250. While possibly alluding to it, he omitted to mention Alan Garrow's *Matthew's Dependence on the Didache*. This study does not need to take a position on Garrow's thesis, although it makes an intriguing and sophisticated argument, but just that there is sufficient evidence to make a strong case is a symptom of the close relationship between the documents.

finds parallels in Luke 6:27–33. While sometimes ordered and conjugated differently, some 36 percent of Matthew's and some 23 percent of Luke's words are found in the *sectio*. More noticeably, where the words do differ, the equivalent concepts are present in all three documents. A table comparing the three texts in this regard is below. The words of the *sectio* shared with Matthew and Luke are in bold.

Didache[11]	Matthew	Luke
1.2 Ἡ μὲν οὖν ὁδὸς τῆς ζωῆς ἐστιν αὕτη·	22:37	10:27 ὁ δὲ ἀποκριθεὶς εἶπεν·
πρῶτον **ἀγαπήσεις τὸν θεὸν** τὸν ποιήσαντά σε,	**Ἀγαπήσεις** κύριον **τὸν θεόν** σου	**Ἀγαπήσεις** κύριον **τὸν θεόν** σου ἐξ ὅλης τῆς καρδίας σου
δεύτερον	39 **Δευτέρα** δὲ ὁμοία αὐτῇ· **Ἀγαπήσεις**	καὶ ἐν ὅλῃ τῇ ψυχῇ σου καὶ . . . καὶ
τὸν πλησίον σου ὡς σεαυτόν·	**τὸν πλησίον σου ὡς σεαυτόν.**	**τὸν πλησίον σου ὡς σεαυτόν.**
πάντα δὲ ὅσα	7:12 **Πάντα** οὖν **ὅσα**	6:31 καὶ καθὼς
ἐὰν θελέσῃς μὴ γίνεσθαί σοι,	**ἐὰν θέλητε** ἵνα ποιῶσιν ὑμῖν οἱ ἄνθρωποι, οὕτως	**θέλετε** ἵνα ποιῶσιν ὑμῖν οἱ ἄνθρωποι,
καὶ σὺ ἄλλῳ μὴ **ποίει**.	**καὶ** ὑμεῖς **ποιεῖτε** αὐτοῖς·	**ποιεῖτε** αὐτοῖς ὁμοίως.
1.3 Τούτων δὲ τῶν λόγων ἡ διδαχή ἐστιν αὕτη·	5:44	6:28
εὐλογεῖτε τοὺς καταρωμένους	**ἀγαπᾶτε τοὺς ἐχθροὺς**	**εὐλογεῖτε τοὺς καταρωμένους**
ὑμῖν καὶ προσεύχεσθε ὑπὲρ	**ὑμῶν καὶ προσεύχεσθε ὑπὲρ**	**ὑμᾶς, προσεύχεσθε** περὶ
τῶν ἐχθρῶν ὑμῶν,		
νηστεύετε δὲ ὑπὲρ τῶν	**τῶν**	**τῶν**
διωκόντων ὑμᾶς·	**διωκόντων ὑμᾶς·**	ἐπηρεαζόντων ὑμᾶς.
ποία γὰρ χάρις,	5:46	6:32
ἐάν ἀγαπᾶτε τοὺς	**ἐὰν** γὰρ **ἀγαπήσητε τοὺς**	Καὶ εἰ **ἀγαπᾶτε τοὺς**

11. Text per Ehrman (LCL).

Didache[11]	Matthew	Luke
ἀγαπῶντας ὑμᾶς;	**ἀγαπῶντας ὑμᾶς,**	**ἀγαπῶντας ὑμᾶς,**
	τίνα μισθὸν ἔχετε;	**ποία** ὑμῖν **χάρις** ἐστίν;
	5:47	
οὐχι καὶ τὰ **ἔθνη**	**οὐχὶ καὶ** οἱ **ἐθνικοὶ**	καὶ γὰρ οἱ ἁμαρτωλοὶ
τοῦτο **ποιοῦσιν;**	**τὸ αὐτὸ ποιοῦσιν**; . . .	**τοὺς ἀγαπῶντας** αὐτοὺς ἀγαπῶσιν.
ὑμεῖς δὲ φιλεῖτε τοὺς μισοῦντας ὑμᾶς,	5:48	6:35
καὶ οὐχ ἕξετε **ἐχθρόν**.	Ἔσεσθε οὖν ὑμεῖς **τέλειοι**	πλὴν ἀγαπᾶτε τοὺς **ἐχθροὺς ὑμῶν**. . . καὶ ἔσεσθε υἱοὶ Ὑψίστου,
1.4 ἀπέχου τῶν σαρκικῶν ἐπιθυμιῶν.	5:39 ἐγὼ δὲ λέγω ὑμῖν μὴ ἀντιστῆναι τῷ πονηρῷ·	6:29
ἐάν τίς σοι δῷ	ἀλλ' ὅστις σε	
ῥάπισμα εἰς τὴν δεξιὰν σιαγόνα,	**ῥαπίζει εἰς τὴν δεξιὰν σιαγόνα,**	τῷ τύπτοντί σε ἐπὶ **τὴν σιαγόνα**
στρέψον αὐτῷ καὶ τὴν ἄλλην,	**στρέψον αὐτῷ καὶ τὴν ἄλλην·**	πάρεχε **καὶ τὴν ἄλλην**,
καὶ ἔσῃ **τέλειος·**	5:48**Ἔσεσθε** οὖν ὑμεῖς **τέλειοι**	
ἐάν **ἀγγαρεύσῃ σέ** τις **μίλιον ἕν**,	5:41 καὶ ὅστις **σε ἀγγαρεύσει μίλιον ἕν,**	
ὕπαγε μετ' αὐτοῦ δύο·	**ὕπαγε μετ' αὐτοῦ δύο.**	
ἐάν ἄρῃ τις τὸ **ἱμάτιόν** σου, δὸς αὐτῷ	5:40 καὶ τῷ θέλοντί σοι κριθῆναι	καὶ ἀπὸ τοῦ αἴροντός σου τὸ **ἱμάτιον**
καὶ τὸν χιτῶνα·	**καὶ τὸν χιτῶνά**	
ἐάν **λάβῃ** τις ἀπό σοῦ τὸ σόν, **μὴ ἀπαίτει·**	**σου λαβεῖν**, ἄφες αὐτῷ **καὶ τὸ ἱμάτιον·**	**καὶ τὸν χιτῶνα**
οὐδὲ γὰρ δύνασαι.		**μὴ κωλύσῃς**.
1.5 παντὶ **τῷ αἰτοῦντί σε δίδου**	5:42 **τῷ αἰτοῦντί σε δός,**	6:30 **παντὶ αἰτοῦντί σε δίδου,**

Didache[11]	Matthew	Luke
καὶ	**καὶ** τὸν θέλοντα ἀπὸ σοῦ δανίσασθαι	**καὶ** ἀπὸ τοῦ αἴροντος τὰ σὰ **μὴ ἀπαίτει.**
μὴ ἀπαίτει· . . .	**μὴ ἀποστραφῇς.**	
καὶ οὐκ **ἐξελεύσεται ἐκεῖθεν,**	5:26 οὐ μὴ **ἐξέλθῃς ἐκεῖθεν**	
μέχρις οὗ **ἀποδῷ**	ἕως ἂν **ἀποδῷς**	
τὸν ἔσχατον κοδράντην.	**τὸν ἔσχατον κοδράντην.**	

The foregoing table is not intended to establish any literary affinity between the various texts, and the following features speak against it. While the Didache's *sectio* is one sustained passage, its material is found in multiple pericopes in the each of the Gospels—Matt 5, 7, 22; and Luke 6 and 10. In particular, though, it is the material of Did. 1.2 that is scattered, whereas the material of Did. 1.3–5 is grouped together in both Matthew and Luke, although the order of both Gospels differs to some extent from the Didache's. The following table puts it more succinctly:

Didache	Matthew	Luke
1.2	22:37, 39; 7:12	10:27; 6:31
1.3	5:44, 46, 47, 44	6:28, 32, 35
1.4	5:39, 48, 41, 40	6:29
1.5	5:42	6:30

What becomes quite clear from the two charts above is the relative independence of each document, with no consistent agreement between any two against a third. Secondly, where in some instances the vocabulary of a saying remains the same, the syntax varies. Thus Did. 1.4 ἐάν ἀγαπᾶτε τοὺς ἀγαπῶντας ὑμᾶς becomes ἐὰν γὰρ ἀγαπήσητε τοὺς ἀγαπῶντας ὑμᾶς in Matt 5:46 and Καὶ εἰ ἀγαπᾶτε τοὺς ἀγαπῶντας ὑμᾶς in Luke 6:32. Also, the same words are not always used, so where the same saying is recorded in Did. 1.5, Matt 5:42 and Luke 6:30, both Didache and Luke agree with μὴ ἀπαίτει against Matthew's μὴ ἀποστραφῇς which significantly changes the meaning.[12] Such variations point to either multiple literary sources, a common literary source not strictly adhered to by all authors, the use of oral tradition, or some combination of these. As Perttu Nikander has argued, "instead of a source critical investigation, one should try to find other ways to define the history of the Sectio Evangelica."[13] The point of these observations is to argue that the specific wording used by the Didache is not merely a product of the source, but also of the redactor's understanding of that source.

The fact that the Gospels share this material and identify it as Jesus' words corroborates the suggestion that the Didachist used it to attribute the Lord's authority to his teaching. All three documents treat the material of the *sectio* as a distinct body of teaching and evidently the Didachist saw it as eminently significant and appropriate as his insertion into the Two Ways material. While this is not controversial, the specific significance of this body of teaching can be seen in that Matthew, Luke, and the Didachist all use this same material in the context of their similar affirmations of the Torah, as will now be shown.

The majority of Didache scholars accept significant affinities between Matthew and the Didache, sometimes viewing them as products of the same milieu.[14] John Welch has tabulated over 100 "words, phrases, and distinctive concepts or elements common" to both the Didache and Matthew in the Sermon on the Mount alone.[15] Matthew's signal emphasis on the Law accords well with the Didache's own assertion of its authority. It is in this context that Matthew uses the same material as the *sectio*, but its position within the Sermon is also instructive. It cannot be divorced from its context, being placed following an extended discourse that begins with Jesus' forceful affirmations of the Torah's permanence and authority in Matt 5:17–20 and then continuing in a discourse in Matt 5:21–48 comprising six antitheses, each beginning with ἠκούσατε ὅτι ἐρρέθη and upholding "a more penetrating appreciation of and obedience to the law."[16] It is the end of this series, the last two antitheses, where the material of the *sectio* appears, the climax

12. At this point I have to differ from Garrow, who argues that "the number of agreements against the *Didache* makes pure coincidence unlikely," *Matthew's Dependence on the Didache*, 227, as the two Gospels do not have as great a number of agreements against the Didache as he supposes.

13. Nikander, *The Sectio Evangelica*, 292.

14. Foremost in this vein are the two multi-author works edited by H. Van de Sandt: *Matthew and the Didache* and *Matthew, James, and the Didache*.

15. Welch, *From the Sermon to the Didache*, 337, 355–61.

16. Saldarini, *Matthew's Christian-Jewish Community*, 162. See also Cuvillier, "Torah Observance and Radicalization in the First Gospel," 148–55.

of Matthew's affirmation of the Torah that ends with the statement "You therefore must be perfect, as your heavenly Father is perfect,"[17] warranting the fuller discussion which is to be found in chapter 10.

In a less pointed way, the same argument can be made from Luke. Just as Matthew used this set of Jesus' sayings in a context that asserts Jesus' authority as a teacher of the Torah, so did Luke. In Luke 6, the same sayings cited by the Didache in the *sectio* come shortly after halakhic statements regarding fasting and the Shabbat.[18] Similarly to Matthew 5, these present Jesus' interpretation of the Torah as distinct and superior to those of other teachers. In Luke these halakic passages set the stage for the calling of the Twelve; the assembling of a multitude; blessings similar to Matthew's macarisms and complementary woes. In conjunction then with Jesus' halakic authority is the separation of followers who accept it.

As Jacob Jervell states, in his Gospel Luke was at pains to avoid "any criticism of the law or parts of it by Jesus."[19] This accords with Luke's presentation of Paul in Acts as conspicuously upholding the Law.[20] While Luke does not arise from the same milieu as Matthew's *intra muros* community, like Matthew, Luke's use of the *sectio* is intrinsically tied to Jesus' authority. Like the Didachist, Luke employs these Jesus sayings in a manner that affirms the authority of the teaching being presented.

In summary, the common implementation of the material shared between the *sectio* and the two gospels points to a common understanding regarding its relationship to the authority of the Lord's teaching regarding the Torah. The Didachist has used his position as an influential teacher and also co-opted, as it were, the Lord's authority via the *sectio* in order to bolster the authoritativeness of his Torah mandate. In this the apostles, who are never again mentioned in the Didache and not to be confused with the itinerants of Did. 11–14, are merely part of the chain by which the Torah is transmitted to the Didachean community.

The *Sectio* as the Words of Jesus

While intensely practical in its subject matter, the Didache is also a Christological document, invoking the name of the Son in its baptismal formula in 7.1, 3; identifying Jesus as the holy vine of David in 9.2; and as the Lord's

17. Matt 5:48.

18. Luke 5:33–39 and 6:1–11.

19. Jervell, "The Law in Luke–Acts," 27. See also Wilson, *Luke and the Law*, 12–58.

20. I follow David Rudolph's line of thinking in this regard, as set forth in his book *A Jew to the Jews*, 54–67.

child, also in 9.2 and 10.2, 3. A high Christology is also suggested, as in Did. 16.7 the Didachist conflates the images of the Lord Jesus and the Lord God in describing his appearance in the clouds. The Didache is congruous with the Gospel of Matthew, of which Andrew Chester wrote: "Jesus is the one who brings in the divine, eschatological kingdom, and along with this, he is also the eschatological judge, and the one who speaks with divine authority."[21] The following paragraphs make the case that the Didache's interpolation of sayings understood to be characteristic of the Lord (Jesus) functions to bolster the authority of its Two Ways teaching.

In Did. 1.3b–6, which is called the *sectio evangelica* the Didachist chose to use words that are elsewhere explicitly attributed to Jesus. That these sayings were widely known to be uttered by Jesus is quite evident, as Justin Martyr cites much of the same material in *1 Apol.* 16, presumably with the Gospels as his source, directly attributing it to Jesus, as does Tatian's *Diatessaron* 9.7–11.[22]. Among Two Ways texts, these sayings are unique to the Didache and its textual descendants. None of the earliest Two Ways texts include them. They are not found in the *Doctrina* or Barnabas, although they are found in the fourth-century Apostolic Constitutions, which in Apos. Con. 7 is an embellished copy of the Didache.

Viewing the *sectio* in context, there is a commonality between these Jesus sayings and a distinction between them and the rest of the Way of Life. This distinction lies in the repetitive pattern within these paragraphs as in three cases the command is accompanied by a promised reward for observing it. But in the *sectio* the repetitive pattern stands out, as the following chart illustrates:

Injunction	**Reward**
εὐλογεῖτε τοὺς καταρωμένους ὑμῖν . . . (Did. 1.3 = Luke 6:28)	. . . καὶ οὐχ ἕξετε ἐχθρόν (Did. 1.3)
ἀπέχου τῶν σαρκικῶν ἐπιθυμιῶν . . . (Did. 1.4, Matt 5:39; Luke 6:29)	. . . καὶ ἔσῃ τέλειος (Did. 1.4a)
παντὶ τῷ αἰτοῦντί σε δίδου . . . (Did. 1.5, Luke 6:30)	. . .ἀθῷος γάρ ἐστιν (Did. 1.5)

21. Chester, *Messiah and Exaltation*, 505.

22. This is not always the case, as in Clement of Alexandria's *Protrepticus* 10, where the Double Love Command and to turn the other cheek are attributed to God (θεός).

The pattern of injunction and incentive is reinforced and its intent demonstrated by a second, sonal pattern. Nikander has demonstrated that the *sectio* is "full of aural repetition of certain sounds and links,"[23] underscoring its oral origins and the need to make the teachings memorable. Unsurprisingly, the sonal "units" that Nikander identifies match the table above, as the sonal units each correspond to a discrete topic. Blessing one's enemies in Did. 1.3 is rewarded by not having an enemy; putting away fleshly desires in Did. 1.4, is rewarded by perfection; and unreserved giving in Did. 1.5 results in the reward of innocence. In the context of a Didachean oral presentation with a teacher animating the teaching, the connection between command and reward in each unit would be further accentuated. In this way the content, sonal patterns and performance of the *sectio* each contribute to a distinctive pattern of command and reward.

In this respect the Jesus sayings hark back to the macarisms of the Beatitudes. Draper noted this in his 1983 dissertation,[24] finding a parallel in *Serek* 4.2–8, which counsels that fearing the laws (משפט) of God brings humility, patience, abundant compassion, and a host of desirable traits and rewards culminating in "a crown of glory with majestic raiment in eternal light."[25] Ephesians (if not the apostle Paul himself, as its authorship is disputed) demonstrates an early Christian sensitivity to promise in the context of commandments, as it singles out honoring one's parents as "the first commandment with a promise."[26] In notable contrast the remainder of the Way of Life contains commands, but does not offer any specific reward for keeping them, with the exception of the injunction ἴσθι δὲ πραῢς of Did. 3.7 which is comparable to Matt 5:5 μακάριοι οἱ πραεῖς, where both texts are accompanied by the reward of inheriting the earth. The sectio therefore adds a motivational component not found in the original Two Ways material. In addition, the Didachist's use of Jesus sayings is an implicit authentication of the entire Two Ways material as congruent with the Lord Jesus' teaching.

Linking command and reward, in a manner that Jesus was known for, as in the Beatitudes, the Didache has reinforced its *sectio* to its audience as the words of Jesus. Functionally, the *sectio* serves to accentuate the higher standards by which Jesus' followers are to live and to define the community in contrast to the "gentiles."[27] In this sense it sets its readers apart from the nations on the basis of their adherence to its teachings in

23. Nikander, *The Sectio Evangelica*, 309.

24. Draper, "A Commentary on the Didache," 76–78.

25. Martinez and Tigchelaar, *Dead Sea Scrolls Study Edition*, 77.

26. Eph 6:2.

27. Did. 1.3.

a way comparable to Israel and the Law. Rather than detract from the Torah, it incentivizes it, in the distinct saying of Did. 1.5b "Happy is the giver according to the commandment" (ἐντολή). Whereas the rest of the Two Ways is in the second person, this incentive is marked by a shift to the third person, warning the hearer regarding correct giving and receiving, and regulating their behavior. As a clarifying statement with a switch of person and language not found in the Gospels, it is apparently an addition by the Didachist, as Niederwimmer also surmises.[28] If so, this strengthens the sense that the Didachist has Torah in mind.

In summary, while the Didache is a Christological document, the *sectio* distinctly sets forth the words of Jesus in a manner that highlights both injunction and incentive. This is evident in the *sectio*'s structure and corroborated by its aural and performative aspects.

Conclusion

The Didache's *sectio evangelica* is a special contribution to the Two Ways tradition in the early church, not witnessed in other early and related Two Ways treatises. This is consonant with the nature of the Two Ways as a Jewish topos, being transmitted by Jews from within that tradition, thus highlighting the significance of the *sectio*. From there, unsurprisingly, the *sectio* is demonstrably to be viewed in the context of a Torah mandate, as a comparison with Matthew and Luke corroborates. Further, the vocabulary of the *sectio*, evidently drawn from Jesus sayings, is characterized by a distinct pattern of injunction and incentive. This was framed for its audience both in its structure and aural features which would have been apparent in a performative context.

That the *sectio*'s Jesus sayings should emerge from a document seated within nascent Judaism and more specifically the stream of Christian Judaism demonstrates that the Didache deemed Jesus' teachings wholly congruent with that. We have not noted any contrast being made between the two. The special significance of the *sectio* is seen in its affinity to the Gospels of Matthew and Luke, and it is noteworthy that both Gospels are affirmative of the Torah in general, and use the same material as the *sectio* in a manner which affirms it.

28. Niederwimmer, *The Didache*, 82.

8

The *Sectio*, Jesus, and the Two Ways

Introduction

THE PREVIOUS TWO CHAPTERS have demonstrated from the *inscriptio*, the Two Ways distinction, and the Double Love Command that the Didache imposed a stark, decisive choice upon its recipients, leaving them no realistic alternative but to adopt the Way of Life. This "choice" was inextricably linked with the authoritative words of the Teacher—Jesus—via the *sectio evangelica* of Did. 1.3b–6.

This chapter begins with an analysis of the Double Love Command and Golden Rule's prefatory remarks to the *sectio*, and then a series of arguments and observations of structural features that make a tight connection between the *sectio* and the following Way of Life. From there, thematic linkages are also highlighted, all of which build a cumulative case that the *sectio* is no mere afterthought or clumsily executed insertion, but well considered and placed to emphasize and underscore the Torah taught in the subsequent Two Ways teaching.

The Placement of the *Sectio*

The first sign that the *sectio* is a carefully crafted prelude to the Two Ways material the Didachist had at hand is revealed in its placement directly following the Double Love Command and the subsequent Negative Golden Rule, which thereby serve as an introduction. This chapter does not digress to a full redactional analysis as the underlying methodology is to work with the text as it is presented to us in H, presumably its final redaction, but it must be noted that the Double Love Command belongs to a sequence of redactions of a *Vorlage* witnessed not only by the Didache but also the Apostolic Church Order (ACO), the Epitome, and *Doctrina apostolorum*.

Among these texts the Didache is the only one to include the subsequent *sectio*, which is then found in texts dependent upon it, namely the Apostolic Constitutions and *P.Oxy.* 1782.

With the *sectio* placed where it is, the Double Love Command functions as the primary statement upon which the *sectio* ultimately depends and seeks to interpret for its reader. The Didache's insertion of the *sectio* is notable in that it culminates and intensifies a clear and logical progression from 1) the Two Ways *Vorlage* and its introductory statement regarding the divergent Ways of Life and Death; to 2) the interpretative Double Love Command which defines the Way of Life; to 3) the added Golden Rule; to 4) the inserted *sectio*; and then 5) the resumed Two Ways *Vorlage*. The progression is as follows:

The Placement of the *Sectio*

1.	*Two Ways Vorlage*	There are two ways; one of life and one of death, and the difference is great between the two ways. The way of life then is this:
2.	Double Love Command	First love the God who made you; second, your neighbor as yourself.
3	Golden Rule	And anything which you would not wish to happen to you, do not do to another.
4	*Sectio*	Didache 1.3b–6
5	*Resumed Vorlage*	Didache 2.1—6.2

Immediately following the Rule, Did. 1.3 continues with the introduction to the *sectio* "And these the words of the teaching are this." This is a progression that Niederwimmer only partly notes, portraying the Golden Rule "as an interpretation of the commandment to love the neighbor."[1] Milavec is in basic agreement, hailing the "Negative Golden Rule" as the definition of the Double Love Command, but his view that the Double Love Command "summarizes positively what must be done" while the Rule "summarizes negatively what must be avoided"[2] while correct, neglects the relationship between the command to love one's neighbor and the subject of the Rule, which is also one's neighbor which is significant to the argument being made here.

1. Niederwimmer, *The Didache*, 66.
2. Milavec, *The Didache: Text*, 46.

It demonstrates the Didache's focus on the horizontal relationships between people rather than vertical, between people and God.

While not given enough attention in scholarship, this progression from the Double Love Command to the Rule to the *sectio* and then on to the Two Ways material itself is important as each component ties back to the Double Love Command which in turn is itself rooted in Torah. This contrasts sharply with Barnabas. Based on a different version of the Two Ways *Vorlage*, Barnabas fits in with this wider pattern characterized by Christian adoption of the Double Love Command that primarily emphasized its commands without stressing elements that would harken back to the Torah. In that respect the writer omitted the key markers πρῶτον and δεύτερον[3] which has the effect of muting any allusion to the tables of the Decalogue and the Torah.

This is consistent with Barnabas' interpretation of "the new law of our Lord Jesus Christ, which is without the yoke of compulsion."[4] Support for this view is also found in Carleton Paget's characterization of Barnabas' intent as being to "interpret the law in the right way," with appeal to Barn. 10.12 where Barnabas declares that having a "righteous understanding" he announces "the commandments as the Lord wished."[5] In this Barnabas is possibly countering Christian-Jewish interpretations of the "yoke of the Lord" as in Did. 6.3 and therefore has no intention of reinforcing a doctrine supporting the ongoing obligation of the Torah for Christians. Draper also sees the possibility of a polemic from Barnabas against a "torah oriented Christian-Jewish us[e] (sic) of the Two Ways."[6]

Among the Gospels, the most similar account of the Double Love Command to that of the Didache is found in Matt 22:36–40, but there are notable differences. Whereas the Didache uses the terms πρῶτον and δεύτερον, in Matt 22:38–39 (agreeing with Mark 12:29–30) the first commandment is not merely designated as πρῶτον, but as ἡ μεγάλη καὶ πρώτη ἐντολή, putting the emphasis on the greatness and priority of the first command, and thus the first table of the Torah. Further, for Matthew the second command is subsumed into the whole in that Jesus' subsequent reference to "all the Law and the Prophets" places the emphasis not so much on the relationship between the two tables of the Torah as on the fact that they summarize the Torah as a whole. In this regard in Matt 22:40 the reader is specifically informed that Jesus teaches ἐν ταύταις ταῖς δυσὶν

3. Barn. 19.2

4. Barn. 2.1 and also Barn. 10.11–12. Ehrman (LCL).

5. Paget, *Barnabas*, 62.

6. Draper, "The Two Ways and Eschatological Hope," 232–34.

ἐντολαῖς ὅλος ὁ νόμος κρέμαται καὶ οἱ προφῆται. Jesus thus answered the question regarding the "great" commandment in such a way that the whole (ὅλος) of the Torah might be addressed in his reply, turning the emphasis away from first command, the ἐντολὴ μεγάλη which he had been asked about, and to the totality of the Law.

As Luz observes, Jesus "does so without being asked" so "it is important."[7] In Saldarini's words, "For Matthew, the Double Love Commandment (22:37–39) gives meaning and direction to the whole Torah."[8] This fits neatly with Matthew Thiessen's thesis that Matthew's emphasis on the Law has an apologetic element to it, countering those who would claim that Jesus was abolishing (καταλύω) the Law and that he and his followers were therefore responsible for divine punishment and "the destruction of Jerusalem."[9] For the Didache, the promulgation of the Torah among gentiles is part of the Matthean concern for the Law insofar as it pertains to its Christian audience. The Didache's distinctive treatment of the Double Love Command is more concise and clear than Matthew in its use of both terms πρῶτον and δεύτερον to enunciate the Double Love Command of God and one's neighbor. Whilst the Torah itself is not explicitly referred to, the implicit reference to the two tables of the Torah serves to compensate.

The Didache's version of the Double Love Command is distinct from the Gospels and contemporaneous literature in that it places the emphasis on the second command. It has something in common with b. Šabb. 31a, where Hillel cited the Golden Rule (which, we have already noted, bears on the second command) to a gentile who wished to convert to Judaism. In doing so he is recorded as having omitted any reference to the first command. Hillel's instruction "What is hateful to you, do not to your neighbor: that is the whole Torah, while the rest is the commentary thereof; go and learn it." As a text explaining what Hillel (or the rabbis later reporting this interchange) believed was required for converts to learn, the parallel to the Didache and its use of the Golden Rule is striking. Significantly, while the Two Ways "motif" is "pervasive" in Barnabas,[10] the Rule is not found, one of the features indicating that the latter is based on a different and possibly earlier redaction of the Two Ways material.

In summary, the Double Love Command has roots in the Torah and Jewish tradition and the Golden Rule ties that Torah tradition to the second table of the Law. In later Christian texts it is tied most strongly to the first

7. Luz, *Matthew: A Commentary*, 3:83.

8. Saldarini, *Matthew's Christian-Jewish Community*, 57.

9. Thiessen, "Abolishers of the Law," 554.

10. Kraft, *Barnabas and the Didache*, 5–6.

command, to love God. However, in Matthew and Mark, it is tied to both tables of the Torah with the two commandments as an encapsulation of the whole. The Didache is distinct in its citation of the Double Love Command with emphasis on the second table of the Torah. In this it bears comparison with Hillel's dictum, which without reference to the first table, also applied the second table to the gentile convert.

Harmonizing *Recueil* or Structured Prologue?

While the *sectio* has already been treated at length in chapter 7, at this point the question regards its purpose and how it fits into the structure and progression of the Didache's Two Ways material. Directly following the Double Love Command and the Golden Rule, the *sectio* continues in the form of positive admonitions. In contrast, the subsequent Way of Life, starting in Did. 2.2, takes the form of negative prohibitions, which serves to draw attention to the Way of Life's affinity to the Decalogue.

Various suggestions have been made concerning the purpose of the *sectio*. We argue here that while there is a Christianizing element to the interpolation of the *sectio*, its purpose was to prepare the reader for the Torah-centric character of the following Two Ways material. It reveals that the Didachist not only wanted to impute the Lord's authority to the teaching, but also to put the emphasis on the neighborly relations characteristic of the second table of the Law.

The common characterization of the *sectio* as a "Christianizing" interpolation carries with it the tendency to minimize or altogether miss the *sectio*'s significant role as a preface to the Didache's Two Ways material. Found only in the Didache, the Apostolic Constitutions and subsequent dependent documents which have utilized the Didache, the *sectio* was clearly of marked importance to the redactor. Milavec's theory concerning its role is that the *sectio* prepares the disciple to "withstand the hostility of family and friends" and that subsequently "the Decalogue and its extensions are considered as the rules for living revealed by the Father."[11] This fits with Milavec's view of the Didache as a pastoral document, but is inadequate in that it fails to address the choice of location of the *sectio* between two passages that are demonstrably tied to the Torah; the Double Love Command and Did. 2.

Bentley Layton's study of the *sectio* utilizes source analysis and examination of its "deliberate constructive formal devices" such as rhetorical figures and literary forms for his extensive evaluation of it as a "harmonizing

11. Milavec, *The Didache: Faith*, 103.

recueil."[12] Layton thereby suggests that the Didachist's "purpose in doing so" is reflected in the "formal structures of the individual verses."[13] Despite the questionable nature of a methodology which rests on the *sectio*'s presumed basis in written sources, his observation that the *sectio* seems more elaborate than the Gospels and most likely "interpolated into an edition of the *Didache* which had been previously published"[14] has merit. However, Layton's methodology does not yield any clear answer as to the "purpose" of this "harmonizing *recueil*" other than to suggest that the redactor was plagiarizing canonical Christian sources "for the composition of a pseudonymous 'Apostolic' teaching."[15]

Perttu Nikander has speculated that "Regarding its placement, the Sectio Evangelica would fit better topically in the context of the *anawim* sayings in Did. 3.8–10 and the rules for life and society in Did. 4 and not before the first vice list in Did. 2."[16] There is merit in this in that the *sectio* is neither a list of commands as in Did. 2 nor a list of vices as in Did. 5, suggesting that the Didachist's primary concern was other than to find the most harmonious location for its insertion. While Nikander does not set out to discern the purpose of the *sectio*, its placement is telling.

Nikander's analysis of the *sectio* is particularly helpful as it highlights the role of aurality in its composition. Drawing attention to the *sectio*'s "repetition of certain sounds and links," Nikander suggests that the *sectio* came into its present form as the result of repeated interaction between speaker and audience.[17] This observation is akin to Draper's observations regarding the Two Ways section in Did. 2–5 in which on the basis of mnemonic markers and the commonality between the Two Ways' vices to those cited by Paul, he strikingly suggests that "it is not the content that is particularly unique to the Two Ways tradition, but the order in which the material is arranged."[18]

While it is necessary to give these elements their due weight, a further consideration remains, which is the evident relationship between the insertion of the *sectio* and the command at the end of the Two Ways to take on the "entire yoke of the Lord" in Did. 6.1–2 (see chapter 10 below). It is a

12. Layton, "The Sources of Didache 1.3b–2.1," 344–45.

13. Layton, "The Sources of Didache 1.3b–2.1," 350.

14. Layton, "The Sources of Didache 1.3b–2.1," 350. See also Wengst, *Didache (Apostellehre)*, 19–20.

15. Layton, "The Sources of Didache 1.3b–2.1," 349–50, 372, 79.

16. Nikander, *The Sectio Evangelica*, 296.

17. Nikander, *The Sectio Evangelica*, 309.

18. Draper, *Vice Catalogues*, 133.

relationship of which Audet stated "on notera, en outre, l'exactitude de la correspondance de 1:2–3a et de 6:1, du point de vue de la composition, de même que celle de παρεκτὸς θεοῦ [6.1] avec le titre Διδαχὴ κυρίου qu'a dû recevoir très tôt le *Duae viae*."[19] Its relevance to the Didache's presentation of Torah requires further comment however, for the *sectio* and the epilogue of 6.1–2 are closely related not only to the Two Ways but also to Jesus' application of the Torah as it appears in the Gospels.

As seen above in chapter 7, the *sectio* appears in Jesus' application of the Torah in the Gospels of Matthew and Luke, and as will be seen below in chapter 10, the very reference to a "yoke" is not only a recognizable nod to the saying preserved in Matt 11:28–30, where Jesus says "Take my yoke upon you," but a term closely related to observance of the Torah. It is unlikely to be coincidence that as prologue and epilogue, both of the passages identify the "teaching" (ἡ διδαχή/τῆς διδαχῆς) as their subject, which is specifically the Two Ways section between them. Combined, they both frame the intervening material and stress its importance, putting it both in the context of Christ's teaching and that of the Torah itself.

In summary, both Layton and Nikander highlight aspects of the *sectio*'s structure, and while their analyses do not provide a firm conclusion regarding its purpose, there is enough evidence to argue that the *sectio* is more than a mere Christianizing interpolation or harmonizing *recueil*. This is confirmed when one examines the placement of the *sectio* in relationship to what we might then call the *conclusio*.

The *Sectio*: Double Inclusion

A further structural sign of the *sectio*'s integration with the following Two Ways material is provided by means of two inclusios, bracketing devices, that occur at the beginning and end of the *sectio*. If we are correct in viewing the *sectio* as interpolated by the Didachist, which is a fairly sure assumption, the Didachist has deliberately included phrases in the *sectio* which he or she observed later on in the material.

The first is found in Did. 1.2 which teaches the recipient to love the "God who made you" (τὸν ποιήσαντά σε). While not overt and possibly unconscious on the part of the Didachist, this phrase finds its complement in Did 5.2 (=Barn. 2.2) which states that those who are on the Way of Death do not know their maker (τὸν ποιήσαντα αὐτούς). Milavec links Did. 1.2 to God's development of the fetus in the womb, as described in Ps 139:13–16.[20] However, it is

19. Audet, *La Didachè*, 352.

20. Milavec, *The Didache: Faith*, 108.

most likely God as Creator of everything that is in view, as seen in the reprise of the theme in Did. 10.3 where the after-meals blessing acknowledges God as the Creator of all things (ἔκτισας τὰ πάντα). This is supported by Philo's observation in *Decalogue* 50–51 that the first table of the Decalogue begins its five commands with "God and Father and Creator of all."[21] Against the pantheon of gods that gentile Christians had previously honored, this assertion of God as Creator emerges as a concern of the Didache, at the beginning and end of the Two Ways material. As both occurrences of this inclusio are in redactional passages, the use of the device indicates an emphasis and underscores the role of the Torah in the *sectio*.

The first bracket of the second inclusio is found in Did. 1.4. It is the second of a series of three promises that begin with the *sectio*'s first phrase εὐλογεῖτε τοὺς καταρωμένους with its motivating result καὶ οὐχ ἕξετε ἐχθρόν being the positive reward of living according to the ideal presented. The disciple is secondly promised that by living up to the ideal of turning the other cheek, he or she ἔσῃ τέλειος (Did. 1.4). A third promise is made for generosity in the phrase μακάριος ὁ διδοὺς (Did. 1.5), which is not repeated later in the Two Ways. Of these three promises, it is that regarding τέλειος which is repeated later in the Two Ways section.

It is not the Torah related overtones of the term τέλειος, as will be discussed in chapter 10, but that it returns as a reprise in Did. 6.2, that catch the reader's attention. This leads Khomych to the natural conclusion that the two occurrences form "some sort of inclusio."[22] Unlike the first inclusio, where the Didache has appropriated an existing theme from Did. 5.2, both brackets of this inclusio occur in redacted passages. In the latter bracket of this inclusio then, τέλειος is the promised result for bearing the "whole yoke of the Lord," a phrase that Niederwimmer takes as a "sicher redaktionellen Stück,"[23] as the phrase is absent in Barnabas, Apostolic Constitutions, and all other texts.

As with the first inclusio, this one also resonates later in the Didache, being found in 10.5 and 16.2. However, there is a striking difference in that the two occurrences related to the Two Ways material both present τέλειος in the context of promise and reward.[24] In the later occurrences, 10.5 is a prayer that God would perfect his church, and 16.2 admonishes faithful participation in the church as a prerequisite for perfection. The use

21. Colson, (LCL)

22. Khomych, "Perfection in the Didache," 5.

23. Niederwimmer, *Die Didache*, 94. Also Sandt, *Bearing the Entire Yoke*, 340.

24. Rordorf and Tuilier see this as being by the hand of the same redactor. *La Doctrine Des Douze Apôtres*, 32–33.

of τέλειος in both the *sectio* and Did. 6.2, part of a redactional bridge to the ensuing chapter on baptism, indicates that the term is significant and that the device was used with intent. By the fact that they are part of the inclusio, the natural implication is that the teachings of the *sectio* are as much a part of this "yoke" as the Torah Lists.

The Didache's use of inclusios has repeated precedent in the Torah and its legal code, Leviticus, and several examples of this are worth mention. Firstly, Lev 25:1 begins an extended discourse concerning possession of the promised land with a fitting locative reference to Mount Sinai (אל־משה בהר סיני) from whence the Lord gives Moses laws regarding the Land. The section likewise concludes in 26:46 (בהר סיני ביד־משה). Secondly, Lev 11:3–6 and 45 arguably are an inclusio surrounding the food laws. Thus, "the singular use of maʿăleh in Lev. xi 45 is explained" by its occurrences in prior use to describe animals that chew the cud.[25] Thirdly, Michael Fishbane further points out that the legal-ritual material of Lev 11–15 is "closed off by means of an historical *inclusio*," namely the death of Aaron's sons in Lev 10 and a second reference to it in Lev 16:1.[26] A fourth example is in the Lev 18 catalogue of prohibited sexual relationships with the bracketing declaration "I am the LORD your God" in 18:2 and 18:31. This is then followed by Lev 19:19–37, a catalogue of laws that begins with "you shall obey my statutes" (את־חקתי תשמרו) and ends with "you shall obey all my statutes" (ושמרתם את־כל־חקתי). David Stewart sees the entire chapter as a "mini-Torah" set within an inclusio formed by 19:2b and 36b surrounding fourteen legal sections marked off by the "nominal self-identification clause" (אני יהוה (אלוהיכם in reduced form.[27]

While not conclusive, the creation of inclusions by the Didachist gives the appearance of intent. Consciously or unconsciously, the same convention found in the Levitical code has been used and the Didache has bound the *sectio* to the entirety of the Two Ways section by means of inclusios.

In summary, with the Didache's two inclusios, the phrase τὸν ποιήσαντά σε/ αὐτούς and the term τέλειος binding the *sectio* to the Two Ways material as a whole, the legal nature of the *sectio* becomes apparent. While parenetic and hortatory styles pervade the Two Ways, in this regard its structure harkens back to Israel's legislative code.

25. Rendsburg, "The Inclusio in Leviticus XI," 419.

26. Fishbane, "Biblical Colophons," 439.

27. Stewart, *Leviticus 19 as Mini-Torah*, 310–11.

The Second δεύτερον

A further hallmark of the *sectio*'s integration with the Two Ways material is found in the direct progression from the *sectio* to the second chapter of the Didache by means of an insertion between the two sources. The insertion is the term δεύτερον in Did. 2.1, a striking repetition of the δεύτερον in Did. 1.2 since there is no parallel to the πρῶτον of 1.2. We will suggest that it is an error of minimization to hold Kloppenborg's position that the "framework" provided by πρῶτον and δεύτερον merely "suggests some familiarity with the Christian tradition."[28] Rather, this awkward structure is best explained as the result of the Didachist's view of the Two Ways as Torah. Niederwimmer nevertheless judges this "ein notdürftiges Konstrukt, hinter der keine tiefsinnige theologische Konzeption, sondern lediglich ein literarisches Ordnungsprinzip steht. Das Konstrukt hat keine weitere Bedeutung als diese, den Anschluß an das Zitat der Vorlage widerherzustellen."[29] *Pace* Niederwimmer, the construct (Did. 2.1), while simply Δευτέρα δὲ ἐντολὴ τῆς διδαχῆς, is neither artless nor without significance.

The Repeated Stress on Δεύτερος

Did. 1.2	πρῶτον ἀγαπήσεις τὸν θεὸν . . . δεύτερον τὸν πλησίον σου . . .
Did. 2.1	Δευτέρα δὲ ἐντολὴ τῆς διδαχῆς·

In reality, this bridge at the end of the *sectio* further signals its role in the entire Two Ways section. Whereas the preceding Double Love command explicitly uses the terms πρῶτον and δεύτερον, in the *sectio* there is no introductory πρῶτον, but in what gives the appearance of a *non-sequitur* the term δεύτερα is employed in its concluding bridge to the following list of prohibitions in Did. 2.2–7. The omission is pronounced, and requires an explanation. Either the Didachist was exceptionally clumsy, leading to the assumption that this is just carelessness, incompetence, or an accident on the part of the Didachist, or there was a purpose in the omission. The first possibility gives the appearance of being an argument from silence, or at best a presumption, whereas the second possibility opens up an opportunity for investigation.

28. Kloppenborg, *The Transformation of Moral Exhortation*, 98.

29. Niederwimmer, *Die Didache*, 115.

In light of the Didache's omission of a second πρῶτον, Garrow notes the "confusion" created by δεύτερα, and with reference to the literature asks "Does the interpolation interpret the first commandment . . . or is it a primary interpretation of the second command?"[30] Given the content of the *sectio*, which reflects only the second table, the answer is given by the text. It follows that since the Didachist was aware that the content of the *sectio* was founded upon the second table of the Torah and its focus on loving one's neighbor, it was entirely appropriate not to insert πρῶτον prior to the *sectio* as the *sectio* also reflected the concerns of the second table rather than the first.

The bridge in Did. 2.1, serving to introduce the prohibitions of Did. 2, is therefore not employed to contrast the "second commandment of the teaching" with what has just been said, but rather to stand in parallel with the introductory phrase "τούτων δὲ τῶν λόγων ἡ διδαχή" in Did. 1.3, signifying that both the *sectio* and Did. 2 are the same "teaching." In both phrases the particle δέ is used, but the context does not substantiate any idea that the Didachist intended to imply a contrast. The *sectio* thus leads directly to the prohibitions in Did. 2.2–7 which stand in the text as commands to be interpreted in sympathy with the *sectio*. The *sectio* is therefore in parallel, not in contrast, to Did. 2. This is reflected in Ehrman's translation which translates the particle δέ in a complementary sense: "And now the second commandment," thus implying that the Didache is proceeding from the first to the second.[31] In this vein, the evidence supports Audet, who sees no break and translates the phrase simply as a header: "Deuxième commandement de l'instruction."[32] This accords with the third-century *Doctrina apostolorum*, "Interpretatio autem horum verborum haec est."[33]

Lastly, a thematic integration of the *sectio* to the Two Ways material must be noted, particularly in regard to its admonitions regarding three categories of relationships. The initial command to love God and one's neighbor in Did. 1.2 is echoed in the words of 4.1–3 where the teacher is to be honored as a way of giving honor to the Lord, and the "presence of the saints" is to be sought out every day. The second type of relationship is with those who are hostile, and take advantage of the disciple. Tellingly, it has reconciliation as its objective, for if the disciple follows the instructions given "you will not have an enemy." This is the topic of Did. 1.3–4, which

30. Garrow, *Matthew's Dependence on the Didache*, 69.

31. Ehrman (LCL). In contrast, Lake (LCL) translated it as "But." Ehrman has moved away from this sharp contrast.

32. Audet, *La Didachè*, 227.

33. Schaff, *The Oldest Church Manual*, 219.

presages 2.7: "Do not hate anyone, but reprove some, concerning whom you should pray, but some you should love over your own soul." Thirdly, charitable relationships are dealt with in Did. 1.5 which advocates giving and warns against taking advantage of others' generosity. This theme, clearly a prominent part of community life, is a prominent part of the Two Ways, occurring in 2.3a and 4.5–8. The neighbor also figures prominently in 2.6, "Do not accept evil council against your neighbor," and communal relations are the overriding concern throughout Did. 4.

In summary, the signposting of Did. 2.1 is best regarded as intentional and informed, linking the *sectio* tightly to the following Two Ways material. The thematic integration of the *sectio* also evidences careful composition. While the *sectio* prefaces the Two Ways material, it is therefore intentionally counted part and parcel of the whole. This further suggests that the Didachist saw the entirety of the material as related to the second command—the second table of the Torah.

ἐπιθυμία and Its Connotations

In addition to literary and redactional connections between the *sectio* and the Two Ways, a number of thematic continuities exist between the two sections. Most notable is the *sectio*'s use of the term ἐπιθυμία which connects it to the Didachist's concern with the prohibitions of ἐπιθυμία in the Two Ways section. Of all of the commands thrice repeated in the Two Ways section, this is the only one that occurs in the *sectio*. This might be unremarkable except for the curious way in which it is listed in those three instances.

The concern with the "lusts of the flesh" is a recurrent focus in both the Pauline and Catholic epistles as seen in Rom 13:14; Gal 5:16, 24; Eph 2:3, 1 Pet 2:11; 2 Pet 2:18; and 1 John 2:16. Such uses of the term with a negative connotation are comparable to Philo's use in *Spec. Laws* 4.93–94 where such desire (ἐπιθυμία) is the antithesis of reason, grounded in animal nature and exemplified by "food taking and copulation."[34]

Contrastingly, ἐπιθυμία is not a focus point for other, earlier New Testament renderings of the Decalogue's commands, which generally omit coveting altogether. Romans 13:9 is the exception, with Paul's Decalogue-based declamation Οὐ μοιχεύσεις, Οὐ φονεύσεις, Οὐ κλέψεις, Οὐκ ἐπιθυμήσεις. This makes it the more remarkable that the Two Ways material turns to ἐπιθυμία so quickly in its lists. While Niederwimmer thinks that this "motif" was introduced to the text as a gloss,[35] his evidence by

34. Colson (LCL)

35. Niederwimmer, *The Didache*, 104.

way of parallels in 1 Pet 2:11 and Tit 2:12 is not sufficient to refute that the *sectio* was framed with an awareness of this "motif" in the Two Ways and its origins in the Decalogue.

Internal to the Didache's Two Ways, in all three lists the order of the final two commands regarding ψευδομαρτυρία and ἐπιθυμία is reversed in comparison to the order in both the MT and LXX, with ἐπιθυμία being placed before, rather than after ψευδομαρτυρία. Further, in the latter two lists the two commands no longer remain adjacent to each other in the order (when other interjecting commands are removed), but are interspersed with the others. This reordering has two observable features, the primary one being the heightened prominence of ἐπιθυμία in all three lists.

Secondly, the greatest divergence from the original order occurs in Did. 3.3, where ἐπιθυμία is raised to second place after φόνος. This prohibition of wrongful desire emerges as the greatest disruption to the Didache's Two Ways' otherwise faithful representation of the second table of the Torah. In the midst of this structure therefore, the prohibition of ἐπιθυμία appears of special interest to the Didachist.

As in the *sectio*, the second occurrence of ἐπιθυμία in Did. 2.3 addresses relations with one's neighbor. In the phrase οὐκ ἐπιθυμήσεις τὰ τοῦ πλησίον, its language closely follows the prohibitions in the LXX translation of Exod 20:17 and Deut. 5:21, although without the Torah's specificity regarding the objects not to be coveted. Niederwimmer contends that the phrase belongs with οὐκ ἔσῃ πλεονέκτης in Did. 2.6,[36] but this supposition is simply based on the two phrases' common theme. One might ask why, if the two phrases so obviously go together, did the Didachist so clumsily separate them? Rather, its early placement in the Didache's lists of Torah commands is consistent with all three lists in the Two Ways material.

This leads to the third occurrence of ἐπιθυμία, in Did. 3.3, in which a distinct shift in the usage of the term can be observed. In Did. 3.3, rather than being faced with a stark list as in the previous and following lists, the inductee is given sapiential advice concerning how to keep each of the commands. As has been frequently noted,[37] in this respect the Two Ways material bears comparison to the later rabbinic Derek Ereṣ Zuṭa. Both texts frequently reflect the same protection of the Torah by providing a "fence" around it in the manner referred to in 'Abot 1.1:

> Moses received the Law from Sinai and handed it down to Joshua, and Joshua to the elders, and the elders to the prophets, and

36. Niederwimmer, *The Didache*, 90.

37. E.g. Draper, "A Commentary on the Didache," 67; Milavec, *The Two Ways as a Rabbinic Training Manual*, 4.

> the prophets handed it down to the men of the Great Assembly. They said three things: Be deliberate in judgment, raise up many disciples, and make a fence round the Law.[38]

While not a Two Ways text, Derek Ereṣ Zuṭa, which begins with the words דרדן של תלמדי (lit: The ways of scholars) is often viewed as coming from a similar source to the Two Ways and reflects similar concerns to the Didache. It is also quite possible that its first four chapters come from the Tannaitic period, which encompasses the date of the Didache's composition.[39] Its form of instruction, similar to that of the Didache's Two Ways τέκνον section (Did. 3–4), is typified in Der. Er. Zuṭ. 1.12 "Keep aloof from anything that may lead to sin" and (2.7) "Keep aloof from anything which may bring you to sin. Recoil from [even] a minor sin that it may not lead you to a major sin."

In Did. 3.3, not only does ἐπιθυμία prominently occupy second place after φόνος, but its significance is fleshed out for the convert in terms of sexual morality. Thus, the passage cautions the convert: τέκνον μου, μὴ γίνου ἐπιθυμητής, ὁδηγεῖ γὰρ ἡ ἐπιθυμία πρὸς τὴν πορνείαν. The emphasis on the term's bearing on sexual behavior is marked, exceeding that of Der. Er. Zuṭ. 1.4, which reflects the warning concerning desirous looks related to ἐπιθυμία in Did 3.3 saying, "Do not be enticed into sin by your eyes, because enticement into sin is caused only through the eyes." Here the concern is muted, and not repeated again. Its usage in Der. Er. Zuṭ. is neither necessarily sexual in nature nor exclusive of it and bears comparison to its usage in the *sectio* in which Did. 1.4 commands 'ἀπέχου τῶν σαρκικῶν ἐπιθυμιῶν." As does Der. Er. Zuṭ., the *sectio* puts the command in a wider context, with the following context instructing the convert how to endure oppression from one's neighbor. If used as a reference point, Der. Er. Zuṭ. therefore reflects a comparable adaptation of the command.

The fourth and final occurrence of ἐπιθυμία between the *sectio* and the Two Ways section is in Did. 5.1. There the list of characteristics of the Way of Death begins with φόνοι, μοιχεῖαι, ἐπιθυμίαι, πορνεῖαι, and κλοπαί. By its proximity to μοιχεία and πορνεία, ἐπιθυμία is here clearly associated with sexual indiscretions rather than coveting, as in the Decalogue. This follows the Didachist's pattern of grouping similar commands together in the Way of Death list, in which for example μαγεῖαι and φαρμακίαι (magic arts and potions) are grouped as well as θρασύτης, ὕψος and ἀλαζονεία (brazenness, pride and pretension), among other groupings.

38. Blackman, *Mishnah*, 4.489.

39. Ginsberg, *Derek Ereṣ Zuṭa: Introduction*, Minor Tractates, 58a (1).

Thus both the third and fourth occurrence of the term are in the sexual context. This contrast between the first two occurrences of ἐπιθυμία and the latter two was observed by Audet in connection with Did. 2.2, where Audet pointed out that Did. 2.2 has more to do with property and that this contrasts with the "sexuel" context of Did. 3.3.[40]

The possibility must be entertained that the Didache, as a Jewish text, reflects contemporaneous Jewish prejudices concerning gentile vices, using what Burton Easton called "a regular 'form' for denouncing Gentiles, in which idolatry was linked with the habitual perpetration of various grossly atrocious deeds."[41] It should be noted that in the New Testament vice lists the term is only found in Col 3:5; Titus 3:3; and 1 Pet 4:3. However, as can be seen in Siegfried Wibbing's statistical overview of all the terms in the New Testament lists, sexual sins are the most frequently proscribed vices among them.[42] For whatever reason, whether or not there was an "Urkatalog"[43] from which the Two Ways material constructed its vice lists, this concern emerges as primary, and such a concern in a teaching addressed to new converts from paganism should not be surprising. In concurrence with this, the later material of the Didache no longer addresses the issue and the term ἐπιθυμία does not recur.

To summarize, the Didache's Two Ways treat the prohibition of ἐπιθυμία in a curious manner. In the *sectio* and Did. 2 it is related to loving one's neighbor. In Did. 3 and 5 it is related to sexual indiscretions. In the Torah lists (to be discussed in more detail below) it emerges not merely as the last command of the Decalogue, but is brought forward in each list suggesting its importance in the mind of the Didachist. The Didache's stress on ἐπιθυμία, the most prominent thematic link between the *sectio* and the Two Ways section, underscores its significance to the Two Ways material and while not definitive proof in and of itself, correlates with the nature of the document as instruction for new gentile converts.

The Thematic Linkage between the *Sectio* and Two Ways

Further thematic continuity between the *sectio* and the Two Ways section is found in the topic of giving and generosity. While not one of the commands of the Decalogue, charity is a significant concern of the Torah, as exemplified in Lev 19:9, 23:22; and Deut 15:11. In the *sectio* (Did. 1.4), the

40. Audet, *La Didachè*, 306.

41. Easton, "New Testament Ethical Lists," 4.

42. Wibbing, *Die Tugend- und Lasterkataloge im Neuen Testament*, 87–88.

43. McEleney, "The Vice Lists of the Pastoral Epistles," 217.

concern is evident in terms of the teaching regarding relationships between the disciple and those who would abuse and take advantage. This is continued in Did. 1.5–6, which gives rules regarding charity for the disciple and the needy. In the Two Ways material, instruction regarding charity and the poor is given in all three sections: 2.6; 4.5–8; and 5.2.

In the *sectio* the instruction to give is not restricted to members of the community, as the disciple is told παντὶ τῷ αἰτοῦντί σε δίδου.[44] At the same time the disciple is told to give with discretion, γνῷς, τίνι δῷς,[45] which well might suggest putting a priority on members.[46] This instruction is more than mere instruction, but a command. In a key phrase, the *sectio* declares μακάριος ὁ διδοὺς κατὰ τὴν ἐντολήν, the key word ἐντολή potentially providing a link not only to the following Two Ways Torah, but a common understanding of charity as a responsibility enjoined by the Torah. This is both a general principle, as in Lev 23:22 with the command to leave the corners of the field for the poor and the stranger, and specific, as in Deut 15:7–11 which requires direct charity for the poor. The phrase also recurs in Did. 13.5 and 13.7, and in each context it is connected to the instruction to give, using the same verb (δίδωμι).[47] This suggests an association between the phrase and the command to give. Regardless of the saying's source, it is a link between the *sectio* and the latter material of the Didache, a further indication that the redactor had the work as a whole in mind as he fashioned the interpolation, and within that certainly the Two Ways material he was prefacing. The *sectio* thus serves to introduce the Two Ways' emphasis on generosity and giving.

In support of this connection between giving and Torah, CD 6.14–21 provides a helpful point of comparison within Second Temple Judaism: "act in accordance with the exact interpretation of the law . . . to abstain from wicked wealth which defiles . . . to set apart holy portions according to their exact interpretation . . . to strengthen the hand of the poor."[48] The same sentiment is reflected in Sirach 29:9 (NRSV): "Help the poor for the commandment's sake, and in their need do not send them away empty-handed." In this respect ill-gotten wealth, tithing and charity are all matters of "the law" (התורה).

44. Did. 1.5.

45. Did. 1.6.

46. Draper contrasts this to the Essenes, suggesting from CD that they would only give to members of their community "A Commentary on the Didache," 43.

47. Possibly this phrase is linked to Jesus' words "it is more blessed to give than to receive" as quoted by Paul (in Luke's account) in Acts 20:35, per Niederwimmer, *The Didache*, 82. This backs up Luke's portrayal of the Jerusalem church as giving its resources to all who were in need (Acts 2:45).

48. Martinez and Tigchelaar, *Dead Sea Scrolls Study Edition*, 559.

A further statement in the sectio states ἀθῷος γάρ ἐστιν, to affirm that the one who gives according to the commandment is "innocent." The implication is that if the one who gives according to the commandment is innocent, the one who does not must be guilty. Both this teaching and that of Did. 4.5–8, which warns the disciple "μὴ γίνου πρὸς μὲν τὸ λαβεῖν ἐκτείνων τὰς χεῖρας, πρὸς δὲ τὸ δοῦναι συσπῶν" parallel to *4QInstruction*, a substantial sapiential text from the DSS, which states in 3.2–5 (=4Q118.9–10) "remember that you are poor [. . .] and your need you shall not find, and in your disloyalty you [. . .] . . . entrusts you, you shall not stretch out your hand to it, lest you be scorched [and] your body be burned by its fire. A[s] you [have received] it, thus give it back, and you will have joy if you are innocent from it."[49] The shared emphasis on the outstretched hand and the attribution of innocence to those who do not stretch out their hands in greed correlates to the texts' shared theme of giving. Not only do the *sectio* and the Two Ways share the theme of giving, but the theme of giving is associated with the commandments of the Torah.

In summary, this section has demonstrated the close integration of the *sectio* with the earlier material of the Two Ways. The Double Love Command and Golden Rule make a connection to the second table of the Law in a manner that is distinct to the Didache. The *sectio* is characterized by an internal structure that points to careful composition and evident purpose. This is borne out by two *inclusios* that bind it to the Two Ways section, and a purposeful second δεύτερον again placing the stress on the second table of the Law. The theme of ἐπιθυμία, the only command of the Decalogue that is common to the *sectio* and Two Ways evidences that this is a significant concern of the Didache related to new converts from paganism. Finally, the theme of charity and greed provides a further connection to the Torah.

Conclusion

This chapter has demonstrated a number of features regarding the placement of the *sectio* in the Didache, of which it is a defining feature. Directly following the Double Love Command, in conjunction with the Golden Rule, it serves to emphasize the second table of the Torah. As a prologue that bears comparison to the Two Ways "yoke of the Lord" epilogue, it places stress on the Torah as mediated by Jesus. This "bracketing" of the Two Ways material is furthered by the presence of two inclusios tying the *sectio* to the Way of Life, one of which teaches love for God as our Creator, the second of which teaches the reward of perfection for the obedient

49. Martinez and Tigchelaar, *Dead Sea Scrolls Study Edition*, 851.

disciple. The character of this Way of Life is marked by the use of the word δεύτερον, again denoting the second table of the Torah. This linkage is again evident in the prominence of the word ἐπιθυμία, which first occurs in the *sectio* and then is elevated in each of the Two Ways material's Torah lists. Lastly, the Didache's concern for charitable giving also provides a complementary thematic linkage, leaving little doubt that the *sectio* is more than a clumsy insertion, but a carefully considered composition intended to buttress the Didache's Torah.

9

The Torah and the Two Ways

Introduction

As this chapter will show, the Two Ways of the Didache has a close affinity not only to the Torah, but specifically to the Decalogue. That affinity provides insight into the Didache's reception of the Decalogue, which is emblematic of its reception of the Torah as a whole. Andrew Chester points to four possible attitudes to Torah in the early Christian movement: intensification, fulfilment, new Torah, and rejection.[1] None of these fit the reception of the Torah in the Didache, however. As seen in chapter 6, it is modelled after the Deuteronomic choice between life and death that was presented to Israel, within that form there is a tripartite repetition, or Decalogue structure, and markers in the text that present and teach it as Torah. This chapter will synthesize existing research into these two aspects and advance it further to demonstrate the Didache's perception of its teaching as Torah for the Christian gentile.

The Decalogue and the Structure of the Two Ways

Chapter 1 has noted that various paradigms have been advanced to express the relationship between the Two Ways and the Torah. Since the earliest days of Didache research, scholarship has recognized a relationship between the content and structure of the Two Ways material and that of the Decalogue. At this point a closer look at the Decalogue as it is presented within the Two Ways will not only demonstrate the Didache's intentionality in adapting the Decalogue's form, but also suggest its foundational concern related to the

1. Chester, *Messiah and Exaltation*, 533–35.

crises the community was facing. Subsequently, this concern will be further clarified in comparison to contemporary ethical lists.

The Two Ways Structure and the Torah

While it is common for scholars to recognize a relationship, scholarship has not paid enough attention to the implications of the structure of the Didache's Two Ways section and its concomitant stress on the Decalogue. Niederwimmer's commentary is representative of this evaluation, as regarding Did. 2.1ff he simply notes that "If necessary, one may further acknowledge the second table of the Decalogue as furnishing the basic structure for the whole." While acknowledging the manner in which the Decalogue carries through the Two Ways, he states that "The catalog of vices in 5.1–2 is (not in form but certainly in content) a doublet of this one."[2]

In contrast to views of the Two Ways as a Christian ethnicization or adaptation of the Torah, the structure of the Two Ways and the sequence of the replicated injunctions from the Decalogue point to a more serious and intentional purpose in the Didache's Two Ways.

The Two Ways section of the Didache has a distinct and purposeful structure, which permits insight into the Didachist's reception of the Torah. This structure has been acknowledged and recently surveyed at length in Shawn Wilhite's doctoral dissertation on apocalypticism in the Didache's Two Ways.[3] Wilhite's summary pays particular attention to the framework of the Two Ways, with the introduction to the Way of Life in 1.2a and its conclusion in 4.14c, then the introduction to the Way of Death in 5.1a and its conclusion in 5.2b.[4] This overall framework provides an entrée to the yet more intricate structure within the Two Ways, as noted at the start of chapter 4. For our purposes, such a careful structure directs attention not so much to the means by which it might have been refined—through oral repetition or careful redaction—but to the authorial intent in its redaction.

Within this overall framework, the Two Ways exhibits a tripartite form, marked by orderly repetition of prohibitions from the Decalogue, evidencing a consistent underlying motif. A summary of the commands in the tripartite Two Ways section, compared to those of the LXX for Exod 20:13–17, is given in the following chart as a basis for further illustrating the Two Ways as the Didache's Torah based instruction. These commands, specifically from the second table of the Torah, are shown in each of the

2. Niederwimmer, *The Didache*, 88–89.

3. Wilhite, *One of Life and One of Death*, 139–63.

4. Wilhite, *One of Life and One of Death*, 163.

Didache's three lists in the order that they occur, minus intervening commands that are not found in the Decalogue.

Sequence of the Decalogue's Commands in Each Part of the Two Ways

Exod 20:13–17; Deut 5:17–19				
BHS	LXX	Did. 2.2–7	Did. 3	Did. 5
לא תרצח	μοιχεία	1—φόνος	1—φόνος	1—φόνος
לא תנאף	φόνος	2—μοιχεία	ἐπιθυμία	2—μοιχεία
לא תגנב	κλοπή	3—κλοπή	2—μοιχεία	ἐπιθυμία
לא־תענה	ψευδομαρτυρία	ἐπιθυμία	ψεύστης	3—κλοπή
לא תחמד	ἐπιθυμία	ψευδομαρτυρία	3—κλοπή	ψευδομαρτυρία
Sequence: 1 2 3 4 5	2 1 3 4 5	1 2 3 5 4	1 5 2 4 3	1 2 5 3 4

As seen above, in all three lists, Did. 2, 3 and 5, the commandments regarding murder (φόνος), adultery (μοιχεία), or theft (κλοπή) are presented in the same sequential order (albeit with intervening commands), and in the order of the Hebrew Text as represented by the extant MT. In contrast, the Septuagint (LXX) records the order as μοιχεία, φόνος, and then κλοπή. The natural implication is that the Didachist may have been more familiar with the Hebrew version than the Greek. This brings to mind Draper's assertion that the variation of order in the Didache's five prohibitions is in fact due to the difference between the Hebrew and Greek Decalogue.[5] The picture is somewhat more complex however, for as the Didache's lists uniformly follow the Hebrew text for the first three commands it then uniformly reverses the order of both the Hebrew and the Greek for the final two, making coveting (ἐπιθυμία) precede false witness (ψευδομαρτυρία) each time.

The apparent order in the Didache's lists, where the first three commands of the Decalogue as attested to in the MT never go out of sequence, even though the final two are reversed and interspersed between them, is intriguing and indicative. This is all the more so, for as Gerald Lanier's comprehensive tabulation of the Decalogue in the ancient versions and citations demonstrates, the first three commands frequently occur in various sequences, but the other seven (the five of the first table and the final two) do not.[6] The final two commands, as noted in the study of ἐπιθυμία,

5. Draper, *Vice Catalogues*, 120.

6. Lanier, "Scriptural Inspiration and the Authorial "Original," 71.

disrupt the order, and in doing so are independent of both the Hebrew and LXX. The order of the first three commands does, however, suggest that the redactor is most comfortable with the order of the Hebrew text and has held to it. Even though other commands intervene in Did. 3 and 5, the order of the first three does not deviate.

In terms of the Decalogue's use in the New Testament, Ulrich Schmid writes that such passages "had been taught, recited and probably memorised. Therefore, most certainly they involve issues of orality."[7] On this point, it is apparent that while it is eminently arguable that the Didache is fundamentally an oral production that was committed to writing, rather than a literary production that formed the basis for oral instruction, its relationship to the established texts of Exod 20:13–17 and Deut 5:17–19 is incontrovertible.

As Kloppenborg points out,[8] following on from Jefford,[9] the Didache and *Doctrina* follow the Masoretic Text. What needs to be noted is that like Matthew and Mark they have done so instead of following the LXX, which makes adultery the sixth command preceding murder, suggesting the Didache's affinity to the Hebrew source.[10] There is yet a further reason to believe that the established text the Didachist had in mind was the Hebrew rather than that of the LXX.[11] If this is the case, the phonetic similarity between לא תנאף and לא תגנב, both with a lingual (נ) and ending in a labial (פ and ב) would naturally have been a mnemonic help. On the other hand, if the Didachist were working with the text of the LXX foremost in his mind, there would have been no such aural sequence to help keep the commands in order.

In summary, all three lists in the Two Ways include all of the second Table of the Decalogue, indicating distinct and purposeful intent. While the lists vary somewhat in the order by which they replicate the commands in the second table of the Torah, there is a discernible inner consistency and structure. In conjunction with the permanent order of the first three commands of the second table of the Law, the final two are variously placed among them, but never displacing the first, φόνος. These two, despite their varying placement in the lists, are consistently in the same order. In all three lists, none of the five are omitted. This careful and consistent adaptation

7. Schmid, *Versions of the Mosaic Law*, 587–88.

8. Kloppenborg, *The Transformation of Moral Exhortation*, 100.

9. Jefford, *The Sayings of Jesus*, 55–56.

10. *Contra* William Varner "The Didache's Use of the Old and New Testaments," 139–40. This is also true of the two key Hebrew Bible quotations later in the Didache, in Did. 14.3 (Mal 1:11, 14) and Did. 16.7 (Zech 14:5).

11. It is worth noting that the extant MT, of course, post-dates the LXX by the greater part of a millennium.

of the second table of the Torah demonstrates the Didache's concern to emphasize it, and in conjunction with that, to particularly emphasize the prohibition against desire, or coveting.

Idolatry

In addition to the five commands of the second table, appearing twice, in the latter two lists of commands, the first table prohibition of idolatry also appears in the Two Ways material. In Did. 3.4 the disciple is warned that "divining," "astrology," and "purifications" all lead to εἰδωλολατρία, which is mentioned twice. Later, in Did. 5.1, εἰδωλολατρία is listed between "theft" and the "magic arts," both characteristics of the Way of Death. It is the same association seen in Gal 5:20, although more often idolatry is associated with fornication and the like. Some, such as Flusser, have associated the prohibition of idolatry with the three "capital sins, idolatry, bloodshed and fornication" which are "frequently mentioned in rabbinic literature."[12] Of these, idolatry in particular distinguished the nations from Israel in the Jewish consciousness, as can be seen in the New Testament.[13]

Rather than ethics, the issue of idolatry is primarily related to cult. As Oskar Skarsaune points out, this is the only instruction prior to those on baptism "concerned with ritual commandments."[14] This is comparable to the issue in Acts 15, where in Myllykoski's view "The speeches of the two apostles clearly show that Luke relates the decree to cult and not to ethics."[15] Thus following the Two Ways material, Did. 6.3 further prohibited the consumption of food offered to idols, giving the reason that to eat such food is service to the θεῶν νεκρῶν. Whether one was going to "be perfect" or not, eating such food was a negation of the true worship of God. Consumption of such food was an acute problem that had to be dealt with as a matter of high importance.[16]

Zetterholm's point, however, even more closely highlights the Didache's concern with the disciples' identity. This is substantiated by the other elements of the decree that indicate that while the presenting issue in Jerusalem was that of circumcision,[17] the discussion quickly turned to the related issue of identity ("no distinction between us and them") in Acts

12. Flusser, *Paul's Jewish-Christian Opponents*, 196.

13. 1 Cor 12:2; 2 Cor 6:16; 1 Thess 1:9.

14. Skarsaune, *In the Shadow of the Temple*, 361.

15. Myllykoski, *Without Decree*, 432.

16. Zetterholm, *The Didache, Matthew, James, and Paul*, 89.

17. Acts 15:5.

15:9 and James' appeal in Acts 15:16–18 to LXX Amos 9:11–12 "that the remnant of mankind may seek the Lord, and all the gentiles who are called by my name."[18] For the Didache, the same concern is evident, first from the association of εἰδωλολατρία with pagan superstitious practices, but also from the close association between the Way of Life with the rubric of loving "the God who made you" in 1.2. This is later borne out in Did. 6.3's prohibition of any connection to the worship of "dead gods,"[19] which associates Christian identity with their renunciation.

The addition of the first table prohibition of εἰδωλολατρία can thus be seen as a fitting complement to the commands of the second table, which have been systematically set forth for the disciple. This prohibition has implications not only for the cult, but also the new identity of the disciple.

The Two Ways and Contemporary Ethical Lists

Not only do the structure of the Two Ways section, and signs within it, substantiate a strong relationship to the Decalogue, but also the Two Ways section's relationship to ethical lists in the New Testament and contemporary literature.

It is a natural assumption to make that Jews, at least generally, did not have a negative attitude to lists of prohibitions, the Decalogue itself being one such list. However, contemporary ethical lists from the Jewish world did not always include the commands of the Decalogue. Philo cautions his reader in *Sacrifices* 32, concluding with a recommendation of "the virtues," listing no less than 146 vices. These are carefully arranged in related groups of three, prefaced by the warning "Know then, my friend, that if you become a pleasure-lover you will be all these things."[20] In them there is no reference to the Decalogue nor its specific injunctions. This lack of correspondence is also evident in Josephus' *War* 2.8.7 (=2.139–42) which describes the entrance requirements for the sect of the Essenes. Whereas the sect had a high regard for the Torah and stringent interpretations concerning adherence to it, Josephus' record is of a list of oaths for proselytes. Of the Decalogue's stipulations, only piety towards God (εὐσεβήσειν τὸ θεῖον) and theft (κλοπή) are mentioned.

18. As Carl Holladay notes, only "the Greek version, not the Hebrew, supports James's contention that the mission to the Gentiles is part of God's original intention. This shows that James's speech is a Lukan composition based on the Septuagint rather than a summary of a speech delivered in Aramaic and based on the Hebrew text." *Acts: A Commentary*, 301–2.

19. See 1 Cor 8:4; 2 Clem. 3.1; *Diognetus* 2.

20. Colson (LCL).

It must be kept in mind that this is not a Two Ways teaching, but also that it demonstrates that distinctions were made, and while some lists included reference to the Torah, others, for other purposes, did not.

In regard to the New Testament, scholars have frequently viewed its ethical lists as founded in the ethical teaching of the Stoa, as Easton suggested.[21] While this connection is fraught with some difficulty, even so Easton's argument demonstrates the fact that generally New Testament lists do not closely follow the Decalogue or other Torah forms.[22] In our view then, the connection between the virtues of the Stoa and the New Testament should not be taken for granted. These examples should suffice to show that within nascent Judaism, neither Stoicism nor the Torah were essential to ethical lists. Particularly in regard to the Torah, this is noteworthy, as the Hebrew scriptures are ubiquitous in quotation and allusion throughout the New Testament. The question as to the extent and manner in which the NT writers used the Decalogue in their vice lists is thus a germane point of reference for the Didache's use of it in its Two Ways section.

In contrast to the above, the Two Ways material as redacted by the Didache proceeds to greatly embellish the five commands of the Decalogue's second table with additional prohibitions, numbering seventeen in Did. 2; thirty-six in Did. 3–4; and thirty-two in Did. 5 (the latter in the framework of a description of the characteristics of those on the Way of Death). This embellishment is comparable to the embellishment of the command against idolatry in *Pseudo-Phocylides*' introductory stanzas, such as "Neither commit adultery nor rouse homosexual passion."[23] Now understood to be a first-century CE or BCE document, Ps.Phoc. has some of the same characteristics as the Didache's Two Ways, this being a case in point: the statement of a command from Torah followed by a contemporary admonition. As discussed above however, the Didache is distinct as in each of its lists the commands from the Decalogue are positioned at the beginning, with few or no vices or prohibitions separating them, suggesting a strong tie to the Decalogue.

21. Easton, "New Testament Ethical Lists," 1–2.

22. The four cardinal virtues, φρόνησις, ἀνδρεία, σωφροσύνη, and δικαιοσύνη (wisdom, courage, prudence, and justice) are part of a holistic value system. A tension exists, however, between Stoic values and ethical lists. Plato therefore seems to have had misgivings about any such approach with laws to follow, and as he has Socrates explain (Republic 4.425b), "For anything laid down by law, verbally or in writing, does not happen in my opinion, nor would it last." This is the view of Siegfried Wibbing, who writes "Tat und Freiheit können in der stoischen Philosophie nicht in einem wesensmäßigen Zusammenhang stehen" *Die Tugend- und Lasterkataloge im Neuen Testament*, 20.

23. Ps.-Phoc. 1.3.

For this reason, the following compilation of NT ethical lists, both of virtues and of vices, takes into account the often omitted lists that include commands from the Decalogue. This table will provide a basis for comparison with the Didache's Two Ways. The lists included comprise three or more virtues or vices with vices listed first as they typically occur first when both occur in close proximity, unlike in the Didache:

Virtue Lists and Vice Lists in the New Testament

Vice Lists	Virtue Lists
Matt 15:19	
Matt 19:18–19	
Mark 7:21–22	
Mark 10:19	
Luke 18:20;	
Rom 1:29–31	
Rom 13:9	
Rom 13:13	
1 Cor 5:10–11	
1 Cor 6:9–10	
	2 Cor 6:6
2 Cor 12:20–21	
Gal 5:19–21	Gal 5:22–23
	Eph 4:2–3
Eph 4:31	Eph 4:32
Eph 5:3–5	Eph 5:9
	Phil 4:8
Col 3:5–8	Col 3:12
1 Tim 1:9–10	
	1 Tim 4:12
	1 Tim 6:11
	2 Tim 2:22

Virtue Lists and Vice Lists in the New Testament

Vice Lists	Virtue Lists
2 Tim 3:2–5	2 Tim 3:10
Tit 3:3	
1 Pet 2:1	
1 Pet 4:3	1 Pet 3:8
1 Pet 4:15	
	2 Pet 1:5–7
Rev 9:21	
Rev 21:8	
Rev 22:15	

In this compilation, Gal 5:19–23 and Eph 4:31–32 are the only instances in which lists of virtues and vices are immediately adjacent, as in the Didache's Two Ways. This suggests that connection or contrast between the two, and particularly the Two Ways topos, was not foremost in the New Testament writers' minds. Further, as can be seen in the table below, Eph 4 does not cite any of the prohibitions from the Decalogue. This leaves Gal 5 as the only passage both listing virtues and vices, and including prohibitions from the Decalogue.[24] This serves as evidence that while the Two Ways metaphor can be found in the New Testament, as in Jesus' depiction of the narrow and broad paths[25] and James' assertion that "friendship with the world is enmity with God,"[26] the Two Ways as a mediation of the Decalogue cannot.

Keeping in mind this point that apart from these examples the New Testament does not feature virtue and vice lists together, a compilation of those vice lists that include the specific prohibitions found in the Decalogue are quite numerous, as the following table shows:

24. If one were to consider Ephesians a pseudo-Pauline letter, the absence of dual virtue and vice lists in the NT (excepting Gal 5) is even more notable.

25. Matt 7:13–14.

26. Jas 4:4. See Sandt, "James 4,1–4 in the Light of the Jewish Two Ways Tradition 3,1–6," 38–40.

Prohibitions from the Two Tables of the Law in New Testament Vice Lists

Third Command: εἰδωλολατρία	Gal 5:20; Col 3:1–8; 1 Pet 4:3
Fifth Command: τίμα	Mark 10:19; Luke 18:20; Rom 1:30
Sixth Command: φόνος	Matt 15:19; Mark 7:21–22, 10:19; Luke 18:20; Rom 1:29; Rom 13:9; 1 Pet 4:15; Rev 9:21, 21:8
Seventh Command: μοιχεία	Matt 15:19; Mark 7:21–22; 10:19; Luke 18:20 1 Cor 6:9–10; Rom 13:9
	πορνεία in Matt 15:19; Mark 7:21–22; 1 Cor 5:10–11; 2 Cor 12:20–21; Gal 5:19–21; Eph 5:3–5; Col 3:5–8; 1 Tim 1:9–10; Rev 9:21; 21:8; 22:15
	κοίτη in Rom 13:13.
Eighth Command: κλοπή	Matt 15:19; Mark 7:21–22; 10:19; Luke 18:20; Rom 13:9; 1 Cor 6:9–10; 1 Pet 4:15
Ninth Command: ψευδομαρτυρία	Matt 15:19; Mark 10:19; Luke 18:20
	ψεῦδος in Rev 21:8; 22:15
	ψεύστης in 1 Tim 1:9–10
Tenth Command: ἐπιθυμία	Rom 13:9; Col 3:5–8; Tit 3:3; 1 Pet 4:3, 15

From the above table it is apparent that at least some of the five prohibitions of the second Table are frequently represented in New Testament lists. Much less commonly, select commands from the first Table are cited, but never more than one in any given vice list. A further breakdown reveals that six of the lists contain three or more of the second Table's five commands: Matt 15:19; 19:18–19; Mark 7:21–22; 10:19; Luke 18:20; and Rom 13:9. Other than Mark 7:21–22 these texts add few or no other vices to their lists.

The lists found in Matt 15:19 and Mark 7:21–22 provide a helpful comparison, as they record the same occasion and saying of Jesus where he lists the things that proceed from within a person and defile them. Mark, by most accounts the earlier of the Gospels, lists thirteen vices, and so on first blush seems most comparable to the Didache. Yet unlike the Didache's three lists, Mark only includes three of the table's five commands: πορνεῖαι, κλοπαί, φόνοι, μοιχεῖαι, (πορνεῖαι and μοιχεῖαι representing the same command). Further, unlike the Didache his list does not begin with φόνος. Yet of Mark's twelve terms, six appear in Did. 2, six in Did. 3, and seven in Did. 5. From these observations, it would appear that while Mark shares much with the

Didache's Two Ways in content, feasibly but not demonstrably from the same extant Two Ways material, Mark's concern was not to represent the second table with its concomitant relationship to the Torah.

In contrast, Matthew replicates four of the second table's commands, maintaining the same order as the Hebrew and the Didache's lists: φόνοι, μοιχεῖαι, πορνεῖαι, κλοπαί, ψευδομαρτυρίαι. Curiously, it is the enigmatic ἐπιθυμία which features prominently and unpredictably in the Didache's lists, which is not included. Nevertheless, Matthew shows a greater affinity to the Didache in terms of its more extensive reproduction of the commands of the table, and its faithfulness to the Hebrew order. Further, while representing more of the second Table, Matthew has also included remarkably few other "vices" in his list, in which μοιχεία is embellished with πορνεῖαι, and ψευδομαρτυρία with βλασφημίαι, both hardly additions, but clarifications of the Decalogue's terms. If Matthew has redacted Mark's longer list as William Hendriksen suggests,[27] in doing so he has brought it into greater conformity to the ideals of the Didache, placing greater emphasis on the Torah as the basis of the vices being prohibited.

The lists found elsewhere in the New Testament, mainly in the Pauline corpus, are also useful as points of comparison. Unlike the Didache there is little to connect these lists to the Torah, with the exception of Rom 13:9, where the Law is explicitly referenced. The terms used are, however, comparable to those in the Didache's lists. In regard to Did. 5, Draper thus points this out in his statement that "There is a remarkable overlap between the content of this list and the commonplace vices cited by Paul."[28] Confirming this, a review of René López' study of Pauline passages with vice lists gives ample demonstration of their detachment from the content and thematic progression of the Decalogue. For López, this demonstrates that while these lists describe the conduct of non-Christians, they serve as lists of vices Christians should avoid.[29]

It therefore appears that when the Torah was in view, New Testament authors (with the exception of Mark 7:21–22) did not typically flesh out their lists with the traditional lists of vices that other Jewish authors were wont to use. On the other hand, as has been illustrated, the Torah was not the foremost element of most NT ethical lists. In contrast, the Torah seems to be what Matthew has in view, in common with the Didache, even though it is not specifically called out by name in either passage. This raises doubts in regard to Vahrenhorst's contention, mentioned earlier in

27. Hendriksen, *The Gospel according to Mark*, 283.

28. Draper, *Vice Catalogues*.

29. López, "Pauline Passages with Vice Lists," 316.

this chapter, that the Didache could not have the Torah in view because it does not mention the Law.[30]

This commonality between Matthew and the Didache, with its use of the Torah as a starting point, calls into question views that would take the Torah as mere supporting material for its instruction. In this latter view, Wilhite suggests that "the Didachist uses a version of the Jewish Two Ways to ground ethics in Torah-like instruction and communal formation."[31] Likewise, Kloppenborg views the Didache's teachings as the product of "Christians who . . . understood ethical teaching to flow from the Torah, and thereby rearranged the Two Ways material in order to make this assumption clear."[32] In both of these views, the Didache's teachings are grounded in the Torah, which forms the basis for something more extensive.

The Two Ways lists of vices, while using some of the same terminology as NT vice lists, do not relegate the Decalogue, or Torah, to the role of a foundation for a teaching of its own. Rather, the "vices" of the Didache's Two Ways reinforce, interpret, and apply the second table of the Decalogue to its recipients. In this way, the Didache actually presents the Torah, namely the second table of the Decalogue. Thus, the Didache has used both the Torah and contemporary paraenetic material in conjunction with each other to make a point.

Further comparisons may be made with the *Serek*, *Doctrina apostolorum*, and Melito's *Peri Pascha*. *Serek* 4 is similar to the Didache in its multiple listing of virtues and vices. Following the introductory "These are their paths in the world,"[33] the true path is described as characterized by the:

> spirit of meekness, of patience, generous compassion, eternal goodness, intelligence, understanding, potent wisdom which trusts in all the deeds of God and depends on his abundant mercy; a spirit of knowledge in all the plans of action, of enthusiasm for the decrees of justice, of holy plans with firm purpose, of generous compassion with all the sons of truth, of magnificent purity which detests all unclean idols, of careful behaviour in wisdom concerning everything, of concealment concerning the truth of the mysteries of knowledge.[34]

In contrast, the "spirit of deceit" is characterized in terms very similar to that of Did. 5, the Way of Death. To it belong:

30. Vahrenhorst, *The Presence and Absence of a Prohibition of Oath*, 372.

31. Wilhite, "One of Life and One of Death," 6.

32. Kloppenborg, *The Transformation of Moral Exhortation*, 104.

33. *Serek* 4.2, as comparable to Did. 1.2a.

34. *Serek* 4.2–6. Martinez and Tigchelaar, *Dead Sea Scrolls Study Edition*, 77.

> greed, sluggishness in the service of justice, wickedness, falsehood, pride, haughtiness of heart, dishonesty, trickery, cruelty, much insincerity, impatience, much foolishness, impudent enthusiasm for appalling acts performed in a lustful passion, filthy paths in the service of impurity, blasphemous tongue, blindness of eyes, hardness of hearing, stiffness of neck, hardness of heart in order to walk in all the paths of darkness and evil cunning.[35]

Remarkably, despite the close similarity of form, these lists do not reflect either table of the Decalogue, either in their structure or content. Rather, these lists reflect the concerns of the *Serek* for those who would join the community.

A comparison may also be made with the *Doct. apos.* While based on the same source, the Doctrina does not follow the MT/LXX order as diligently as the Didache. The prohibitions of *Doct. apost.* 2.2 (=Did. 2.2) in order are adultery, murder, false witness, fornication, and covetousness, or a 2–1–4–x–5 sequence versus the Didache's 1–2–3–5–4.[36] In other words, while *Doct. apost.* reflects much of the content of the second table, it has replaced the prohibition of theft with the prohibition of fornication not found in the Decalogue and made little attempt to reflect the order of the commands. Again, in the equivalent verses to the Didache's τέκνον section (=Did. 3) the only two commands from the Decalogue that are repeated in *Doct. apost.* are murder and theft, which are the first and last in the Didache's list. Finally, in the Way of Death (=Did. 5), the order is adultery, murder, false witness, wrongful lusts, and then theft. Here the sequence is 2–1–5–4–3. For a document most probably based on the same Two Ways *Vorlage* as the Didache, *Doct. apost.* does not reflect the Didache's concern to replicate the general order of the second table of the Torah. Amongst Two Ways traditions based on a common source, the Didache evidences a unique emphasis on and replication of the five latter commands of the Decalogue.

Finally, a more distant comparable is seen in *Peri Pascha*, a work that bears much resemblance to a Passover Haggadah in its Christological application of the Passover to the Eucharist. Composed c. 160 CE, *Peri Pascha* was written by the Bishop of Miletus who is described by Polycrates (according to Eusebius' record in *H.E.* 5.24) as of Jewish birth. In *Peri Pascha* 50 and 51, two short lists of vices have a substantial affinity to the lists of Did. 3 and 5. Thus the list of *Peri Pascha* 50 refers to μοιχεία, πορνεία, φιλαργυρία, and φόνος,

35. *Serek* 4.9–11. Martinez and Tigchelaar, *Dead Sea Scrolls Study Edition*, 77.

36. The *Doctrina apostolorum* has been translated into English by Alistair Stewart-Sykes, *On the Two Ways*, 50–52.

four out of eight vices mentioned. In turn the list of three vices in *Peri Pascha* 51, while not using the same terms as the Didache's Two Ways, replicates the condemnation of Did. 5 in its description of the evil as murderous and in pursuit of evil. While the actual form, or topos, of the Didache's Two Ways is not evident, its general contours and content is present in this work and again there is no attempt to replicate or teach Torah.[37]

In summary, the Two Ways section of the Didache is founded upon and presents the commands of the Torah with additional prohibitions. This has variably been viewed as a Christian exposition of the Decalogue and a "fence" around the Torah. Contemporary Jewish ethical lists such as those of Philo and Josephus may have owed much to Greek thought, and did not necessarily base themselves on the Torah. This is also reflected in the New Testament that does not always include the Torah in its vice lists. Other lists from various sources also serve to highlight the distinctiveness of the Didache in its emphasis on Torah. Nevertheless, particularly in Matt 15:19 there is a particular affinity not only to the Torah but to the vice lists of the Didache. This survey suggests that the Didache employed both traditions—from Hellenism and the Torah to teach Torah to its recipients.

The Torah Markers of the Two Ways

Having established a relationship between the Didache's Two Ways and the Torah, specifically for the Didache a teaching of Torah observance based on the structure of the Decalogue, this section proceeds to examine other syntactical features that bolster the argument that the Didache does indeed view its teaching as Torah interpreted for gentiles. These are the terms "full of cursing" in Did. 5.1, the prohibition not to add or take away

37. A fascinating record indicating the extent to which the Didache's Two Ways teaching may have spread is found in the Jesus Messiah Sutra, left by seventh-century Nestorian missionaries. The Sutra declares in verse 44 that there are two ways: the "wicked-Way-Hell" and the "Way to Heaven." Repeatedly the Lord of Heaven is referred to, identifying its precepts with the Lord God. A connection between the "laws of the Lord of Heaven" is made in verse 74 as the one who lives by them is said to be "a man who 'received the teaching of the Lord of Heaven.'" Reflecting Did. 11.2, *Jes.* (75) warns against the one who "constantly commits evil deeds himself but also teaches others to do the same," although such is not said to be a teacher. *Jes.* (95) instructs that "Those who have 'received the Law and Teaching' of the Lord of Heaven should not act contrary to 'the precepts.'" These precepts are described as ten "vows" and include prohibitions reflective of the Ten Commandments including adultery (107), theft (108) and coveting (109). Significantly, the Nestorian Monument, which records the history of Christianity in China, repeatedly refers to the religion as "the Way," which evokes both the Way of Life and the name by which the early Jerusalem Jesus movement was called. Saeki, *The Nestorian Monument in China*, 163–77.

in Did. 4.13b, and the glaring omission of the first table of the Decalogue (excepting idolatry) throughout.

Scribal Convention: Don't Add or Take Away

The relationship of the Didache's Two Ways to the Torah is further indicated by its concluding prohibitory note to the Way of Life in Did. 4.13b. "Do not forsake the commands of the Lord, but guard what you have received, neither adding nor taking away." The statement parallels and has literary affinities to Deut 4:1–2 (also 12:32 (13:1 MT, LXX)). In that passage, Moses warns Israel to listen to the "statutes and the rules" (אל־החקים ואל המשפטים) he is giving and not to "add to the word that I command you, nor take from it, that you may keep the commandments of the Lord your God that I command you." The consequence of obedience, as in the Didache, is life, underscoring the relationship between the texts.

Did. 4.13	Deut 4:1–2
do not forsake the commands of the Lord	listen to the statutes and the rules that I am teaching
οὐ μὴ ἐγκαταλίπῃς ἐντολὰς κυρίου	שמע אל־החקים ואל־המשפטים אשר אנכי מלמד
guard what you have received	that you may keep the commandments of the Lord your God that I command you
φυλάξεις δὲ ἃ παρέλαβες	לשמר את־מצות יהוה אלהיכם אשר אנכי מצוה אתכם
don't add or take away	not add to the word . . . nor take from it
μήτε προστιθεὶς μήτε ἀφαιρῶν	לא תספו על־הדבר אשר אנכי מצוה אתכם ולא תגרעו ממנו

Both parallel commands begin with a parenetic injunction to adhere to the commands. In the Didache, this is a negative command, whereas in Deuteronomy it is in the positive. Both injunctions however, ἐγκαταλείπω and שמע, emphasize adherence and acceptance of the commands. Both injunctions also include a clear instruction to adhere to the "commands" (Didache), and "statutes and the rules" (Deuteronomy) which are the subject of their teachings. Tellingly, although in Greek, in using the verb φυλάσσω the Didache is using a word that directly corresponds with the Hebrew שמר. Both verbs can just as well be translated "guard," and the LXX translates שמר in that very way, and thus like the Didache uses φυλάσσω. Most recognizably, the command not to add or take away is at the culmination of each passage, in which the Didache uses the same terms that the LXX uses to translate the Hebrew יסף (to add) and גרע (to take away). In light of these strong connections, it therefore seems that Niederwimmer is a bit too hesitant in saying that Deut 4:2 "ist wohl" the model, as there is a high degree of likelihood.[38]

Similar formulations are also found elsewhere in the Hebrew Bible, suggesting that the Didache was also drawing upon a traditional convention. The closest in form is Deut 12:32, but other similar formulations exist, as in Prov 30:5–6 (LXX), Eccl 3:14, and Jer 26:2. This tradition re-emerges in the NT and other Jewish literature, as in Rev 22:18–19, 1 Enoch 104.11, and *Ant.* 1.17, but these examples differ substantially not only in their form, but in their function in the text, as a cursory reading shows and as W. C. Van Unnik has documented.[39]

Such instructions also have well known precedent elsewhere in the ancient Near East, thus Van Unnik quotes the Maxims of Ptahhotep, variably dated from the sixth or twelfth Egyptian dynasties, as advising "Nimm kein Word weg und füge keines hinzu."[40] Simpsons' more recent translation of the passage (prose 18.8 = maxim 43) renders it "Do not say something and then go back on it."[41] The context of Did. 4.13b however, puts it in a framework that is specifically related to the Torah, so such a broad meaning to the phrase is highly unlikely, as this phrase too is specifically related to the stipulations of the Torah.

Often, such statements are associated with ancient suzerainty and international treaties, and as in Deuteronomy are associated with an "inscriptional curse" as Meredith Kline describes.[42] As Bernard Levinson argues, there is a literary origin in the Assyrian king Esarhaddon's vassal treaties of the seventh century BCE. This is seen in the context of the demand for fidelity to the treaty in Vassal Treaty 5.410–13 "(You swear that) you will not alter (it), you will not consign (it) to the fire nor throw (it) into the water . . . nor sweep (it) away."[43] The literary tradition can be seen in later texts such as Rev 22:18–19,

38. Niederwimmer, *Die Didache*, 145.

39. Unnik, "De la Regle" 10–23.

40. Unnik, "De la Regle" 23.

41. Prose 18.8 (= maxim 43). *The Maxims of Ptahhotep*, 147.

42. Kline, *The Structure of Biblical Authority*, 35–37.

43. Wiseman, *The Vassal-Treaties of Esarhaddon*, 60. Levinson also cites Vassal

Ant. 1.17 and 1 En. 104.9, but it is in the Didache's Two Ways setting that the topos occurs most consistently with its Deuteronomic context, as in the Temple Scroll לוא תוסיף עליהמה ולוא תגרע מהמה.

The Didache is quite clear that the commands of its concluding note are the "commands of the Lord."[44] The identity of the Lord is not made clear, although the Lord Jesus may be inferred from the *sectio* and the Lord God from the Two Ways material's content and structure. As I have argued elsewhere, the Didache typically means Jesus when it speaks of the Lord.[45] In this regard, and specifically in the context of the Two Ways, Pardee has rightly specified that "there are no instances in the Two Ways where κύριος requires the translation of 'God' over 'Christ.'"[46] It is reasonable to conclude therefore that the Didache, knowing that its readers and teachers would see both the Lord Jesus and the Lord God in the text, intended this identification of the Son with the Father. As the Sectio, with its close connection to the following ways indicates, this Torah, a rendition of the Mosaic Law, is consonant with the teaching and authority of Jesus. Finally, it has to be noted that while the Didache carefully follows the Deuteronomic convention, Barn. 19.11 entirely omits the warning not to forsake the commands of the Lord, highlighting the differences in their approaches to the Torah.

In summary, the concluding prohibitory note to the Way of Life is intentionally Deuteronomic in form. Its relationship to the Torah is confirmed as the Didache's consistency in reproducing the Deuteronomic form contrasts with other contemporary uses. It is in this context that the words of Pardee, who without developing a case intuitively stated that in her view the Didache uses this formula "because the Way of Life is the law of Moses for gentiles."[47]

Compliance and Confession

For the Didache, the Torah was to be taken with the utmost gravity. Didache 3.6–8 symbolically puts the disciple in the place of Israel in the wilderness, and even before the Mountain of the Lord from whence the Torah was given. Before arriving at the Mountain of the Lord, Israel grumbled.[48]

Treaty 5.397–398 "[whoever changes, neglects or transgresses the] [oaths of this tablet or erases it . . .]," which unfortunately is essentially reconstructed text and less certain.

44. Did. 4.13a.

45. Nessim, *Didache and Trinity*, 3–8.

46. Pardee, *Genre and Development*, 116.

47. Pardee, *The Didache and Oral Theory*, 326.

48. Exod 16:2, LXX διεγόγγυζεν

The disciple is warned not to grumble with similar language in Did. 3.6, μὴ γίνου γόγγυσος. In case this might appear incidental, the passage continues with the admonition to tremble "at the words you have heard."[49] Here the language hearkens back to the language of Israel in the wilderness, for while the LXX doesn't use τρέμω, the picture is that of Israel afraid at the Mountain, requesting Moses speak to God for them, "lest we die."[50] In *Serek* 4.2, this trembling is directly associated with fear of heart (לפחד לבב) before the commandments (משפטי) of God.

The instruction to guard the Teaching, and not to add or take away from the instructions of the Way of Life is directly followed by the instruction in Did. 4.14: ἐν ἐκκλησίᾳ ἐξομολογήσῃ τὰ παραπτώματά σου, καὶ οὐ προσελεύσῃ ἐπὶ προσευχήν σου ἐν συνειδήσει πονηρᾷ. αὕτη ἐστὶν ἡ ὁδὸς τῆς ζωῆς.[51] Ambiguity regarding the meaning of παραπτώματα is evident in the way translators treat it. Ehrman translates the word as "unlawful acts,"[52] in contrast to Bruce Brooks' choice of "wrongdoing."[53] As is discussed here, the meaning of παραπτώματα in this context reflects upon the Didache's reception of the Torah, particularly as it relates to the πονηρά and κατάρας[54] of the Way of Death. In this light, failure to obey the Didache's mediation of the Torah in the Two Ways was, in effect, failure to keep the Torah.

Such confession of sins was indeed clearly linked to failure to keep the Torah, among other things, as demonstrated in the *Serek*, as in 1.21–24 where after "the levites have recited the iniquities of the children of Israel. . . . Those who enter the covenant shall confess after them."[55] Likewise, in CD 15.3–4, in the context of covenant both with the community and the Torah, the text states that "If the judges adju[re] (someone) by the curses of the covenant . . . If he transgresses, he will be guilty and will have to confess and make amends."[56] The same elements found in Did. 4.14—5.1 are present here: transgression, confession, and curse. In a further affinity to the Didache, which stresses the Teaching of the Lord through various teachers, in CD 20.28, confession is linked with listening "to the Teacher's

49. Did. 3.8, τρέμων τοὺς λόγους, οὓς ἤκουσας; also Barn. 19.4; Isa 66:2 LXX "τρέμοντα τοὺς λόγους μου."

50. Exod 20:18.

51. My translation: "In assembly, you should confess your transgressions, and not come to your prayer in consciousness of evil. This is the way of life."

52. Ehrman (LCL).

53. Brooks, *Before and After Matthew*, 269.

54. Did. 5.1.

55. Martinez and Tigchelaar, *Dead Sea Scrolls Study Edition*, 71.

56. Martinez and Tigchelaar, *Dead Sea Scrolls Study Edition*, 563.

voice."[57] As Draper suggests, this tradition continues into later prayer practices, as in the sixth benediction of the daily Amidah סְלַח לָנוּ, אָבִינוּ, כִּי חָטָאנוּ, מְחַל לָנוּ, מַלְכֵּנוּ כִּי פָשָׁעְנוּ ("Forgive us, our Father, for we have sinned, pardon us, our King, for we have transgressed").[58]

In summary then, the Didache's injunction to confess one's sins in the assembly bears comparison to the *Serek*'s admonition to confess unlawful behavior, which is also reflective of later Jewish prayer.

Conclusion

This chapter has demonstrated the affinity between the Two Ways of the Didache and the Decalogue. This has been seen in its distinct and purposeful structure characterized by order and repetition which demonstrate an underlying rationale. When compared to contemporary ethical lists, Jewish, Stoic, and in the New Testament, it is seen that the Decalogue was not a necessary or even common component in any of these genres. The same is seen in the *Serek*, *Doctrina*, and *Peri Pascha*. In contrast, the Didache's Two Ways carefully utilizes the second table of the Decalogue. The connection between the Two Ways and the Torah is confirmed by repeated Deuteronomic injunctions to adhere to its teachings, guard and keep them, and not to add nor take away from them; scribal conventions that echo ancient treaty language. Finally, the seriousness of the Torah thus taught was underscored by the provisions made for confession, an acknowledgement of the Torah's claim upon the individual.

57. Martinez and Tigchelaar, *Dead Sea Scrolls Study Edition*, 581.

58. Draper, "A Commentary on the Didache," 111–12.

10

The Yoke of the Lord

Introduction

In the conclusion to the Two Ways section, the Didachist invokes the metaphor of a ζυγός, a term that is laden with implications for the Didache's reception of the Torah. In Niederwimmer's words, this is the "crux interpretum" of the Didachist's quotation of the Two Ways.[1] The term hardly comes in isolation however, appearing in an instructional matrix of meanings, the interpretation of which has yielded no universally accepted thesis. The purpose of this chapter is to confirm that the "yoke of the Lord" conclusion to the Two Ways has a clear and demonstrable intent to mandate the Torah for the disciple.

In order to accomplish this, it is necessary to determine the point at which the Two Ways section ends. Subsequently, the meaning and implications of τὸν ζυγὸν τοῦ κυρίου can be interpreted partly in that light. Further signs of the Didachist's intent will also be seen in the content and role of the following transitional material.

The Two Ways Conclusion

Like the prefacing *sectio*, the conclusion of the Two Ways is integrated at various levels with the intervening material, supporting its character as Torah teaching. Comparisons with related Two Ways conclusions further illustrate this, as the Didachist pointedly intended the Two Ways section to culminate in his command to adhere to the teaching and to bear the "whole yoke of the Lord" as seen in Did. 6.1–2: εἰ μὲν γὰρ δύνασαι βαστάσαι ὅλον τὸν ζυγὸν τοῦ κυρίου, τέλειος ἔσῃ· εἰ δ' οὐ δύνασαι, ὃ

1. Niederwimmer, *Die Didache*, 153.

δύνῃ, τοῦτο ποίει. In the following paragraphs, I will argue that Did. 6.1–2 forms the conclusion of the Two Ways section with its emphasis on adherence to the Way of Life as Torah.

Views against Did. 6.2 as the Two Ways Conclusion

Rather than taking the view that the Two Ways section of the Didache concludes with 6.2, the majority scholarly opinion has long been that the Two Ways concludes with Did. 6.2–3.[2] The position that Did. 6.3 is part and parcel with 6.2 is considered almost a foregone conclusion by some commentators. Thus in his otherwise comprehensive commentary Niederwimmer does not even note the parallel περὶ δέ that begins both Did. 6.3 and 7.1, ignoring this prominent device that links 6.3 with the following rather than the preceding text.[3]

More recently, Milavec and others have concluded that the Two Ways ends with Did. 6.2. Following a methodology based on the presumed unity of the text and its oral transmission to a trainee, Milavec holds to the "internal coherence" of Did. 1.1—6.2 as the "Training Program in the Way of Life."[4] Somewhat undermining his argument, however, he later points out that the "second person singular prevails in the Way of Life and in 6:1–3."[5] The observation is, of course, correct, but serves better to highlight the change to the plural when baptismal instruction is introduced in 7.1. It is not surprising then, that Pardee has critiqued his assertion that 6.3 belongs with the preceding verses as "unconvincing" and "convoluted."[6] She thus points out the disparity between Milavec's structural analysis of the text and his hypothesis about its flow as an oral teaching. In fact, it is Pardee's later observation that 7.1 refers to the Two Ways as an entity of its own (ταῦτα πάντα προειπόντες) that has led Pardee to suggest that "the text beginning at 7.1 represents a new redaction of a *Didache* that had concluded originally at 6.1–2."[7]

While Milavec's approach is thus problematic, Pardee is nevertheless of the view that Did. 6.2 is the conclusion to the Two Ways material. Recently, Shawn Wilhite has also argued that Did. 6.2 concludes the Two

2. Sandt, *Bearing the Entire Yoke*, 332.

3. Niederwimmer, *The Didache*, 123–24.

4. Milavec, *The Didache: Faith*, 58–59.

5. Milavec, *The Didache: Faith*, 245–46.

6. Pardee, *Genre and Development*, 56–57.

7. Pardee, *Genre and Development*, 76. See also Brooks, *Before and After Matthew*, 259, 283.

Ways in his doctoral dissertation, having analyzed the text in terms of its discourse and the boundary marker περὶ δέ at the beginning of Did. 6.3.[8] In his view, "6.2a and 6.2c are joined together and serve to strengthen collectively the argument in 6.1."[9]

The position that Did. 6.2 is part and parcel with 6.3 in concluding the Two Ways of the Didache has erroneously led writers to connect it to the apostolic decree of Acts 15 in terms of its lenient requirements for gentile Christian practice, three out of four of which pertain to dietary restrictions. In this, they are in company with the fourth-century Apos. Con. 7.20, which expands upon and reinterprets these. Sandt and Flusser entered into an extended exposition of 6.2–3 in this regard, linking not only to Acts 15 but Judaism's Noachide laws,[10] and Alan Garrow points to the "shared interest" that Did. 6.2 and 6.3 have in "doing what you are able" in reference to the yoke of the Lord.[11] On this same basis, Audet in his commentary on Did. 6.2–3 stated "il est impossible de lire 6.2–3 sans penser au vaste problème des rapports de l'évangile et de la Loi tel qu'il s'est posé dans la mission aux gentils."[12]

A connection to the decree is nevertheless doubtful. Niederwimmer himself agrees that there is "no special reference to the 'apostolic decree'" at this point.[13] If there was indeed a relationship to Acts 15, it is curious that there is no reference to "things strangled" or to "blood" in Did. 6 or elsewhere in the Two Ways, which could be expected. It therefore suggests that the food prohibitions of Acts 15 are not in view, and that there is no expansion upon them because the Didachist either did not know of them or did not find them relevant. Didache 6.3 thus prohibits "that which is offered to idols" but does not refer to the "blood" or "what has been strangled" of Acts 15. In other words, the Didache does not evidence influence from the Apostolic Decree at this point.

In addition to promoting a false identification of the conclusion with the Apostolic Decree, the view that the Two Ways ends with Did. 6.3 has also minimized the effect of the Two Ways conclusion, which emphasizes the yoke of the Lord; the consequential reward of perfection; and the accommodation for the disciple's possible inability to keep the commands. These will be discussed in the following pages.

8. Wilhite, "One of Life and One of Death," 153–59.

9. Wilhite, "One of Life and One of Death," 153.

10. Sandt and Flusser, *The Didache*, 238–70.

11. Garrow, *Matthew's Dependence on the Didache*, 97–101.

12. Audet, *La Didachè*, 353. See also Alan Segal, *Jewish Christianity*, 331.

13. Niederwimmer, *The Didache*, 123 n. 38.

Comparisons with Other Texts

The location of the Two Ways conclusion as well as the Didachist's peculiar leanings become apparent when is set alongside the conclusions of other independent witnesses. Specifically, in both Barn. 21.1 and *Doct. apost.* 6.1–4, there are comparable endings to the Two Ways, in which both adjure compliance with the previous teaching. These texts have been selected due to their early dates and close relationship to the Two Ways *Vorlage*.

Conclusions to the Two Ways

Didache 6.2	*Doctrina apostolorum* 6.1, 4	Barnabas 21.1b
Ὅρα, μή τις σε πλανήσῃ ἀπὸ ταύτης τῆς ὁδοῦ τῆς διδαχῆς, ἐπεὶ παρεκτὸς θεοῦ σε διδάσκει. εἰ μὲν γὰρ δύνασαι βαστάσαι ὅλον τὸν ζυγὸν τοὺ κυρίου, τέλειος ἔσῃ· εἰ δ' οὐ δύνασαι, ὃ δύνῃ, τοῦτο ποίει.	Et uide, ne quis te ab hac doctrina auocet, et si minus, extra disciplinam doceberis. 4. Haec in consulendo si cottidie feceris, prope eris uiuo deo; quod si non feceris, longe eris a veritate.	Καλὸν οὖν ἐστὶν μαθόντα τὰ δικαιώματα τοῦ κυρίου, ὅσα γέγραπται, ἐν τούτοις περιπατεῖν. ὁ γὰρ ταῦτα ποιῶν ἐν τῇ βασιλείᾳ τοῦ θεοῦ δοξασθήσεται· ὁ ἐκεῖνα ἐκλεγόμενος μετὰ τῶν ἔργων αὐτοῦ συναπολεῖται.
Watch, lest someone deceive you from the way of the Teaching, for he teaches you away from God. If then you are able to bear the whole yoke of the Lord, you will be perfect, and if you are not able, that which you can, do that.	1. See to it that no one leads you astray from this instruction, since [the person who would do so] teaches apart from the [right] instruction. 4. If you will act with this in mind every day, you will be near to the living God, [but] if you will not act so, you will be far from the truth.[14]	And so it is good for the one who has learned all the upright demands of the Lord that have been written to walk in them. For the one who does these things will be glorified in the kingdom of God. The one who chooses those other things will be destroyed, along with his works.[15]

While the wording differs somewhat the sense is the same as five features common to these Two Ways conclusions can be observed. There is: 1) the initial endorsement of the previous teaching; 2) the value placed upon following that teaching; 3) the exhortation to abide by that teaching; 4) the promise accompanying compliance; and 5) the warning associated

14. Sandt and Flusser, *The Didache*, 130.

15. Ehrman (LCL).

with non-compliance. Following this conclusion, each of the documents proceeds in a manner characteristic of its particular emphasis. In Did. 6.3 the Didachist uniquely turns to the topic of acceptable food, and prohibits food offered to idols. In contrast, but also changing to a different topic, the *Doct. apost.* continues with the words "*Put all this in your mind and you will not be deceived in your hope.*"[16] Likewise, Barnabas changes the topic and theologizes "This is why there is a resurrection."[17] This comparison therefore substantiates the hypothesis that Did. 6.2 is the intended conclusion to the Two Ways section of the Didache. Through to the end of the equivalent to Did. 6.2 each of these passages have the same form and follow the same sequence of instructions. At the same point, each of the passages diverges to a different topic.

Commensurate with the Didache's emphasis on Torah in the Two Ways, its warning associated with non-compliance is markedly different from *Doct. apost.* and Barn. in that while the latter texts are negative in form, the Didache is framed positively: ὃ δύνῃ, τοῦτο ποίει. Uniquely, the Didache does not state any negative consequences for non-compliance, but assumes that the disciple seeks to do what they can to "bear the whole yoke of the Lord" and "be perfect." Vokes has pointed in general to this as a "double standard" being "found in I Cor vii,"[18] an "aristocratic division"[19] between bishops and deacons and the rest of the community. This, however, does not accurately represent the text, which applies the Two Ways to all disciples without discrimination. We thus agree with Niederwimmer, who states that the Didachist "Über den Radikalismus der Gebote des Herrn macht er sich keine Illusionen; wer die Gebote nicht voll zu verwirklichen vermag, soll wenigstens tun soviel er kann."[20] In this regard, our point is that the Didache's injunction to do so is unique and fitting in terms of its signature emphasis on the Torah.

It is possible, but highly unlikely, that both *Doct. apost.* and Barn. have independently truncated the Two Ways conclusion at the same point, removing Did. 6.3. Likewise, the possibility that Did. 6.3 was added to Did. 6.2 at some point in the development of the Two Ways *Vorlage* which the Didache used, and that did not occur in the textual tradition(s) which *Doct. apost.* and Barn. relied upon, cannot be ruled out. However, it is a simpler and more likely solution, that Did. 6.3 is a supplement added by

16. Sandt and Flusser, *The Didache*, (italics original) 130.

17. Barn. 21.1 (Ehrman, [LCL]).

18. Vokes, *The Riddle of the Didache*, 96, 132, 143.

19. Vokes, *The Riddle of the Didache*, 148.

20. Niederwimmer, *Der Didachist*, 77, 156.

the Didachist in joining the Two Ways material to the instructions that follow. This following material is closely linked to the food restrictions of Did. 6.3, as Did. 8–14 are particularly concerned with food in prayer (Did. 8), communal meals (Did. 9–10), the feeding of prophets (Did. 11, 13), and the Eucharist (Did. 14). My position therefore is that regardless of its textual history, Did. 6.2, and not 6.3 is intended to be a conclusion to the Two Ways material.

In summary, a comparison of the conclusions to the Two Ways material in the Didache, the *Doctrina*, and Barnabas has shown that all three documents conclude in remarkably similar fashion and have a similar point of departure at the end of what in the Didache is 6.2. Remarkably, the documents continue with strikingly different teachings. This highlight's the Didache's stress on the yoke of the Lord, and the Didache continues with its base assumption that the disciple will at least attempt to take it upon himself and thus be "perfect." Other possibilities have not been examined in depth, but the most straightforward solution for the role of Did. 6.3 is that it was added by the Didachist, but not as an integral addition to the conclusion.

The Yoke of the Lord

The Two Ways, presented as Torah by the Didache, is concluded with a striking affirmation of the "yoke of the Lord," a term that both requires definition, and placement, in its literary and historical context. Its position at the end of the Two Ways material fits its role as a conclusion, in the series of parenetic admonitions that follow the Way of Death that are noted above. However, the term ζυγὸν τοὺ κυρίου contrasts with the Doctrina's *disciplina* and Barnabas' δικαιώματα τοῦ κυρίου.

The term ζυγὸν τοὺ κυρίου is immediately evocative of Jesus' two uses of the term ζυγός in Matt 11:28–30. In that passage, Jesus teaches that those who accept his yoke "will find rest for your souls. For my yoke is easy, and my burden is light." He does not, however, make it clear exactly what the burden he would relieve his listeners of is. Other NT texts do provide some definition however. Thus Paul opposes the freedom of Christ to a "yoke of slavery" in Gal 5:1. That he is referring to the Torah is given in the previous verses in his polemic for "Jerusalem" rather than "Mount Sinai," the place where the Torah was given.[21] The same sentiment is expressed, with the reference to the Law of Moses in Acts 15:10, which describes it as an attempt to place a ζυγὸν ἐπὶ τὸν τράχηλον τῶν μαθητών ὃν οὔτε οἱ πατέρες ἡμῶν οὔτε ἡμεῖς ἰσχύσαμεν βαστάσαι. Again, 1 Tim 6:1 speaks of bondservants as under a

21. Gal 4:25–31.

yoke. The usage in the NT thus shows that ζυγός is consistently associated with it being a burden, although not always the burden of the Law. Its general usage then, contrasts with Jesus' easy and light yoke, supporting the possibility that Jesus' words were not directly referencing the Torah, particularly as the immediate context in Matthew is to do with Jesus' relationship to the Father rather than Torah. Cynthia Deutsch's extensive study confirms that the yoke is often "a symbol for Torah in the apocrypha, pseudepigrapha, and among the Tannaim, as well as for obedience to God."[22]

As would be expected then, the term is widely attested to in nascent Judaism, but not always in terms of the Torah. Sirach 51:25–26 speaks of putting one's neck under the yoke of wisdom, similarly referring to it as a voluntarily accepted and beneficial burden. Differently, 4Q389 (=4Q*Pseudo-Moses*), an apocalyptic fragment, warns of the "heavy yoke in the lands of their exile,"[23] suggesting that the exile would be a burden. Subsequent to the Didache, rabbinic b. Ber. 14b records a discussion regarding the import of the phrase "bind and write" in Deut 6:8–9 in which R. Simeon b. Yochai reasons that "One . . . should first accept upon himself the yoke of the kingdom of heaven and then accept the yoke of the commandments." A similar use of the term is found in *Sifre* Deut 323.1.2.C (to Deut 32:19–31) "And what did he say to them? 'Accept upon yourselves the rule of Heaven, and let one subdue the other in fear of heaven, and conduct yourselves with one another through acts of unrequired love.'"[24] This representative selection of texts suggests that Deutsch's assertion that "In Second Temple and tannaitic literature, the image of a 'yoke' symbolizes Torah or wisdom, which is identified with Torah,"[25] while it has some merit, cannot be assumed to be correct in all cases.

While a direct reference to the Torah in Did. 6.2 cannot be assumed on the basis of the term ζυγός alone, there are a number of indications in its setting that substantiate the relationship. The first indication is that the Didache unapologetically assumes that its yoke is a heavy burden. As noted above, this contrasts with Matthew's presentation of an easy yoke, and the concern of Acts 15:10 that a heavy yoke should not be placed upon the gentiles. As Jefford puts it, "the Didache shows no awareness of . . . a historical need to explain the easy nature of the 'yoke of the Lord.'"[26] On the face of it, this suggests

22. Deutsch, *Hidden Wisdom and the Easy Yoke*, 130. See also Stuiber, "Das ganze Joch des Herrn."; Draper, "Torah and Troublesome Apostles."

23. Martinez and Tigchelaar, *Dead Sea Scrolls Study Edition*, 781.

24. Neusner, *Sifre to Deuteronomy*, 361.

25. Deutsch, *Hidden Wisdom and the Easy Yoke*, 133.

26. Jefford, *The Sayings of Jesus*, 95. See also Sandt, *Bearing the Entire Yoke*, 334.

the possibility that the Didache does not have the yoke which Jesus promises in Matt 11:28–30 in view, but something else. However, as Hendriksen prefers, a better translation of χρηστός is "kindly" rather than "easy,"[27] which significantly changes the nuances of the passage in Matthew. The two passages therefore are not irreconcilable, for as Philip Sigal argued on the basis that Jesus was teaching halakha that went beyond the requirements of the Law, "What Jesus is cited as saying at Matt 11:28–30 is not meant to lead his followers to believe it will be easy to attain the aim of 5:48."[28]

The second indication provided by the context is the adverb ὅλος (whole), in the phrase "whole yoke of the Lord." Jens Schröter relates this to the *sectio* on the basis of the conclusion's emphasis on perfection, stating that the "'entire yoke of the Lord,' therefore, entails all radical commandments of the *sectio* necessary to keep for attaining perfection."[29] While somewhat justifiable, this is still a bit of a leap, and it is more likely that the Didachist is referring to the whole of the material taught thus far in the Two Ways, including the *sectio*. A similar leap is taken by Sandt who writes that it refers to the "entire Torah" since the phrase "is found in the context of the restrictions on idol-meat in 6:3."[30]

Since the command to take up the "whole" yoke of the Lord implies that others may not take up the "whole" yoke, various commentators have suggested that those who do take it up are the "ascetic" ideal. The concept was notably set forth by Rudolf Knopf,[31] and was partly echoed in agreement by Stuiber[32] and Draper,[33] although I would argue that this view lacks substantiation in the text of the Didache, particularly in light of its early date, before asceticism took hold in the church. The emphasis remains on the promise of perfection to those who can "bear the whole yoke of the Lord." To Draper, this promise introduced a "double standard" between the command to keep the "whole law" of God and "the radical ethical demands" of Jesus.[34] This is reading into the text, however, as the Didachist betrays no awareness of such an implication in his teaching. There is no reason to think

27. Hendriksen, *The Gospel according to Matthew*, 505.

28. Sigal, *The Halakhah of Jesus of Nazareth*, 95. Sandt relates this to Matt 28, and in doing so he attempts to harmonize its meaning with the Didache, suggesting that "Matthew's community pursues a greater righteousness" which "involves exceeding the legal requirements of the Torah." *Bearing the Entire Yoke*, 337.

29. Sandt, *Jesus Tradition in Matthew, James, and the Didache*, 249.

30. Sandt, *Bearing the Entire Yoke*, 337.

31. Knopf, *Die Lehre der Zwölf Apostel*, 21.

32. Stuiber, "Das ganze Joch des Herrn," 325–26.

33. Draper, "A Commentary on the Didache," 134.

34. Draper, "A Commentary on the Didache," 136.

other than that he has done his best to teach the Torah as far as it pertains to gentiles, and views it as the standard of perfection.

More substantive justification is found in the preceding phrases, which similarly employ comprehensive terms. Thus, the way of death is described in conclusion as πανθαμάρτητοι, and is immediately followed by the warning ῥυσθείητε, τέκνα, ἀπὸ τούτων ἁπάντων, in what is clearly a look back at the evil characteristics of those on the way of death in Did. 5.2. Directly after, Did. 6.1 looks back at the preceding ὁδοῦ τῆς διδαχῆς, again referring to the preceding Two Ways, while neither including or excluding the *sectio*. Further justification is found in the subsequent phrase ταῦτα πάντα προειπόντες (Did. 7.1) where the preceding teaching is presented as a prerequisite for baptism. The conclusion therefore is that ὅλος, modifying ζυγός here, is intended to denote that the "whole yoke of the Lord" is the entirety of the Two Ways teaching. That Two Ways teaching, as argued in chapter 9, is indeed founded on and identified with the Torah.

The Didache's "yoke" is also identified as the "yoke of the Lord." As determined in chapter 5.2 the Lord in this text is most closely identified with the Lord Jesus, the Lord of the *incipit* and the *sectio*. Again, this does not imply that the Lord Jesus' teaching differs from that of the Lord God or is not to be identified as the Torah. Here our argument does not depend entirely on the identity of the Lord, as Jesus' teaching in the *sectio* is used to support, not to detract from the Torah taught in the subsequent Two Ways section. As argued in chapter 5.2, Jesus' authority is intended to add his authority to the Torah presented.

Finally, this assertion that gentile converts were to take on the "whole yoke of the Lord" can hardly have been easily or universally accepted in light of early church writers' typical reinterpretation of the Law. In this vein, 1 Clem. 2.8 refers to the "commandments and righteous demands of the Lord [which] were inscribed upon the tablets of your heart."[35] Ignatius, *To the Magnesians* 8.1 warns against living "according to Judaism," which could be a reference either to its traditions or covenant nomism. Barnabas potentially provides a notable external witness to the Didache's yoke in a passage where the readers are encouraged to "commit" themselves to seeking out "the righteous acts of the Lord." Barnabas argues against the sacrificial cult, concluding with the strong words of Isa 1:14: "incense is loathsome to me. I cannot stand your new moons and sabbaths."[36] Following those words, Barnabas continues to assert "And so he nullified these things that the new law of our Lord Jesus Christ, which is without the yoke [ζυγός] of compulsion

35. Ehrman, (LCL).

36. Barn. 2.5. Ehrman (LCL).

. . . ."[37] As Draper opines, this could well be Barnabas' response to the Didache.[38] If that were so, it would be symptomatic of a debate continuing in Christian Antioch well beyond the days of the Didache.

In summary, while it is commonly assumed that the "yoke" of Did. 6.2 refers to the Torah, the record does not allow for absolute certainty. On the other hand, the assertion that the yoke is a burden, in harmony with NT usage, suggests that it is the Torah, and does not contradict the Gospel's statement that Christ's yoke is χρηστός. Further, the term ὅλος, again in context, refers to nothing other than the preceding teaching, which as has already been argued is to be identified with the Torah.[39]

The Lord's Yoke and Its Effects

The context in which the Lord's yoke is prescribed is one in which Deuteronomic themes come to the fore. Three elements, with their associated terms ἐντολή, ἄνομος and τέλειος substantiate these themes and the yoke's relationship to the Torah.

In this regard the first of these themes emerges in the identification of the Way of Life as a commandment (ἐντολή). Reference to the ἐντολή occurs five times in the Didache, three of those being in the context of the Two Ways: 1.5, 2.1, and 4.13. The *sectio* refers enigmatically to τὴν ἐντολήν in Did. 1.5, a sign that its definition was self-evident. Following this the Way of Life begins with ἐντολή as the title of teaching, "implicitly" making "the commandments in the *sectio* the πρώτη ἐντολή and the following commandments the δευτέρα ἐντολή."[40] The Way of Life is then rounded off by Did. 4.13 which warns 'οὐ μὴ ἐγκαταλίπῃς ἐντολὰς κυρίου.' While not an *inclusio* for the entire Two Ways as are those discussed in chapter 8.3, its use at the very beginning and end of the Way of Life[41] does bracket the entire section.

This Way of Life in its *inclusio* is followed by three admonitions: 1) to guard what "you have received, neither adding nor taking away;" 2) to

37. Barn. 2.6. Ehrman (LCL).

38. Draper, *Do the Didache and Matthew Reflect an "Irrevocable Parting of the Ways" with Judaism?* See also Sandt and Flusser, *The Didache*, 241, n.

39. While it is difficult to say with any certainty, a final reflection of this understanding may possibly be found in various early Christian writings such as Barn. 2.6 which gives the appearance of a refutation of the Didache's teaching regarding the yoke of the Lord.

40. Niederwimmer, *The Didache*, 86.

41. Did. 2.1, 4.13.

"confess your transgressions" in the assembly;[42] and 3) not to enter prayer conscious of "evil." While the latter two injunctions clearly have a liturgical purpose, the first of these devices establishes and reinforces commitment to the commandments of the Lord. In this, Deut 4:2 bears comparison, as discussed in chapter 9.2: "You shall not add to the word that I command you, nor take from it, that you may keep the commandments of the LORD [יהוה] your God that I command you," signifying the Torah. In corroboration of this, as discussed in chapter 2.5, the Didache is closely related to the Matthean milieu, and in Matt 5:17–19 ἐντολή is used to refer to the Torah as a whole in the context of a severe warning against relaxing the least of its commandments. In all other occurrences of the noun in Matthew, its usage is closely related to that of the Didache. In particular, Matt 19:17 directly links keeping the commandments with "life" as Jesus tells an enquirer "if you would enter life, keep the commandments." We conclude then, that with the term ἐντολή the Didachist is identifying the instructions of the Way of Life with the Torah.

The significance of ἐντολή is a redoubled one, as its occurrence in 4.13 (ἐντολὰς κυρίου) is also in the context of a conclusion, that of the Way of Life. Andrew Chester notes this connection between the conclusions of 4.13 and 6.1–2, and to him they give the impression of a "'new law' for the kingdom or church" but he does not go so far as to ascertain whether this "new law" is Torah or not.[43] The reason he gives for the reference to a "new law" or "law of Christ" is that this is what has been set out in the *sectio*, but as I have argued in chapter 7, the *sectio* was not intended to reframe or reorient the following Two Ways Torah, but to lend authority to it. Nevertheless, Chester's observed connection between the two texts demonstrates the consistency of the Didache's message.

In the second of the thematic terms, in like manner to the use of ἐντολή to complete the Way of Life, the Didachist uses the term ἀνομία in the penultimate conclusion to the Way of Death in Did. 5.2 where those on the Way of Death are described as πενήτων ἄνομοι κριταί. The implications of the term are intensified by the following phrase regarding those who are lawless and therefore of the Way of Death. They are πανθαμάρτητοι, and the related admonition is to be "freed . . . from all of these." The gravity of lawlessness is confirmed in the second reference to it in Did. 16.4, which is generally considered to belong to the same layer of the Didache

42. Did. 4.14.

43. Chester, *Messiah and Exaltation*, 509–12.

as Did. 1–6. In light of this, Willy Rordorf and André Tuilier's translation *juges iniques* is perhaps not strong enough.[44]

The reference to ἁμαρτία, which the lawless are full of, has the potential to cloud the meaning of ἀνομία which it modifies, as its NT usage has been variously viewed as either a reference to lawlessness in the sense of disregard for the Torah, or in the more general sense, to sinfulness. Its uses in Matt 7:23; 13:41; 23:28; 24:12; Rom 4:7; 6:19; 2 Cor 6:14; 2 Thess 2:7; Tit 2:14; Heb 1:9; 8:12; 10:17; and 1 John 3:4 permit no simplistic definition. Nevertheless, the non-Pauline texts do better support an identification with the Torah than the Pauline. In this regard, in each of the four Matthean pericopes where ἀνομία occurs, the term refers to unrighteous behavior within a distinctly eschatological context connected to God's judgement upon evildoers.[45] Ἀνομία also may be contrasted to its antonym. Sim's argument in this regard is that "Given the importance of the law (νόμος) for Matthew, one can hardly believe that he intended ἀνομία in any other way than as the opposite of Torah-fulfilment according to the definitive exegesis of Jesus."[46] Thus, the two concepts of law-breaking and sinfulness are not as far apart as might be supposed. In the words of 1 John 3:4, Πᾶς ὁ ποιῶν τὴν ἁμαρτίαν καὶ τὴν ἀνομίαν ποιεῖ, καὶ ἡ ἁμαρτία ἐστὶν ἡ ἀνομία.

Not only was the Way of Life a suitable vehicle for instruction, and not only was it presented as an imperative choice, but it was also presented as the means to perfection (τέλειος).[47] In light of ἐντολή and ἄνομος the term τέλειος (perfect) gains in significance. Its singular form, as the Didache addressed the individual disciple, is in accord with the entirety of the Way of Life and indicates a personal aspect to perfection. In contrast, its later use of plural forms in Did. 10.5 and 16.2 reflects a communal aspect, as Taras Khomych demonstrated.[48] However, in Did. 6.3 that aspect of the notion is not explicit, neither is the eschatological element that comes to the fore in 16.2.

44. Rordorf and Tuilier, *La Doctrine Des Douze Apôtres*, 169.

45. Matt 7:23; 13:41; 23:28 and 24:12.

46. Sim, *Apocalyptic Eschatology in the Gospel of Matthew*, 212.

47. Wilhite advances the thesis that perfection "refers not to moral perfection but to a Graeco-Roman virtue system. To be perfect means to lack any deficiency . . . . As the Didachist combines a virtue and vice list with the outcome of τέλειος, the Didache links arms with part of the Graeco-Roman τέλειος-ἀνὴρ setting and with part of the Jewish inner-*shalom* tradition." *The Didache*, 161. This position is largely founded on Philo's use of the term (159–60) in conjunction with Graeco-Roman usage. While feasible, the greater weight I give to the Jewish sources and religiously Jewish milieu of the Didachist leads me to relegate any such meaning to an undercurrent in the Didache's use of τέλειος.

48. Khomych, "Perfection in the Didache," 5–7.

A comparable usage of τέλειος is found in the Qumran literature, where the Hebrew equivalent (תם) appears in several documents, more often than not in conjunction with the equivalent of ὁδός (דרך). It is this frequent pairing of תם and דרך that provides data on the meaning of τέλειος in the Didache's Two Ways. In this regard *Serek* 1.8 advocates that the "instructor" become "attached to all good works" and the "covenant of kindness" and "walk in perfection" (התהלך לפניו תמים). In response, *Serek* 1.13 states that the "sons of light" are to walk "in accordance with his perfect paths" (תם דרכיו). The path is portrayed here as an ideal, and in confirmation, *Serek* 11.11 later refers to the "perfection of the path" (תום הדרך). This juxtaposition of perfection and the Way is most notably found also in *Serek* 3.9–10; 4.22; 5.24; 8.10; 18, 21, 25; 9:2, 5, 6, 8, 9, 19; 10:21; 11.2; 1QH; 4Q256; 4Q258; and 4Q259. In addition to its general connotations of behavior fully in accordance with the Torah and the community's rules, to be perfect also requires an attitude of the heart, as *Serek* 11.7 states "without you no behavior [path] is perfect."

In NT usage, Matthew's Gospel provides a reference point as the term occurs twice: in Matt 5:48 and 19:21. As van de Sandt points out, τέλειος doesn't occur anywhere else in the Gospels.[49] However, as in the Didache, on both occasions where it does occur in Matthew it occurs in close relationship to ἐντολή. In the first of these passages it appears as the culmination of the teaching introduced by Matt 5:19, which identifies the commandments with τὸν νόμον and τοὺς προφήτας, sternly warning that "whoever relaxes one of the least of these commandments and teaches others to do the same will be called least in the kingdom of heaven." The subsequent six Antitheses culminate with the key term τέλειος in 5:48, which occurs at the end of Jesus' intensification of the Torah and in similar fashion to the Didache concludes the Torah teaching by presenting perfection as the goal. This, as Anthony Saldarini states, comes in the context of an interpretation which provides "a correct understanding and fulfillment" of biblical Law.[50] The usage of τέλειος in Matthew 5:48 therefore echoes that of Did. 6.3 which likewise follows the Torah-interpretive material of the *sectio* and the original Two Ways section.

In the second Matthean use of the term, in 19:21, perfection is again held up in the context of the Torah and the teaching of Jesus, which goes beyond the Torah's requirements. There a "young man" is given the answer to his question regarding ζωὴν αἰώνιον and told that if in addition to keeping the commandments (ἐντολάς, 5:17) he were to give his possessions to the

49. Sandt, *Bearing the Entire Yoke*, 339.

50. Saldarini, *Matthew's Christian-Jewish Community*, 162.

poor he would be "perfect." In this case τέλειος is given soteriological weight by Matthew, that is not so overt in the Didache, but the legal context is once again related to Jesus' mediation and interpretation of the Torah. In contrast, the later version of the Didache's Two Ways found in Apos. Con. 7.2 (as noted in chapter 2) omits any reference to perfection, suggesting a later playing down of the Didache's emphasis on Torah.

In relationship to the conclusory nature of Did. 6.2, the function of the Two Ways' conclusion is underscored, as Audet has noted,[51] by its repetition of the term τέλειος, which has already been set forth as an ideal in the *sectio.* As noted in chapter eight, when used in Did. 1.4, this repetition forms an *inclusio* showing the care with which the Didachist framed his teaching. Not only is the word repeated, but in an identical phrase in reverse word order. As Khomych has written, the "linguistic similarity of the two passages (ἔσῃ τέλειος//τέλειος ἔσῃ) is worth noting."[52] A closer look at the two passages further suggests the deliberate repeated use of the term in the first recognisable words of the Teacher. The second occurrence at the end of the Two Ways section directly follows an admonition to remain faithful to the teaching given, the warning against teachers who might not uphold it, and the characterisation of that teaching as the "yoke of the Lord." In both cases τέλειος is thus linked to the Lord's teaching as set out by the Didachist. Together the two passages complement and uphold the imperative nature of the Way of Life as it has been treated earlier. The relationship between the imperative nature of this Way and the "yoke of the Lord" remains to be discussed following a clarification on the function of Did. 6.3.

It is in relationship to τέλειος that Draper clearly states his view of the Torah in the Didache, one with which we are largely in agreement. For Draper, the one who is "perfect" is the "one who keeps the whole Torah according to Christian *halakah*" and for whom "the goal of the Christian life was full compliance with the Jewish Torah, under the aegis of the Messiah."[53] A goal of this dissertation is to accumulate evidence and set forth the systematic way in which the Didache has been composed to teach this. Functionally, however, the reference to τέλειος adds to the impact of the mandate that the Didache is imposing, and this is where we would both go further but yet not as far as Draper, who concludes that at "the end of the day, it is required of him/her [the gentile proselyte] that he/she become a full Jew in order to attain salvation."[54] As has been argued in

51. Audet, *La Didachè*, 353.

52. Khomych, "Perfection in the Didache," 5.

53. Draper, "Torah and Troublesome Apostles," 367.

54. Draper, "Torah and Troublesome Apostles," 368.

chapters 5 and 6, the Torah is authoritatively mandated, and set forth as a prerequisite and goal, but the Two Ways does not assert a new national or ethnic identity for the convert neither does it mention Judaism or Jews, as will be shown in more detail in chapter 11.

It is in light of this that the Didache's seemingly conciliatory injunctions ὃ δύνῃ, τοῦτο ποίει and ὃ δύνασαι βάσταυον must be revisited. The taking up of the "whole" yoke of the Lord and then the apparent concessions by the Didache then highlight not the Didache's permissiveness, but rather its Torah. In context, the Didache is acknowledging the reality of non-observance, but is not condoning it. In the subjunctive, the term ὃ δύνῃ has no special weight attached to it, simply indicating one's ability to act or not (e.g. Mark 9:23; Luke 16:2; Hermas 18.8, 23.4). The imperative form of τοῦτο ποίει is unmistakable and has to be taken seriously. The fact that there is "L'esprit de concession"[55] in this passage does not negate the importance of observing the teaching given, only an acceptance of the convert's social reality.

Comparison has and should be made with Did. 4.13, where the end of the Way of Life concludes with an uncompromising command not to "forsake the commands of the Lord." The difference between Did. 4.13 and 6.2 is the intervening Way of Death, and while the Way of Death also replicates the second table of the Torah, like the *sectio*, it goes beyond it and treats not mere deeds, but describes in 5.2 the characteristics of the lawless. Here a high bar has been set for the disciple, as in the *sectio* and the Sermon on the Mount. The disciple can aspire to be completely free from these things, but in what Milavec calls the Didache's "pastoral genius" the Didache acknowledges that perfect success may be beyond reach. Thus the phrase at the end of the Way of Death: ῥυσθείητε, τέκνα, ἀπὸ τούτων ἁπάντων, in the aorist passive.

In summary, the three terms ἐντολή, ἄνομος and τέλειος as used in the Two Ways section all contribute to the significance of its conclusion in Did. 6.2, and all substantiate a strong emphasis on the Torah. The first of these, ἐντολή, established a connection to the precepts of the Deuteronomic Law. The second, ἄνομος, points to the relationship between Law-breaking and sin, particularly, if comparable to the Matthean uses of the term, to unrighteousness in an eschatological context. The third and final term, τέλειος, not only establishes the reward for keeping the Torah as taught by the Didache, but also the nature of the Torah. As corroborated by Matthew and its usage in the DSS, perfection is associated with a walk, or path, as in the Didache. It is also associated with an attitude of heart. Overall, these terms set forth an intense view of conformity to the Way of Life, which is identified with the Torah.

55. Rordorf and Tuilier, *La Doctrine Des Douze Apôtres*, 167.

Concerning Food: Postlude or Prelude?

Following the conclusion of the Two Ways, Did. 6.3 occupies a significant but somewhat problematic position in the text. Rather than continuing to address the individual disciple, the chapters of the Didache after Did. 6.3 primarily address communal matters. Didache 6.3, therefore, either functions as a bridge to these following chapters or is part and parcel of the baptismal instructions of chapter 7.

Pardee has acknowledged the "awkward position" of Did. 6.3.[56] Since Did. 6.3 remains placed between the conclusion of the Two Ways and the Didache's extensive discussion of baptism and communal meals, in Pardee's estimation it is an "addition" to the Two Ways teaching.[57] This is supported by the fact, already noted and observed before,[58] that there is no parallel to Did. 6.3 in the *Doctrina apostolorum*. While our argument is not based on analysis of the Didache's redaction, the textual evidence confirms E. Bruce Brooks' view of Did. 6.3 as both a transition and "as the opening of the second main section of the Didache."[59]

Didache 6.3 is demonstrably linked to the following segment in chapter 7 first and foremost by the use of the introductory clause περὶ δέ which is also used in the next verse, Did. 7.1. These two occurrences of περὶ δέ introduce the subject matter of the immediately following text. Thus, Did. 6.3 introduces the topic of food, related to the topic of community meals in Did. 8–10, while Did. 7.1 introduces the topic of baptism, treated in the rest of Did. 7. The same occurs in the two other occurrences of περὶ δέ, in Did. 9.1 which introduces the teaching on thanksgivings at meals, and 11.3, which initiates the teaching on apostles and prophets. This is in keeping with Pauline usage of the same clause. As Alex Cheung notes, the "introduction of various topics by the formula περὶ δέ (Did. 6.3; 7.1; 9.1–3; 11.2) finds parallels in 1 Cor 7.1, 25; 8.1; 12.1; 16.1, 12."[60] In light of its use elsewhere in the Didache, it is therefore reasonable to conclude that Did. 6.3, the admittedly short but coherent teaching on idol foods before the next περὶ δέ of 7.1, is a discrete teaching that stands on its own.

The question then arises as to whether the phrase ταῦτα πάντα προειπόντες in Did. 7.1 includes 6.3 or not. In other words, does it or does it not require that the Two Ways material as well as the instruction regarding

56. Pardee, *Genre and Development*, 55.

57. Pardee, *Genre and Development*, 55, 89, 96.

58. Rordorf and Tuilier, *La Doctrine Des Douze Apôtres*, 210.

59. Brooks, *Before and After Matthew*, 266n, 270–71.

60. Cheung, *Idol Food in Corinth*, 213.

idol food be recounted before baptism? Ταῦτα πάντα προειπόντες is enigmatic partly because the phrase cannot logically include the phrase περὶ δὲ τοὺ βαπτίσματος, οὕτω βαπτίσατε, which has not yet been expanded upon.

Audet's position is that the phrase is attributable to the redactor of the Didache (the Didachist), arguing from a text-critical perspective that "Le plus naturel serait de supposer qu'il ne lisait pas ταῦτα πάντα προειπόντες dans le texte de la *Didachè* qu'il avait sous la main,"[61] The attribution of this phrase to the redactor was also accepted by Rordorf and Tuilier[62] and later on by Niederwimmer.[63] This accords with my position, set out in chapter 2, that the Didachist compiled the Didache with both borrowed sources and original material, composing various bridges to unite the whole into a unified composition.

In contrast to this position, a number of scholars take ταῦτα πάντα προειπόντες to indicate that the Didachist intends to include all the foregoing instruction, up to Did. 6.3. In this case, 6.3 is viewed not as the bridge that it is, but the conclusion to the Two Ways. As seen earlier in this chapter, this is the opinion of Huub van de Sandt and David Flusser[64] as well as Audet.[65] In addition to the points made there, based on the fact that Did. 6.3 is in the singular, 6.3 has been viewed as linguistically linked with the preceding Two Ways material. The case for this is not as secure as it might be, however. Rordorf and Tuilier hold that originally 6.3 was in the plural. If that were so, it would tie 6.3 more closely to the subsequent section. Their evidence is not from the Didache, but from other texts. As they point out[66] in later years both the Apostolic Constitutions[67] and the Ethiopian version of the Didache[68] rendered both verses in the plural. If this is the case, as it seems to be, Did. 6.3 is actually more closely linked to Did. 7.1–4 than the Two Ways, in accordance with its function as a bridge. In this case, even if ταῦτα πάντα προειπόντες is meant to include Did. 6.3, the phrase does not require that the Didachist viewed 6.3 as the conclusion of the Two Ways teaching.

The Didache's teaching on idolatry and idol food has already been treated in chapter 9.1 and has been shown to be a fitting complement from

61. Audet, *La Didachè*, 60.

62. Rordorf and Tuilier, *La Doctrine Des Douze Apôtres*, 35, 170.

63. Niederwimmer, *The Didache*, 125.

64. Sandt and Flusser, *The Didache*, 29, 88.

65. Audet, *La Didachè*, 358.

66. Rordorf and Tuilier, *La Doctrine Des Douze Apôtres*, 169 n. 9.

67. Apost. Con. 7.21.

68. Audet, *La Didachè*, 35.

the first table of the decalogue for the five commands of the second as they are systematically set forth in the Two Ways. While issues surrounding idolatry appear in the Two Ways, this is the first occasion where food is mentioned, giving some insight into the social situation of the disciple. The view that this is a reference to ascetic practices, as suggested by Harnack[69] has been dispensed with by modern scholars such as Stuiber,[70] Draper,[71] and Niederwimmer.[72] Idolatry, specifically in Did. 6.3, relates to the second command of the Decalogue, prohibiting graven images. This is the only occasion in the Two Ways where it is connected with idols and the worship of "dead" gods.

The baptismal prerequisite ταῦτα πάντα προειπόντες therefore, substantiates the view that not only is the yoke of the Lord in view, but also the special emphasis on idolatry in Did. 6.3. The latter five commands of the Decalogue have been stipulated in detail, and in a more general sense, those commands of the first table have also been commanded and are to be accepted by the disciple before baptism. As will be substantiated in the next chapter, such stipulations for inductees have parallels in the rites of the Essene community.

The phrase functions as a summary and logical connection between the Two Ways teaching and that on baptism, and is part of the Didachist's bridge between his two sources. Niederwimmer rightly views this comment as a source of social information, but it does not necessarily follow that its function is merely "within the church's life and especially its missionary activity. . . . In the context of baptismal catechesis, and specifically as instruction before baptism."[73] This would suggest that although preceding, the Two Ways material is subordinate in that sense to the liturgical material that follows. This is a functional subordination in the Didache as we have it, for the Two Ways is, while obviously foundational, the key to full participation in the church. This participation, treated in Did. 7–15 is significantly an insertion within the original 1–6, and 16 "envelope."

To summarize, I have argued that Did. 6.3 is in an "awkward" position, between the yoke of the Lord conclusion and the baptismal instructions of Did. 7. Standing on its own, as is evident from its marking off with the clause περὶ δέ, it makes its own significant contribution to our understanding of the Didache's reception of the Torah. While the five commands of the second

69. Harnack and Gebhardt, *Die Lehre der zwölf Apostel*, 21.

70. Stuiber, "Das ganze Joch des Herrn," 325–26.

71. Draper, "A Commentary on the Didache," 132–33.

72. Niederwimmer, *The Didache*, 123.

73. Niederwimmer, *The Didache*, 126.

table of the Torah have been methodically taught in the Two Ways, Did. 6.3 re-emphasizes and punctuates the command against idolatry, found in the first table, in a way that specifically references the intent of the command related to idolatry in the first table. The instruction of Did. 7.1 further serves to show the Didache's intent, in that it instructs that all the preceding teachings, including 6.3, are to be accepted together as the prerequisite for baptism. The Didachist's hand and his intent are thus made clear.

Conclusion

The purpose of this chapter has been to demonstrate that the "yoke of the Lord" conclusion to the Two Ways was an intentional mandate of the Torah for the disciple. We have argued that it has erroneously been associated with the Apostolic Decree of Acts 15, which has resulted in scholars tending to minimize its legal force. In contrast with *Doct. apost.* 6 and Barn. 21, the yoke of the Lord stands out as a positive injunction, rather than their more generic warnings against disobedience. While "yoke" terminology may imply other than the Torah, as seen in contemporary literature, the Didache clearly treats it as Torah, and does not try to present it as an "easy" burden. The terms related to this yoke, ἐντολή, ἄνομος, and τέλειος, together speak of a whole-hearted observance of this instruction, one that the Didache places no soteriological or covenant value on, acknowledging that not all may be able to bear it. Finally, confirming the importance of the yoke of the Lord but also the Didachist's reception of the Torah, he specifically stresses the teaching regarding idol food in 6.3, which has been shown to be more than a "bridge" but a completion of the instruction required for the baptizand.

This conclusion leads to a final consideration. Does the Didache thereby imply that the disciple is in some sense a convert to Judaism, as part of his shouldering of the yoke of the Lord? This is the topic of the following chapter.

11

The Two Ways Disciple

Introduction

HAVING ARGUED FOR THE Two Ways of the Didache as Torah, taught and mandated for the disciple, it is the aim of this chapter to gain a fresh perspective on the disciple's identity through the lens of the Torah implicit to the Didache's implementation of the Decalogue. This will be evident in the ways in which Torah has been applied specifically to the disciple's circumstance. This chapter will first review the concessionary clause of Did. 6.2 for indications as to its intent. The second part of this chapter will survey the inclusions and omissions of the Two Ways' Decalogue, again, to examine the reasons why. Thirdly, it is to be demonstrated, by a backwards view at previous scholarship and Jewish conversionary requirements, that the Didache is not attempting to convert the disciple to Judaism or lay upon him or her the specifically Israelite provisions of the Torah. Finally, the induction of the disciple into the church via baptism is recast in light of the disciple's identity and the Didache's reception of the Torah.

The Concession and the Yoke

Having established the Torah as the mandatory yoke of the Lord, the Didache's following instruction, in what we will call Did. 6.2b, serves to modify its demand for perfection with the seemingly conflicting instruction: εἰ δ' οὐ δύνασαι, ὃ δύνῃ, τοῦτο ποίει. A *prima facie* reading suggests that the Didachist intended to ameliorate or walk back his hitherto unambiguous line regarding the Torah. The language is remarkable, and as discussed in chapter 9 contrasts starkly not only with Did. 6.1–2a, but also Did. 4.13 and its admonition μήτε προστιθεὶς μήτε ἀφαιρῶν from the "commands of the Lord."

This apparent contradiction is telling, and arguably it would have not escaped the notice of either the teacher or disciple, particularly in view of the likelihood that the Two Ways was the basis for oral instruction as has been suggested at various points in this study. Arguments made by Draper and Milavec in this regard rest in part on the consensus expressed by Pieter Botha, who states that "no one will deny that orality was part of the Greco-Roman world," and continues, "we need to realize to what extent orality was the norm."[1] Further, just as the "concession" is a point of contention today, so it must have been in the days that the Didache was orally taught, particularly against the background of general tension around issues surrounding gentiles in the Antiochene Jesus movement (Acts 15:1–29; Gal 2:11–14; Barn. 2.6; Ign. *Magn.* 8.1). It is in such a context that the inconsistency in these concluding teachings would have raised questions. In what way was this apparent conflict viewed? The interpretation of Did. 6.2b cuts to the heart of the social and religious identity of the Didache's milieu and its expectations of new disciples.

Taking the view that converts were ideally on a path to convert to Judaism, Draper takes ὃ δύνῃ, τοῦτο ποίει to infer that "continued faithfulness and growth in living out the ethical provisions of the Torah will be the yardstick by which one will stand on the last day" and that this would be "an incentive for Gentiles to move towards full acceptance of the Torah."[2] Nathan Mitchell goes further, arguing that the Didache thus "places the gentile believer under intense pressure to become (eventually, at least) an observant Jew who fully accepts the 'whole yoke' of the Torah as interpreted through Christian *halakoth*."[3]

This suggestion of conversion contrasts sharply with Stuiber's view that 6.2–3 is a Jewish "Nachtrag" and "Da das Gesetz zu Israel gegeben ist, ist nur der Israelit zu seiner Beobachtung verpflichtet." For Stuiber, the Didache simply laid moral commands on the gentiles.[4] In this view, conversion was not required, but adherence to the moral law was. Thus Bruce Brooks suggests that Did. 6.2 "had in mind the whole of the ethical injunctions in the preceding Two Ways (not the whole of the Jewish Torah)."[5] With a different but related opinion, Murray Smith surmised that the Didachist "most likely intends 'the yoke of the Lord Jesus.'"[6]

1. Botha, *Orality and Literacy in Early Christianity*, 15.
2. Draper, "Torah and Troublesome Apostles," 368; Tuckett, *Synoptic Tradition*, 480.
3. Mitchell, *Baptism in the Didache*, 237.
4. Stuiber, "Das ganze Joch des Herrn," 327–28.
5. Brooks, *Before and After Matthew*, 260, 283.
6. Smith, *The Lord Jesus and His Coming in the Didache*, 372.

Stephen Finlan, in his study on identity in the Didache community, makes an observation that supports this, as he notes "The Two Ways chapters are full of Torah commandments, but in that material the language of Israel is absent from the group's self-identification."[7] While metaphors that liken the church to Israel do appear later in the Didache in connection with thanksgivings,[8] they are limited to the context of the "kingdom" and the gathering of the church in the eschaton. The language in these texts echoes that of the Hebrew Bible and Matt 24:31; Mark 13:27. Nevertheless, the Two Ways focuses on a change of behavior qualifying the disciple for induction into the community rather than any change of identity.

Rather than framing the matter in terms of conversion, Matthew Larsen and Michael Svigel have put Did. 6.2 in the context of the progression from "repentance to maturity"; maturity being τέλειος as found in Heb 5:14.[9] Here, "do that which you are able" is put in the context of those who no longer need milk, but "solid food," being those who are able to "distinguish good from evil." A similar approach is adopted by Janicki, who compares Did. 6.2 with Matt 19:11; 1 Cor 7:7 to say "The Didache points the Gentile believer in the direction of fuller observance of the Torah in light of the teachings of the Master and the apostles, but at the same time it leaves room for those to whom this would be unbearable and too difficult in their current situation."[10]

This concessionary interpretation was anticipated and developed by Milavec, who argues that "when it comes to defining what constitutes 'the rules of the Lord' (4:13) and 'the way of training' (6:1), there is no room for half measures. When it comes to applying these things to individual persons, however, allowance is made for failure and for gradualism."[11] As Rordorf and Tuilier put it "L'esprit de concession marque tout particulièrement ce passage; on note, en effet, l'emploi réitéré de la seconde personne δύνασαι, qui tempère le caractère impératif des préceptes."[12] Such a concessionary approach is found in Cyprian's treatise *On Jealousy and Envy*: "Imitate good men, if you are able to follow them; but if you are not able to follow them, at least rejoice with them."[13]

7. Finlan, *Identity in the Didache Community*, 22.

8. Did. 9.4, 10.5, and possibly 16.7.

9. Larsen and Svigel, *The First Century Two Ways Catechesis*, 484.

10. Janicki, *The Way of Life*, 250.

11. Milavec, *The Didache: Faith*, 778–79.

12. Rordorf and Tuilier, *La Doctrine Des Douze Apôtres*, 169.

13. *On Jealousy*, 10.17. ANF 5, 490.

The approach of the Didache, uncompromising in its teaching, but aware of the disciples' limitations, was quite possibly driven by doubt that gentiles were "capable of keeping to some basic moral laws."[14] This is Milavec's supposition as he attempts to solve the apparent contradiction by suggesting the Didache's concession was temporary in nature, in hope that "with the passage of time" there would be "a gradual stiffening of the expectations made upon candidates who were passing through the program on their way to baptism."[15] Draper has gone further yet in suggesting that "*the concession concerning perfection in Torah observation was valid only for the time before the coming of the Messiah on the clouds to inaugurate the kingdom on earth.*"[16]

Against the backdrop of the Didache's firm Torah teaching, in which there is no hint of concession, but as in the *sectio*, even of a higher standard as it is mediated by Christ, the position that the Didache is retracting its demands is suspect. In keeping with this broader context, the natural sense of Did. 6.2 is related, as it says, to the ability of the disciple, not the negotiability of the teaching.

Not only is there no hint of "walking back" within the Two Ways material itself, but the Torah affirmative stance is carried forward into the later material of the Didache. Thus, in Did. 11.2 if someone "turns to teach another teaching leading to destruction, do not hear him. But if it leads to righteousness and the knowledge of the Lord, receive him as the Lord." The choice remains clear. The Way of Life leads to righteousness and to the contrary, to disregard it leads to death. Likewise in Did. 16.2 the reader is told "all the time of your faith will not be useful to you, if you are not found perfect in the last time." Here no concession has been made in terms of the Torah, rather an assertion that the disciple must by all means conform to its instructions to the best of his ability.

Finally, the goal of perfection, treated in the previous chapter, can now be more closely defined. Whereas in its first occurrence it is found in the *sectio*, and related to the Lord's commands, now it is in the context of the conclusion to entire Two Ways section. As discussed before, its repetition forms an *inclusio*, and is deliberate. Perfection, as it is being stressed, is a quality that is achieved not merely by keeping the precepts of the Two Ways, but also the commands of the Lord, which preface and provide context for the more traditional Two Ways material.

14. Sandt and Flusser, *The Didache*, 267.

15. Milavec, *The Pastoral Genius of the Didache*, 2, 110.

16. Draper, *Mission, Ethics and Identity in the Didache*. 7, (italics original).

In summary, we have established that scholarship has had a long track record but significant difficulty in dealing with the "concession" of Did. 6.2b. While some have viewed it as pointing towards a moral interpretation of the Law, others have seen it as explicitly pointing towards the Teaching as a prerequisite for conversion to Judaism, or at least Christian-Judaism, if there was indeed significant differentiation between the two at that time. This has raised issues regarding the identity of the new convert, or disciple, in terms of his or her relationship with the Jewish people and Israel. Some more recent approaches have stressed the ongoing validity of the Torah but taken the concessionary wording as indicating a provisional loosening of its requirements. Nevertheless, the Didache neither encourages the disciple to take on a new identity nor to deviate from its commands. Its promise of perfection refers to the entirety of the Two Ways and the *sectio*'s framing of it.

Omissions and Inclusions

The Didache's Two Ways, while tightly following the second table of the Torah, is notable for its omission of two commands from the first. Of the first table, only the prohibition against idolatry with the related issue of idol food is present, as has already been discussed in chapters 9 and 10. However, this command is not part of the Two Ways second table structure. The omission of the other four commands of the first table, in contrast to the specific inclusion of the prohibition of idolatry is the concern of this section.

The Didache does not specify the reasons for this omission, which has naturally drawn attention and speculation. Audet suggested that the Didache has specifically Greek fallibilities in view in its inclusions, saying "les maîtres de morale regardaient volontiers de telles déviations comme une spécialité grecque."[17] But in terms of its omissions he commented that the "omissions de l' «instruction» par rapport au décalogue posent une difficulté un peu plus delicate."[18] He noted in particular the omission of the prohibition against graven images, use of the Lord's Name in vain, the Sabbath, and parental respect. In the following pages Audet attributes this to existing pressure. "On peut donc penser que la pression institutionnelle et sociale dans laquelle le *Duae viae* a vu le jour a été consciemment ou inconsciemment ressentie comme une suffisante indication de la conduite à tenir sur les points qu'on omettait."[19] As has been argued in chapter 3, the Christians in Antioch were indeed under considerable pressure, but

17. Audet, *La Didachè*, 286.
18. Audet, *La Didachè*, 285.
19. Audet, *La Didachè*, 285.

there is no evidence that this would have been cause for them to omit commands. On the contrary, the text evidences a response specifically prescribed for this community under stress, as seen in the advice concerning how to perceive bad things that happen to oneself in Did. 3.10, and what to do when taken advantage of in Did. 1.4b.

Milavec asserts that the first table of the Decalogue was omitted because the Way of Life is an adaptation for gentiles. These commands are therefore not discussed due to redundancy, as their subject matter is treated elsewhere in the Didache, or unworkability in the social situation of its disciples.[20] To Milavec the first command is "redundant" due to a) the acknowledgement of God in Did. 1.2; b) the warning against things that lead to idolatry in 3.4; and c) the warning against eating idol food in 6.3.[21] Milavec holds that the second command against idolatry would have been unworkable for gentiles in pagan society;[22] the third command against taking God's name in vain is redundant due to the Didache's warnings against swearing falsely in 2.3;[23] and the fourth command concerning the Sabbath was unworkable for gentiles and would have "imposed severe economic hardships."[24] Lastly, the fifth command, to honor one's parents, was "suppressed" due to unworkability.[25]

Milavec's points are enlightening, but a number of objections have to be made. In particular, Did. 1.2 is more closely related to Deut 6:4 than the Decalogue, as neither version of the Decalogue speaks about loving God. Secondly, his explanations for the omission of the fourth and fifth commands are greatly affected and supported by his interpretation of the *sectio* as addressing people who are suffering familial persecution. With Christianity as "a minority religion that was forced to recruit members by dividing sons from fathers and daughters from mothers" the fifth command to him was "impossible to imagine."[26] Milavec's suggestion that this is because of the difficulty in honoring non-Christian parents opposed to the Christian faith is also supported by Draper.[27] In Draper's view, one might surmise the convert was given "new fictive parents and new fictive peers."[28] This assumption runs contrary to NT

20. Milavec, *The Didache: Faith*, 212–23; *The Didache: Text*, 53.
21. Milavec, *The Didache: Faith*, 121.
22. Milavec, *The Didache: Faith*, 123.
23. Milavec, *The Didache: Faith*, 123.
24. Milavec, *The Didache: Faith*, 121.
25. Milavec, *The Didache: Faith*, 128.
26. Milavec, *The Pastoral Genius of the Didache*, 2, 108–9; *The Didache: Faith*, 128.
27. Draper, *Children and Slaves in the Community of the Didache*, 98.
28. Draper, "Ritual Process," 124.

evidence where respect for parents is commanded.[29] While this study has argued that the addressees of the Didache were in the midst of various crises, familial alienation is not one of them.

Particularly in the context of the Didache's Torah teaching in the Two Ways, the rationale for its inclusions and omissions from the Decalogue needs further attention. A potential answer is to be found in the Didache's understanding of the unique covenant obligations of Israel and the historical matrix in which that was formed. There is little argument that the Didache celebrates the unity of the church as a whole, and in that sense demonstrates a universal consciousness,[30] particularly in its expectation of the eschaton. In terms of its application of the Torah to its gentile recipients, it is nevertheless somewhat particularistic, congruent with Jewish preconceptions regarding Israel's unique obligations. In both the pre-existing and obviously redactional material that has been examined thus far, this preconception comes to the fore.

In the Qumran literature, the particularistic narrative of Israel and its national salvation-history is indicated explicitly a number of times, particularly in regard to God's redemptive act bringing Israel out of Egypt. 4Q365 (=*4QReworked Pentateuch*) thus connects Israel's festival observances to the exodus. Moses commands in 4Q365.23.1–2: You 'shall live [in hu]ts for seven days . . . so th[at your] gen[erations may know] how I made your fathers live [in hu]ts when I took them out of the land of Egypt. I am yhwh, your God!"[31] Not only is the redemption a key element, but the specific act of the YHWH who thereby establishes his relationship to Israel. The same two features are seen in 1Q22 (=*1QWords of Moses*) with the words in 1Q22.2.5–7: "Moses [spoke] and [said to the sons of I]srael: Forty [years] have passed [from the] day of our dep[arture] from the land [of Egypt, and] to[day Go]d, [our] God, [has caused the]se [wo]rds [to issue] from h[is] mouth [all] his [pre]cepts <[and] all [his] pre[cepts."[32] A third example affirms the redemption from Egypt as foundational to the imposition of the Torah upon Israel, as 11Q19, 64.5–7, 16–17 states: "All the things which I order /you/ today, take care to carry them out; you shall not add to them nor shall you remove anything from them . . . . yhwh, your God, who brought you out from the land of Egypt and redeemed you from slavery."[33] This redemption narrative, connected as it is with the giving and

29. Col 1:20, Eph 6:1–3.

30. Did. 10.5, 16.5.

31. Martinez and Tigchelaar, *Dead Sea Scrolls Study Edition*, 722–23.

32. Martinez and Tigchelaar, *Dead Sea Scrolls Study Edition*, 61.

33. Martinez and Tigchelaar, *Dead Sea Scrolls Study Edition*, 1275.

reception of the Torah, is entirely absent from the Didache's Two Ways despite the fact that other imagery from the Hebrew Bible permeates its later texts. Its absence in such a text harmonizes with the view that its recipients did not share in Israel's historic narrative, rather the meta-narrative provided by the Lord's words in the *sectio*.

To the degree that the Qumranic context reflects more prevalent Jewish conceptions it is entirely unremarkable that the Didache did not focus on the first command of the Decalogue. The same identification of certain commands from the first table specifically with Israel is seen in other sources. The convert's relationship with God had already been distinguished from the Israel-redemptive context by Did. 1.2, where God is described as τὸν θεὸν τὸν ποιήσαντά σε. God's self-identification "I am the Lord your God, who brought you out of the land of Egypt, out of the house of slavery" is the basis for the first command's henotheistic instruction, to have "no other gods before me" for Israel, but not for gentiles whose ancestors did not participate in that deliverance from Egypt. The convert has, however, accepted God the maker of all mankind as per Did. 1.2.

This perspective of the Didache correlates with the similar omission of the third command, "You shall not take the name of the Lord your God in vain." As seen above, Milavec has argued that this command seems to appear in Did. 2.3, which reads οὐκ ἐπιορκήσεις. οὐ ψευδομαρτυρήσεις. However, while there is arguably some equivalency, and Philo takes this command to be a prohibition of perjury (*Spec. Leg.* 2.224), this is not the wording of the MT (לא תשא את־שם־יהוה אלהיך לשוא) or of the LXX which translates it literally (οὐ λήμψῃ τὸ ὄνομα κυρίου τοῦ θεοῦ σου ἐπὶ ματαίῳ). Unlike the other commands of the Decalogue, which are expressed accurately in the Two Ways, the Didache has chosen markedly different language to express this command, undermining Milavec's assertion that it is indeed present in the Two Ways. It seems, therefore, that while there may be a relationship between the Decalogue and Did. 2.3, the Didache is not expressly replicating the command. In this light the omission of the third command is stark.

The fourth and fifth commands return to the theme, specifically present in the first table, of its commands as specifically related to the relationship between God and Israel. Both are presented as positive commands, and while they have intrinsic prohibitions, are not introduced as such. In Exod 20, the command to keep the sabbath day is commanded on the basis of God's rest after creation on the seventh day. Deuteronomy 5, however, gives an entirely different rationale, that of the exodus from Egypt. This serves to clarify that the reason for the day of rest is based in Israel's redemption, and the reason for it being on the seventh day of the week, because that was God's day of rest.[34] Despite Philo's general advocacy of the Sabbath to all humanity,[35] for many Jews of the first century, the Sabbath was something specific to Israel. Jubilees 2.31 is representative of this in regard to the Sabbath, reading "The Creator of all blessed it, but he did not sanctify any people or nations to keep the sabbath thereon with the sole exception of Israel. He granted to them alone that they might eat and drink and keep the sabbath thereon upon the earth."[36] Further, the midrash Mekilta de Rabbi Ishmael, recording early rabbis from the first two centuries, interprets the Sabbath to apply only to the righteous proselyte (גר צדק),[37] leading to the eventual prohibition of Sabbath observance for gentiles in general.[38] However, the evidence of the Didache is that proselytes to Judaism are not being addressed.

This interpretation is corroborated in Exod 31:12–13, "And the LORD said to Moses, 'You are to speak to the people of Israel and say, "Above all you shall keep my Sabbaths, for this is a sign between me and you throughout your generations, that you may know that I, the LORD, sanctify you."'" This text remains part of the ritual of Kiddush, sanctifying of the Sabbath, in Jewish tradition to this day. As a commandment this command is therefore specifically associated with God's covenant with Israel, and not necessarily a universal command. As such, it is unsurprisingly not included in the Didache's instruction for the gentile disciple.

The fifth command, to honor one's father and mother, is particularly striking. Connected with a promise, Exod 20:12 reads "Honor your father and your mother, that your days may be long in the land that the Lord your God is giving you." Here, whether long life is for the individual or nation, the point is that it is connected to life in the land given by God. The Didache nowhere gives a hint of disrespect for parents, but omits this command. The promise associated with this command in the Decalogue, however, is bound up with the blessings and curses of the Two Ways in Deut 30:1–5, where obedience to the Torah is connected to possession of the land. The promise

34. Harold Dressler made a similar point in his survey of the origins of the Sabbath, seeing Deuteronomy as adding "another reason" for the Sabbath. *The Sabbath in the Old Testament*, 26. The broader point as to whether the Sabbath is a "creation ordinance" or not, and whether applicable to all humanity, is not addressed here, as I am simply addressing the relationship between the Decalogue and Jewish understandings of its meaning. As Peter Craigie notes, "The Exodus from Egypt marks in effect the creation of God's people as a nation." *The Book of Deuteronomy*, 157.

35. Philo, *Dec.* 96–98.

36. Charlesworth, *The Old Testament Pseudepigrapha*, v. 2, 58.

37. Mekilta de Rabbi Ishmael, *Baḥodesh* 97.

38. b. Sanh. 98b.

associated with this command of the Decalogue therefore has a particularistic element connected to God's covenant with Israel. In this way, the Didache preconceives a distinction between Jewish and gentile Torah observance. This contrasts with the relatively bold adoption of the command to honor one's parents in Eph 6:1–3, where the promise of the Decalogue is specifically emphasized and applied.

The Didache's neglect to command honor to one's parents is particularly striking in light of the teacher's parental posture in the τέκνον section of Did. 3. The Didachist is indeed concerned with familial relationships, as parents are taught to discipline their children in 3.9, but there the goal is not that children should honor their parents, but learn the fear (φόβον) of the Lord. In line with the authority afforded the teacher, the Didachist arrogates honor (τιμήν) to the one teaching the Two Ways, using the same Greek verb used by the LXX to translate the כבד (honor) due to parents in Exod 20:12.

Finally, returning to the prohibition of idolatry, the Didache's inclusion of this command, which has universal applicability, is specific and clear. It is comparable to the description of "the path of the Black One" and the "path of eternal death" in Barn. 20.1, which begins with idolatry at the head of its list of "those things that destroy people's souls."[39] As in the Didache, Barnabas omits the other commands of the first table of the Torah, but unlike the Didache, there is no tri-partite repetition of the second table. It is possible that Barnabas reflects the division between the universal and the particular commands of the tables, but without the evidence of this stress on the Decalogue and the second table, there is little material present on which to draw a conclusion.

A point of comparison to the Didache is found in the *Didascalia*, the basis for the first six books of the Apostolic Constitutions. It has long been recognized that the author of the *Did. apost.* distinguished between "the true and abiding Law" and the "*Deuterosis* or Second Legislation." Whereas the latter is characterized by the detailed ceremonial law, the true Law was seen as the Decalogue and "Judgements."[40] An early witness to the Didache, it seems to evidence debate over the role and extent of the Law as it applies to Christians.[41] The *Didascalia* does not replicate the Didache's striking pattern of omission of those identity related commands peculiar to the people of Israel. It does however argue extensively for the observance of Sunday instead of the Sabbath, for example.[42]

39. Ehrman (LCL).

40. Connolly, "The *Didache* in the *Didascalia*," 153.

41. Fonrobert, "The *Didascalia Apostolorum*: A Mishnah," 507.

42. *Did. apost.* 53. Connolly, *Didascalia Apostolorum: Syriac*, 235–38.

In summary, this section has shown that the first command to worship God alone has merely been alluded to in the *sectio*, and a potential reason for this is its exclusive connection to Israel's redemption narrative. Likewise, the third command has not been replicated. Definitively, the fourth and fifth commands regarding the Sabbath and filial honor, which have specific relationships to Israel's covenant relationship to God, have been omitted, and we have argued it is for that very reason. In contrast, the second command prohibition of idolatry has been stated clearly. This is more than an *argumentum e silentio* on the basis that the selectiveness of the omissions and inclusions within the matrix of the highly structured Two Ways demonstrates intent. The nature and placement of the omissions from the decalogue contrast to the universality of the inclusions and while it cannot be conclusively proven that the reason for the omissions is their basis in God's relationship to Israel, and the identity of the disciple, who is not of Israel, there is significant evidence that this distinction underlies the Two Ways.

The Gentile Disciple

Having a "concession" that is less than a true concession, and omitting commands that have special relevance to Israel, especially the fourth and fifth commands of the decalogue, there is substantial evidence for the Didache's affirmation of Torah in general, and for the disciple's identity as a non-Jew. The question as to whether the Didache requires conversion to some form of Judaism or Christian Judaism has already been answered in part. The identity of the Christian disciple and his or her relationship to the Torah can now be further clarified.[43]

Gedaliah Alon argued in 1940 that the Didache does not support the idea that it was written "primarily for gentiles who came to convert to Judaism" and makes the salient point that the Didache does not address issues which "all those who wish to convert to Judaism are required to confess to, such as the Sabbath, Holy Days, and forbidden foods etc."[44] That said, early rabbinic records show that these commandments are only the tip of

43. Finlan's aforementioned argument (chapter 2) on the basis of Social Identity Theory that the Didache is written to gentiles supports the position that the Didache is not seeking to convert gentiles to Judaism, even as he relegates issues regarding Torah observance to a secondary status. Finlan concludes that the gentile "Converts to the Didache community are converting first of all to *belief in Christ*, not to membership in Israel." Finlan, *Identity in the Didache Community*, 31. This contribution is helpful, and highlights the perplexing issue of Torah observance in relationship to gentiles.

44. Alon, *The Halacha in the Teaching*. Alon's original article was, "ההלכה שבתורת."

the iceberg in what is required of the proselyte. Gerim 1.3–4 (=Mas. Qeṭ. 60a) specifies that the proselyte is only accepted

> on condition that he will give gleanings, forgotten sheaves, the corner of the field and tithes. As they say this to a man, so they say to a woman that [she is accepted] on condition that she will be particular in regard to *niddah*, *ḥallah* and the kindling of the Sabbath lamp.

Circumcision and immersion was also required, as per Gerim 1.6: "If a proselyte has been circumcised but has not yet bathed [he is a proselyte]; if he has bathed but not yet been circumcised [he is not yet a proselyte]; everything depends on the circumcision. This is the view of R. Eliezer, but R. 'Aḳiba said: Also [the lack of] bathing is a bar." More stringently, b. Yeb. 47a specifies that a convert must be

> informed of the sin [of neglecting the commandments of] Gleanings, the Forgotten Sheaf, the Corner and the Poor Man's Tithe. . . . Furthermore, he is addressed thus: "Be it known to you that before you came to this condition, if you had eaten suet you would not have been punishable with kareth, if you had profaned the Sabbath you would not have been punishable with stoning; but now were you to eat suet you would be punished with kareth; were you to profane the Sabbath you would be punished with stoning."

Ruth *Rabbah* 2.22 further forbids the frequenting of "Gentile theatres and circuses" and stipulates that "daughters of Israel" are not "to dwell in a house which has no *mezuzah*."

Of all requirements incidentally mentioned in the rabbinic record—gleanings, forgotten sheaves, corners of the field, tithes, niddah, challah, Sabbath lights, circumcision, immersion, suet (kashrut), the Sabbath itself, eschewing gentile entertainment, and the mezuzah—there are only three somewhat tenuous parallels to requirements in the Didache. None of them imply that the Didache intended its initiates to convert and assume a Jewish identity.

The first of these is the requirement regarding tithes, and in accordance with b. Yeb. 47a and Gerim 1.6, Did. 13.1–7 instructs the initiate regarding giving. The Talmudic record is notably later than that of the Didache, but the concern for giving is the common to both documents, which permits a parallel. In particular, the command of 13.3–4 is to take one's "first produce" as a gift for the prophets "for they are your high priests" and to give "according to the commandment." In this respect, the

Didache advocates an order outside the Temple order which had only one High Priest.[45] Further, as Milavec notes, the giving of first fruits is distinct from the giving of tithes.[46] Yet further, not only is there is a disruption of the biblical order, but there is no indication that the Didache's prophets are necessarily Jewish themselves. Thus, while inspired by the scriptural command, the Didache is not requiring the disciple to give in accordance with the traditions mentioned in the later rabbinic record. In fact, as Anthony Giambrone describes it, the Didache mandates what Judith considered a "monstrous sin," when she tells Holofernes of her compatriots who had "resolved to spend (*i.e.*, to eat) the firstfruits of the tenths of wine and oil, which they had sanctified, and reserved for the priests that serve in Jerusalem" in Jdt 11:13.[47] Giambrone rightfully asserts that "the *Didache*'s use of ἀπαρχή is 'artfully adopted for gentiles.'"[48]

Immersion, the second feature that is arguably a requirement for conversion to Judaism, is similarly not for the sake of conversion to Judaism in the Didache. There is an ongoing discussion as to whether such immersions were practiced at all within Judaism, based on a paucity of early literary evidence.[49] Later texts do provide evidence that this was a known practice however. Gerim 1.3 (=Mas. Qeṭ. 60a), bears this out, stating that if someone wishes to become a proselyte, he is taken to the "house of immersion" (בית טבילה) where he is told some of the details of the precepts and his obligations regarding "gleanings, forgotten sheaves, the corner of the field and tithes." This is quite possibly a Tannaitic tractate,[50] thus from the same general time period as the Didache. Other later texts unambiguously point to the significance of immersion to conversion. One such is found in *Sifré Bamidbar* 108, quoting Yehudah HaNasi: "Rabbi says, 'Just as an Israelite enters the covenant in one of three ways only, namely, circumcision, immersion and the propitiation of an offering, so proselytes fall under the same rule.'"[51] A distinction between Jewish and Didachean immersions in respect to conversion cannot be drawn on the supposed basis of the non-existence of immersion as a conversion ritual in the Jewish world of the time.

On the basis of internal evidence, the function of baptism in the Didache is tied to the Didachean community itself and the church rather than

45. Lev 16:32.

46. Milavec, *The Didache: Faith*, 497.

47. Giambrone, "According to the Commandment," 461.

48. Giambrone, "According to the Commandment," 462.

49. Hartman, *"Into the Name of the Lord Jesus,"* 5.

50. Cohen, *Preface*, Soncino Talmud, Minor Tractates.

51. Neusner, *Sifré to Numbers*, 2, 148.

to Israel. It is immersion into the ὄνομα of the Father, Son, and Holy Spirit in Did. 7.1, 3, and precedes full involvement in the community's prayer life in Did. 8, and communal meals in Did. 9–10. Clues as to the community's identity are found in Did. 12.1, which states "you shall receive all who come in the name of the Lord," this being the same name that the disciple has been baptized into. Following that, the term "Christian" defines those who are part of the community in Did. 12.4. In the appropriated metaphor of regathering "from the four winds of heaven" in Did. 9.4 and 10.5, it is specifically the "church" that is regathered as in Did. 16.7 with its anticipation of the Lord's return "with all his saints with him." In other words, the baptism of the Didache is not a conversion to Judaism, but to something other; as Audet called it, "un rite d'entrée."[52]

The third comparable between the Didache's requirements for its gentile adherents and those converting to Judaism is that of kashrut, or eating "suet" (*i.e.* forbidden fat) in Did. 6.3: "concerning food, bear what you are able. But particularly abstain from that which is offered to idols." The latter requirement, to abstain from idol food, is a non-negotiable requirement also addressed in Did. 3.4 and 5.1, confirming the Didache's abhorrence of idolatry. Of this Matti Myllykoski surmises, with some justification although no final proof, that eating "idol food is obviously a practice that some gentile members of the communities have not given up."[53] Alex Cheung has helpfully drawn a line between the Didache with its use of the formula περὶ δέ in Did. 6.3 (and also 7.1; 9.1–3; 11.3) and Paul's use of the same phrase in the same way in 1 Cor 7:1, 25; 8:1; 12:1; 16:1, 12.[54] While Cheung views the passages as bearing some similarity however, Paul's approach is starkly different in that he considers the consumption of idol food as a "liberty" (1 Cor 8:9) whereas the Didache permits no such thing.

Regardless, it is not merely the consumption of idol food that is significant in terms of whether the Didache is requiring adherents to convert to Judaism. This requirement also corresponds to the Apostolic Decree of Acts 15, which as Huub van de Sandt and David Flusser have extensively shown reflects both earlier and later Jewish traditions, particularly those of

52. Audet, *La Didachè*, 358. Did. 9.5 is explicit in terms of baptism as a rite of entrance: "Do not let anyone eat or drink from your thanksgiving, but those who have been baptized into the name of the Lord." Nathan Mitchell's unique perspective is not that baptism in the Didache is conversionary, but that it "places the gentile believer under intense pressure to become (eventually, at least) an observant Jew." There is not enough evidence for this.

53. Myllykoski, *Without Decree*, 444.

54. Cheung, *Idol Food in Corinth*, 213.

the Noachide laws.[55] These Noahide laws (and their antecedents) are for all humanity rather than for the sake of conversion.

The Didache's lack of requirements for converts to Judaism, both from the Decalogue and according to tradition, contrasts with Qumran community's requirement for all of its members, including proselytes, to keep all aspects of the Torah. The *Serek*, which while not concerned with proselytism nevertheless addresses the issue of inducting non-Jewish persons into the community. *Serek* 5.6 thus stipulates the "rule for the men of the *Yahad* who volunteer to repent from all evil" is to "atone for all those in Aaron who volunteer for holiness, and for those in Israel who belong to truth, and for Gentile proselytes who join them in community."[56] While there is no specific statement regarding the structure, it can be seen both in Michael Wise's translation and the Hebrew:

Aaron	—	volunteer for holiness (המתנדוים לקודש באהרון)
Israel	—	belong to truth (לבית האמת בישראל)
Gentile proselytes	—	join in community (והנלוים עליהם ליחד)

In this context, Wise's translation of הנלוים as gentile converts contrasts with Martínez and Tigchelaar's "those who join them."[57] Wise's translation, which he uses consistently where the term occurs, is substantiated from the context and the divisions stated: Aaron, Israel, and a third group. Given that Aaron and Israel together comprised the totality of the Jewish people, the third category is clearly outside of Israel. While there is an apparent progression with theological overtones in the three categories, the distinctions climax with the description of the proselytes as those who join the community and subject themselves to its adjudication of disputes (ריב) and regulations (משפט) over against those who trespass against them.

Strengthening this interpretation, CD 14.3–6 has a similar progression and categorization:

> All of them shall be enlisted by their names: the priests first, the levites second, the children of Israel third, and the proselyte [הגר] fourth; and they shall be inscribed by their [na]mes, each

55. Sandt and Flusser, *The Didache*, 246–51.

56. Wise et al., *The Dead Sea Scrolls*, 122, 136.

57. Martinez and Tigchelaar, *Dead Sea Scrolls Study Edition*, 81.

> one after his brother; the priests first, the levites second, the children of Israel third and the proselyte [הגר] fourth.[58]

It can then be seen that similarly to the *Serek*, after the categorization is made in CD, there is likewise the reminder that all alike are subject to the judgement (שפטם) of a learned priest (CD 14.8). Here the proselyte, or *ger*, is specified to be such (גר). Again the question arises as to who such a proselyte might be if not a gentile.

A survey of proselytes in the Qumran literature by Terence Donaldson concludes that proselytes in the texts "are probably to be understood as hypothetical figures" and that it is unlikely that the community itself "actually incorporated Gentile converts."[59] Even if that were the case, and the *Serek* were not envisaging gentile proselytes, its requirements for those entering the community are as strict as for Aaron and Israel.

It is therefore the lenient phrase in Did. 6.3 "concerning food, bear what you are able" that is pertinent. In addition to the record of Qumran, it contrasts with the requirements of the (later) rabbinic record, where as in b. Yeb. 47a, which has been quoted above, dietary stipulations are absolute, and transgression of them carries punishment. The Didache contrasts with the Essene community's strict requirements for its members to only eat "pure" food, as in *Serek* 5.8–9; where the new member is required to "swear with a binding oath to revert to the Law of Moses, according to all that he commanded, with whole heart and whole soul."[60] Even after that a year's probation was required before they might touch the "pure Meal of the congregation"[61] (6.16–17).

The *Serek*'s contrast with the Didache's leniency regarding food is quite marked, if indeed acceptance of the Torah's stipulations in this regard was required of gentiles in the Didachean community. At this point, Draper suggests what seems natural, that the "Jewish ritual food laws are also made desirable but optional."[62] If this is so, the desirability of the ritual food laws serves to demonstrate the fact that they were not mandatory. In other words, the Didache's requirements for converts were not contiguous with these other traditions within Judaism.

In summary, this section has argued that on the basis of early rabbinic records, the Torah taught by the Didache does not correspond with the requirements made of converts to Judaism. The Didache does not require

58. Martinez and Tigchelaar, *Dead Sea Scrolls Study Edition*, 573.

59. Donaldson, *Judaism and the Gentiles*, 215.

60. Martinez and Tigchelaar, *Dead Sea Scrolls Study Edition*, 81.

61. *Serek* 6.16–17. Martinez and Tigchelaar, *Dead Sea Scrolls Study Edition*, 81.

62. Draper, *A Continuing Enigma*, 112.

circumcision, immersion according to Jewish practices (more is to be said regarding this in the next chapter), nor kashrut. A comparison with the requirements of converts in the *Serek Hayaḥad* shows that in the Qumran community, a convert would be required to live by as strict a rule as "Aaron" and "Israel." The omission of these major commands in the Didache substantiates that conversion is not in view.

Immersion and Conversion

On the heels of the Didache's identification of the disciple, its teaching on baptism is striking, memorable, and indicative of the disciple's relationship to the Torah and the community, but not his conversion to Judaism.

Immersion and Virtue

In the ancient world, ritual washings, immersions, and other water cleansing rites were a feature of both pagan religions and Judaism.[63] In both spheres, writers were at pains to counter what was apparently a popular conception (as with Pilate in Matt 27:24) that cleansings with water could cleanse the soul. Ovid wrote against the idea that water itself had any power to spiritually cleanse, he lamented in *Fasti* 2.45–46 that any should think that water could wash away their guilt. Philo, referring to the festivals of the Greeks and barbarians in *Cher.* 95 decried their practices for "they cleanse their bodies with lustrations (λοθτροῖς) and purifications (καθαρσίοις), but they neither wash nor practise to wash off from their souls the passions by which life is defiled."[64] The same connection is made in *Unchangeable* 8, where Philo finds it absurd that people would cleanse their bodies but not their hearts.

The connection between the outward cleansing demanded by Jewish Law and inward purity demanded inward cleansing if the outer cleansing was to have any meaning. Thus, *Serek* 3.7–9 says of the one being immersed that "it is by the holy spirit of the community, in its truth, that he is cleansed of all his iniquities. And by the spirit of uprightness and of humility his sin is atoned. And by the compliance of his soul with all the laws of God his flesh is cleansed by being sprinkled with cleansing waters and being made holy with the waters of repentance."[65] Poetically, the Sibyl-

63. Ferguson, *Baptism in the Early Church*, 25–37.

64. Colson (LCL).

65. The obverse is also true. *Serek* 5.13–14 states that "one is not cleansed unless one turns away from ones wickedness, for he is unclean among all the transgressors of his word." Martinez and Tigchelaar, *Dead Sea Scrolls Study Edition*, 75, 81.

line Oracles, which in Charlesworth's view are "a political oracle from the Hellenistic age updated by a Jew in the late first century A.D.,"[66] include a heartfelt appeal in 4.162–66. There occur the lines: "Ah, wretched mortals, . . . wash your whole bodies in perennial rivers. Stretch out your hands to heaven and ask forgiveness."[67]

As Eyal Regev states, "a profound legacy of Jewish thought about moral impurity was inherited by early Christian communities."[68] In the Jewish world such immersions attained exceptional importance, doubtless because of precedents found in the Law of Moses.[69] According to Josephus, adoption of these rites was an essential prerequisite before new adherents could be accepted into the Essene community, and a full year's probation was required before the initiate was "allowed to share the purer kind of holy water."[70] This level of dedication earned Philo's admiration, causing him to deem them "athletes of virtue."[71] For some, though, no immersion would suffice. In *Serek* 3.4–5, those not willing or strong enough (לוא חזק) to enter the community would not "be purified by the cleansing waters, nor . . . be made holy by seas or rivers, nor . . . be purified by all the water of ablution."[72]

Despite the role of immersion in the induction of new members into the Essene community, evidence that first-century Jews practiced baptism as a rite of conversion is patchy. In this regard, van de Sandt and Flusser argued that there is sufficient evidence to show that immersion was practiced as a rite—but not the "direct proof that proselytes were baptized before the earliest stage of Christian baptism."[73] Later texts, however, unambiguously point to the significance of immersion to conversion. One such is found in Sifré

66. Charlesworth, *The Old Testament Pseudepigrapha*, v. 1, 381.

67. Charlesworth, *The Old Testament Pseudepigrapha*, v. 1, 388. Jonathan Lawrence recently argued further in his survey of washings and the *Yahad*, and concluded that "Since bathing was likely a part of a candidate's life in the *Yahad* even before sharing in the pure food and since bathing is described as part of the process of repentance and readmission to the community in Serek 2.4–9, we may still conclude that bathing was part of initiation even though it is never explicitly stated." *Washing in Water*, 141.

68. Regev, "Moral Impurity and the Temple in Early Christianity," 391.

69. Ronny Reich, in pursuing the relationship between synagogues and *miqwaot* during the Second Temple period in the regions of Judea and Galilee, found that "Next to each of the synagogues dating to the Second Temple period, archaeologists found a *miqweh*" *The Synagogue and the miqweh*, 297. Roland De Vaux documented a "considerable number" of cisterns that would have been fit for purpose. *Archaeology and the Dead Sea Scrolls*, 131.

70. Josephus, *War* 2.138.

71. Philo, *Prob.* 88.

72. Martinez and Tigchelaar, *Dead Sea Scrolls Study Edition*, 75.

73. Sandt and Flusser, *The Didache*, 278.

Bamidbar 108, quoting Rabbi Yehudah HaNasi (simply called "Rabbi" due to his prominence): "Rabbi says, 'Just as an Israelite enters the covenant in one of three ways only, namely, circumcision, immersion and the propitiation of an offering, so proselytes fall under the same rule.'"[74] But here, Rabbi is a second-century source. Gerim 3, quite possibly a Tannaitic tractate and thus from the same general time period as the Didache, bears this out, however, stating that if someone wishes to become a proselyte, he is taken to the "house of immersion" (לבית הטבילה).[75]

In summary, what has been demonstrated is that the fundamental meaning of immersion was the inward purity it represented. Immersions were used as a rite of passage for inductees to religious societies and, quite likely, proselytes. It has not been shown, however, that immersion was an inextricable part of conversion rites. In other words, immersion did not necessarily indicate that a conversion was taking place.

Immersion and Induction

An indication that the Didache's immersion was one that emphasized induction and commitment to its Way of Life over conversion is found in its detailed instructions regarding baptism, part of what has been called the Didache's "Riddle"[76] or "*Enigme*."[77] Whereas the record of first-century

74. Neusner, *Sifré to Numbers*, 2, 148.

75. There has thus been an ongoing discussion as to whether this was the case at all. Hartman, *"Into the Name of the Lord Jesus"*, 5. Writing before the discovery of the Dead Sea Scrolls, Israel Abrahams argued that proselyte baptism was practiced in the first century. *Studies in Pharisaism*, 36–46. Although his sources by which to prove this were limited, he was able to cite y. Pes. 63b.1. While this tractate dates long after the days of the Didache, it attributes the incident to the report of a Tanna, from a date prior to the destruction of the Temple. It reads ותני כן רבי אליעזר בן יעקב אומר איסרטיוטות היו שומרי צירין בירושלם וטבלו ואכלו פסחיהן לערב. "Rabbi Eliezer son of Jacob spoke: 'Soldiers were guards of the treasury in Jerusalem and they immersed and they ate the Passover.'" *Studies in Pharisaism*, 37. Here Abrahams presented a key piece of evidence. The Yerushalmi substituted immersion for circumcision, which in Exod 12:43, 49 is specifically required for a non-Jew to participate in the Passover meal. Similarly, Joachim Jeremias advanced a number of textual evidences for first-century proselyte immersion. However he too struggled to find early sources and admitted that evidence for baptism as part of the induction process in the first century is hard to come by. *Infant Baptism in the First Four Centuries*, 25. It is not surprising therefore that this position was subject to skepticism. Finding Jeremias' citations insufficient and even misquoted, Robert Webb subsequently argued that "proselyte immersion, as described in rabbinic texts such as *b. Yeb.* 46a–47b and *b. Ger* 60a–61b, was most probably not practiced prior to 70 CE." *John the Baptizer*, 62, 128.

76. Vokes, *The Riddle of the Didache*.

77. Giet, *L'énigme de la Didachè*, 149.

Christian-Jewish baptism is scanty outside of the New Testament and the Didache is a key part of the evidence currently available, the baptism it prescribes simply illustrates how little is known for certain. As Nathan Mitchell states, its words on baptism have become "as notable for what they *omit* as for what they contain."[78]

In terms of its execution, the baptism of the Didache refuses to fit into any known paradigm. The Didachist's instructions are not only hard to align with what is known of early Christian practices, but also Jewish.[79] The Didache's provisions distinguish its rite from rites in other Jewish contexts. In contrast, no accommodations were made by the community represented by *Serek* 5.6 (= 4Q256, 4Q258), the *Serek* having otherwise significant points of comparison to the Didache.

Mitchell correctly observes that in comparison with Jewish proselyte baptism or ritual immersions, "neither of these Jewish 'parallels' can be proven to have been adopted by Christians."[80] Therefore, although the Didache uses the word βαπτίζω, adopting the word without qualification can lead to misconceptions as to how it was performed. Wrestling with this from the perspective of Christian Judaism, Eugene Spivak uses different language and refers to the Didache's baptism as "an introductory bath."[81] This simplified term has its merits, yet the Didache's instruction is not necessarily for a bath but also a rite that may be performed by the act of affusion, or pouring. These concessions in Did. 7 serve to demonstrate that in reality, its baptism was not perceived as being for the sake of ritual purity.

The procedures for baptism laid out in Did. 7 are markedly different from those normative in Jewish lustrations. These follow a logical order. Immersion in living water is prescribed in Did. 7.1, followed by a series of progressive concessions in Did. 7.2. From "living" water to "other" water, to "warm" water if cold is unavailable, to "pouring" water over the head three times. A variety of suggestions have been made as to the rationale and meaning of the concessions. Some suggest the rationale is based on practical, health related reasons, or to infant baptism. Thus Vööbus proposes that in winter the water would need to be heated,[82] whereas Adolph Har-

78. Mitchell, *Baptism in the Didache*, 226.

79. Humorously, Philip Schaff writes that "Pædobaptists found in it a welcome argument for pouring or sprinkling, as a legitimate mode of baptism; Baptists pointed triumphantly to the requirement of immersion in living water as the rule, and to the absence of any allusion to infant baptism; while the threefold repetition of immersion and the requirement of previous fasting suited neither party." *The Oldest Church Manual*, 13.

80. Mitchell, *Baptism in the Didache*, 246.

81. Spivak, "A Christian-Jewish School," 15.

82. Vööbus, *Liturgical Traditions*, 24.

nack held that "die Gesundheit des Täuflings es verbietet, kaltes Wasser zu gebrauchen."[83] However, there is nothing in the text that suggests such a reasoning. Georg Schöllgen suggests that "the author wants to solve a particularly pressing question for the communities in waterless regions"[84] but again, there is nothing in the text to suggest this, and it would have to be an extremely waterless region not to have access to some sort of bath where an immersion could be performed. Other suggestions come via critical analysis of the text. Thus Mitchell proposes that in terms of the development of the Didache's tradition, it may that the progressive concessions regarding water are the result of multiple stages of redaction.[85] As Rordorf and Tuilier concluded forty years ago, there is no sure answer.[86]

What the Didache does show is that the ideal of living water (ὕδορ ζῶν, Did. 7.2) was desirable, but not imperative.[87] In contrast CD A, Col. 10.10–11 states that "A man may not wash himself in water that is filthy and too shallow to make a ripple."[88] Thus, the Didache's permission to pour water on the head has little to commend itself from the standpoint of purification. "Water from a vessel (מים שאובים) was not only not to be used for *tebilah*, but it even 'made unclean' if it fell over the head and the greater part of the body of a person."[89] In this light Did. 7 does not so much reflect a softening of requirements from a time when "flowing water was required without exception,"[90] but rather a different understanding of the meaning of the rite, as one not related to purification.

In summary, Did. 7 does not prescribe a conversionary rite according to Jewish norms, in which purification was normally a part. It does not emphasize (although it may presume) commitment to a theological schema, other

83. Harnack and Gebhardt, *Die Lehre der zwölf Apostel*, 23. Schöllgen also suggests that "the rule that warm water may also be used refers not so much to the cold season but rather to sick baptisands"; cf. F. J. Dölger, "Nilwasser und Taufwasser," *ACh* 5 (1936) 175–83 and Benoit, *Le baptême*, 8. Schöllgen, *The Didache as a Church Order*, 46. However, there is nothing in the text to suggest that the infirm are in view.

84. Schöllgen, *The Didache as a Church Order*, 47.

85. Mitchell, *Baptism in the Didache*, 252.

86. Tuilier, *La Didachè et le Problème Synoptique*, 171 n. 6.

87. The term used in Did. 7.1, ὕδατι ζῶντι, is used to translate מים חיים in both Lev 14:5; Jer 2:13 in the LXX and is also used by Jesus in John 17:38 in reference to the benefit of belief in him. The role of such living water (מים חיים) is pre-exilic (Lev 14:5; Jer 2:13) in origin and is used in the Dead Sea Scrolls "as both a technical term for running water as well as a metaphor for God's blessings." Lawrence, *Washing in Water*, 134. See also Mishnah Mikwa'ot 1.1–8 for categories of pure water.

88. Wise et al., *The Dead Sea Scrolls*, 71.

89. Abrahams, "How Did the Jews Baptize?" 611.

90. Niederwimmer, *The Didache*, 127.

than in its baptismal formula itself. It does, however serve in the Didache's framework as a rite of initiation and induction to the Way of Life.

Immersion and Dogma

Among the Essenes, immersion was primarily to mark the acceptance of a set teaching, while it also represented a change of heart, thereby functioning both in support of induction and conversion of new members. In anticipation of a day when it was expected that all Israel would join the *Yahad*, 1QSa 1.5 taught that the new members would hear "[a]ll the precepts of the covenant, and shall instruct them in all their regulations, so that they do not stray in [the]ir e[rrors.]."[91] *Serek* 6.13–15 (see also 1QSa, 1Q28a) reads: "And anyone from Israel who freely volunteers to enrol in the council of the Community, the man appointed at the head of the Many shall test him with regard to his insight and his deeds . . . and he shall teach him all the precepts of the Community."[92]

When conversion of non-Jews was in view, teaching was also an important component. This is also reflected in Josephus' account of the conversion of Helena and her son Izates to Judaism in *Ant.* 20, both of whom had been "instructed by another Jew and had been brought over to their laws." Further, the famous story of a gentile who approached both Shammai and Hillel seeking to convert to Judaism but seeking to learn the entire Torah while standing on one foot (b. Shab. 31a) evidences the necessity of instruction for conversion.

In accordance with these types of approaches to immersion, the induction of new members, and even conversion, the Didache fits quite neatly. In it, as Andreas Lindemann noted, "Die Didache gibt keine explizite theologische Deutung der Taufe."[93] He is correct that the meaning of baptism is not explicit, and one may go further to note that the text of the Two Ways does not convey significant doctrine in other matters either, but rather had thus far conveyed only "such moral instruction as was considered necessary before baptism."[94]

Whereas previously the baptizand was addressed as if the Didachist was teaching, in Did. 7 the Didachist addresses the baptizer. Addressing the teacher in the second person imperative the Didachist emphasizes the preceding teaching as a prerequisite for baptism using the phrase ταῦτα

91. Martinez and Tigchelaar, *Dead Sea Scrolls Study Edition*, 101.

92. Martinez and Tigchelaar, *Dead Sea Scrolls Study Edition*, 85.

93. Lindemann, *Die Taufe in der Didache*, 2, 784.

94. Romestin, *The Teaching of the Twelve Apostles*, 96.

πάντα προειπόντες. The phrase awkwardly interrupts the flow of the text and as a result accentuates the fact that these preceding teachings must not be omitted. While the awkwardness of the phrase naturally raises questions, leading to the possibility that it is the work of the Didache's redactor,[95] that does not diminish its significance. At the very least, if such a redactor was involved, he validates the observation that the preceding teaching of the Two Ways is pre-baptismal teaching.

Such an emphasis on teaching is easily understandable in the context of Jesus' command in Matt 28:19–20 to teach his commands in connection to baptism. This meaning is also on the surface of the text, as not only was acceptance of the Two Ways required, but also the implicit acceptance of His mediation of it. This comes to the fore in the appeal to the "name" (singular) of the Father and of the Son and the Holy Spirit. With very slight variation, this tri-partite baptismal formula is mentioned twice, both ensuring that it is emphasized and that it should not be omitted during the rite.

The source of the formula is clear enough. The first citation uses exactly the same words as Matt 28:19.[96] When the Apostolic Constitutions[97] reproduced this passage of the Didache, it did so with a direct citation of that pericope. The Apostolic Constitutions had picked up on the clear inference of Did. 7.1 that the baptizer has a duty to instruct in advance of baptism. It is thus either from a common source or from Matthew itself. Its purpose is not to present a developed trinitarian doctrine. As Mitchell points out, neither of the formulas require a Christology "where Jesus is identified in essence or substance with God."[98] Neither is this a "trace of the Pauline theology of baptism."[99] While the three persons are all identified as one in "name," the theology is undeveloped. Just as the *sectio* precedes the Two Ways, the trinitarian formula follows it, and regardless of its theological import, it functions to seal the authority of Christ—and the Lord God—over the entire teaching.

Baptism is the gateway into the Didachist's community and occupies a prominent position in the structure of the manual. In Audet's words, "L'instruction sur le baptême occupe la première place, comme il est naturel. C'est un rite d'entréeu."[100] The baptizand was not to be immersed in order to attain ritual purity, or presented with a theological creed but to

95. Rordorf and Tuilier, *La Doctrine Des Douze Apôtres*, 170.

96. Niederwimmer, *The Didache*, 126–27.

97. Apost. Con 7.22.

98. Mitchell, *Baptism in the Didache*, 253.

99. Rordorf, *Baptism According to the Didache*, 222.

100. Audet, *La Didachè*, 358.

mark commitment to the way of life taught in the Two Ways section, and unite with those on that Way who call on the name of the Father, Son, and Spirit. Baptism is a new common entrance to the community just as Sim finds it is in Matt 28:19.[101] This step was to be preceded with fasting, marking the seriousness of the step being taken. New Christians were being taken through a ritual step designed to remove them "permanently from their old (Gentile) society and weld them into a new and permanent (Jewish Christian) community."[102]

Despite the fact that the Didache's instructions regarding baptism are detailed in some respects, there is no indication that baptism was a "relatively new" practice for the Didache community although Zangenberg is right to raise the possibility . Rather, it is the seriousness of its implications and its historical antecedents in Jewish washings that makes the procedure significant. In his or her new life, upon taking the step of baptism the baptizand was at least aspiring to keep the whole yoke of the Lord spoken of in Did. 6.2, if not enthusiastically intending to keep it in its entirety "as interpreted through Christian *halakoth*."[103]

Finally, it is reasonable to suppose that more teaching was given to the baptizand than the words of the Didache alone. Aaron Milavec sees it as an outline of a training "program."[104] In such a case, according to the discretion and leanings of the teacher different emphases may have been drawn out. Nevertheless, its Torah content, as the prerequisite for baptism, was also endorsed and even enforced by it as the baptizand was immersed. It is possible, as Brown and Meier suggest,[105] that at a later time the "pro-Paul" Christians in Antioch desired baptism to replace circumcision and Jesus to replace the Mosaic Law. The Didache's teaching however, while requiring all to be baptized, did not present the Mosaic Law as superseded by Jesus.

In summary, immersion and teaching went hand in hand among Jews in the first century, and the Didache is no stranger to this. In its teaching on baptism, the Didache emphasizes both the previous Two Ways teaching (which we have identified as teaching of the Torah) and imparts further authority to it by appeal to the name of the Father and of the Son and the Holy Spirit. The affinity of this injunction to Matthew, and its relationship counterposed with the *sectio* stress not only its authority but Christ's mediation of it.

101. Sim, *Reconstructing*, 30.

102. Draper, "Ritual Process," 124.

103. Mitchell, *Baptism in the Didache*, 237.

104. Milavec, *The Didache: Text*, 47–48.

105. Brown and Meier, *Antioch and Rome*, 41.

Conclusion

This chapter has argued on the basis of the supposed "concession" of Did. 6.2 that in reality, the Didache neither encouraged deviation from its commands nor the assumption of a Jewish identity. In particular, the specific inclusions and omissions from the Decalogue as it is presented in the Two Ways material, demonstrate strident presuppositions regarding the applicability of the Torah to the reader. The Didache's specific intent is seen in the omission of those commands that had a particularistic applicability to Israel and its covenant relationship based on the redemption from Egypt rather than the nations. Confirming the non-Jewish identity of the new disciple in terms of Jewish conversionary literature from prior to and after the Didache, it is evident that the Didache does not apply the Torah to its disciples in the way that other branches of Judaism did, suggesting that conversion was not in view. The Didache's adaption of the rite of baptism, also, while having parallels to conversionary rites in Judaism, lacks any indication that the convert, though taking upon himself the yoke of the Lord, was intended to convert to Judaism. Baptism was a sign of an inward change of heart and cleansing, but not of ritual cleansing. It was also a sign of complete acceptance of Christ's mediation of the teaching presented in the Two ways via the *sectio* and the trinitarian baptismal formula, this teaching being the Torah mediated for the church.

Conclusion

THIS STUDY HAS AIMED to discern the underlying reception of the Torah in the Didache, and its application of it to its recipients. Following a methodology that has sought to set the Didache in the context of first-century Jewish and Christian literary traditions, I have also sought clues in the social situation, language, and structure of the text which indicate its meaning and intent. This study is the first study devoted solely to understanding the Didache's teaching in regards to the Torah, and as such should provide a benchmark for future scholarship to interact with.

Surveying literature on the Didache since its *editio princeps*, it has been shown that the role of the Torah in the Didache has not been adequately addressed to date, although considerable progress has been made, particularly since the discovery of the DSS. Further research in this area has the potential to enhance our understanding of Christian Judaism and this Torah observant mission to the gentiles. In chapter 2 I established that the Didache was an early document that reflects the Jewish milieu of the early church, and was finally redacted sometime after the destruction of the Temple in 70 CE.

In chapter 3, the social situation of the Didache was further clarified on the basis of an Antiochene provenance. Beset by political and religious turmoil without, the events of the mid to late first-century levant were shown to have caused internal stress for the community as well, necessitating the establishment of generally accepted behavioral norms. As chapter 4 showed, such norms were ready to hand in the Two Ways tradition of the Hebrew Bible which had significant parallels in extant pagan literature. This made the Two Ways topos comprehensible to the gentile disciple, even though he or she may not have fully comprehended its basis in Torah. In order to give its teaching weight, as chapter 5 argued, the Didache leveraged the natural authority accorded religious teachers in the Jewish world, and ultimately the authority of the Lord Jesus himself.

Following these preliminary considerations, a closer look at the text of the Didache demonstrated from the text how these concerns manifested themselves. From the very *incipit* and the following "choice" presented the disciple, the Didache starkly stressed the importance of the Way of Life and defined its character via the Double Love Command and the Golden Rule. Chapter 7 then demonstrated that the *sectio evangelica*, which precedes the Two Ways, had a special affinity for those passages in the Gospels of Matthew and Luke that affirm the validity of the Torah. This teaching was particularly framed in a manner that patterned both injunction and incentive to encourage adherence to its precepts.

In chapter 8, I demonstrated that the *sectio* has a much closer relationship to the Two Ways material than previously supposed. In particular, it is bound to the Two Ways by notable inclusios emphasizing the nature of God as Creator and also the goal of perfection through obedience. Thematic linkages further substantiate the literary relationship. Chapter 9 then proceeded to highlight the features of the Two Ways that point to its emphasis on Torah, both in its structure and its terminology. Particularly, the Didache's use of Deuteronomic prohibitions not to forsake the teaching; to guard it; and not to add or take away from it point to the esteem in which the Two Ways teaching was to be held.

The main point of chapter 10 added more evidence of the Two Ways teaching's authority as Torah, as the yoke of the Lord has been shown to imply not an "easy" burden as in Matt 11:28, but one that not all could successfully bear. The three words related to the yoke of Did. 6.2, ἐντολή, ἄνομος and τέλειος, are all Torah related terms that confirm the importance of taking up the yoke of the Lord. At this point, chapter 11 confirms the identity of the gentile disciple as one not beholden to keep the entire Torah insofar as it was applicable to Jews. The specific omission of most of the first table of the Decalogue combined with silence concerning those requirements normally made of gentiles converting to Judaism was noted. The acceptance of the Torah, mediated for the gentile disciple, was sealed by baptism and the implicit authority of Christ.

This book has not exhausted all that the Didache has to say about the Torah. Its focus has been on the Two Ways material and the induction of the disciple. Further study on how this earlier teaching is incorporated in Did. 8–16 is necessary and should, in my opinion, corroborate the conclusions of this study. Further, more research into the origins, sources, and nature of vice lists in the New Testament would provide helpful insight into the character of moral instruction in the early church, shedding light also on the Didache's Two Ways. This is particularly so as when Easton and

Wibbing's landmark study was published data from the DSS and Nag Hammadi had not yet been adequately studied.

Further study could also place the Didache in the matrix of recent work on Christian Judaism by the likes of David Rudolph, who argues from 1 Cor 7:17–24 that Paul's rule for the churches means the church is to be comprised of practicing Jews and uncircumcised (non-practicing) gentiles for the purpose of mutual blessing within the Body of Christ.[1] Likewise Fredriksen argues that Paul's mission was not Law-free, but held gentiles to the worship commands (worship of God alone, and no idolatry) and the second table of the Decalogue, much as this study argues for the Didache.[2]

The conclusion that the Didache mandated the same Torah followed by the Jewish people for gentiles, insofar as it was deemed to apply to them, has relevance to the modern Messianic Jewish movement, which struggles for theological models by which to accommodate its significant number of gentile participants. Various proposals have been made, foremost among which is the bilateral ecclesiology proposed by Mark Kinzer in his landmark monograph *Postmissionary Messianic Judaism*.[3] This study has not gone so far as to substantiate Kinzer's thesis that the church is a united but two-fold community of Jews and all nations. It has, however, argued that in the eyes of the Didache, gentiles were like the Jews in that they were expected to keep the Torah insofar as it pertained to them.

1. Rudolph, "Paul's "Rule in All the Churches" (1 Cor 7:17–24) and Torah-Defined Ecclesiological Variegation," 21.

2. "He [Paul] insisted that his pagans conform their new behavior precisely to the mandates of Jewish worship, the first table of the Law: no other gods, and no idols. Further, he explicitly urges the Law's second table on the community at Rome (Rom 13:9–10): no adultery, no murder, no theft, no coveting: loving the neighbor fulfills the Law's second table, δικαιοσύνη." Fredriksen, "'Law-Free' Apostle?" 649.

3. Kinzer, *Postmissionary Messianic Judaism*.

Bibliography

Unless noted otherwise:

- All quotations from classical literature are taken from the Loeb Classical Library.
- Talmudic references are based on the Soncino Hebrew–English edition.
- Mishnah is quoted from the Blackman edition.
- All Biblical quotations are from the ESV (UK) unless translated by the author.
- Translations from the Didache are the author's unless noted otherwise.
- Apostolic Constitutions is quoted from ANCF.

Select Primary Sources

Aland, Kurt, et al. *The Greek New Testament*. Stuttgart: Deutsche Bibelgesellschaft, 1983.

"The Apostolic Fathers: With English Translation." In *Loeb Classical Library*, edited by T. E. Page. Cambridge: Harvard University Press, 1965.

Biblia Hebraica Stuttgartensia. Stuttgart: Deutsche Bibelgesellschaft, 1977.

Blackman, Philip, ed. *Mishnayoth: Pointed Hebrew Text, English Translation, Introductions, Notes, Supplement, Appendix, Indexes, Addenda, Corrigenda*. 2nd ed. New York: Judaica, 1963.

Bryennios, P. Διδαχὴ τῶν δώδεκα ἀποστόλων ἐκ τοῦ ἱεροσολυμιτικοῦ χειρογράφου. Constantinople: Boutura, 1883.

Charlesworth, James H. *The Old Testament Pseudepigrapha, Vols 1–2: Vol. 1. Apocalyptic Literature and Testaments Vol. 2. Expansions of the "Old Testament" and Legends, Wisdom and Philosophical Literature, Prayers, Psalms, and Odes, Fragments of Lost Judeo-Hellenistic*. London: Darton, Longman and Todd, 1983–85.

Connolly, Richard Hugh. *Didascalia Apostolorum: The Syriac Version Translated and Accompanied by the Verona Latin Fragments, with an Introduction and Notes by R. Hugh Connolly.* Oxford: Clarendon, 1929.

Copenhaver, Brian P. *Hermetica: The Greek Corpus Hermeticum and the Latin Asclepius in a New English Translation, with Notes and Introduction.* Cambridge: Cambridge University Press, 1992.

Ehrman, Bart D., ed. *The Apostolic Fathers.* Loeb Classical Library. London: Heinemann, 2003.

Goold, G. P., *Josephus.* Loeb Classical Library. London: Heinemann, 1965.

Goold, G. P., and Jeffrey Henderson, eds. *Philo.* Loeb Classical Library. London: Heinemann, 1979.

Grenfell, Bernard Pyne, and Arthur Surridge Hunt. *The Oxyrhynchus Papyri.* 74 vols. Vol. 15. London: Egypt Exploration Fund, 1922.

Henderson, Jeffrey, ed. *Eusebius. Loeb Classical Library.* London: Heinemann, 1926.

Koetschau, Paul, ed. *Origenes Werke.* Die Griechischen Christlichen Schriftseller der ersten drei Jahrhunderte. Leipzig: Hinrichs, 1913.

Martínez, García F., and Eibert J. C. Tigchelaar. *The Dead Sea Scrolls Study Edition.* Leiden: Brill, 1997.

Most, Glenn W. *Hesiod.* Loeb Classical Library; 57, 503. Cambridge: Harvard University Press, 2007.

Neusner, Jacob. *Sifre to Deuteronomy: An Analytical Translation.* [In English.] Atlanta: Scholars, 1987.

———. *Sifré to Numbers: An American Translation and Explanation.* Brown Judaic Studies. Edited by Jacob Neusner. 2 vols. Vol. 2. Atlanta: Scholars, 1986.

Roberts, Alexander, and James Donaldson, eds. *The Ante-Nicene Fathers.* Peabody, MA: Hendrickson, 1994.

Saeki, Peter Yoshiro. *The Nestorian Documents and Religious Monuments.* Tokyo: Academy of Oriental Culture, 1937.

———. *The Nestorian Documents and Relics in China.* Tokyo: Academy of Oriental Culture Tokyo Institute, 1951.

———. *The Nestorian Monument in China.* London: LSPCJ, 1916.

Schaff, Philip, and Henry Wace, eds. Athanasius. "Athanasius: Select Works and Letters." In *Nicene and Post-Nicene Fathers: Second Series.* Peabody, MA: Hendrickson, 1994.

Septuaginta: Id est Vetus Testamentum Graece Iuxta LXX Interpretes. Stuttgart: Deutsche Bibelgesellschaft, 1979.

Simpson, William Kelly, ed. *The Maxims of Ptahhotep.* The Literature of Ancient Egypt: An Anthology of Stories, Instructions, Stelae, Autobiographies, and Poetry, 129–48. New Haven: Yale University Press, 2003.

Stählin, Otto, ed. *Clemens Alexandrinus.* Die Griechischen Christlichen Schriftseller der ersten drei Jahrhunderte. Leipzig: Hinrichs, 1906.

Stewart, Alistair C. *On Pascha: With the Fragments of Melito and Other Material Related to the Quartodecimans.* Translated by Alistair C. Stewart. Popular Patristics Series, 2nd ed. Yonkers, NY: St Vladimir's Seminary Press, 2017.

Vermès, Géza. *The Complete Dead Sea Scrolls in English.* New York: Penguin, 1997.

Wise, Michael Owen, et al. *The Dead Sea Scrolls: A New Translation.* San Francisco: HarperCollins, 1996.

Wiseman, Donald J. *The Vassal-Treaties of Esarhaddon*. Translated by Donald .J. Wiseman. Iraq Vol. 20.1. London: British School of Archaeology in Iraq, 1958.

Secondary Works

Abrahams, Israel. “How Did the Jews Baptize?” *JTS* 12 (1912) 609–12.

———. *Studies in Pharisaism and the Gospels*. Cambridge: Cambridge University Press, 1917.

Adams, Edward. *The Earliest Christian Meeting Places*. London: Bloomsbury, 2013.

Aldridge, Robert E. “The Lost Ending of the *Didache*.” *VC* 53.1 (1999) 1–15.

Allen, George Cantrell. *The Didache: Or the Teaching of the Twelve Apostles Translated with Notes*. London: Astolat, 1903.

Allen, Pauline. “The *Jewish War* as a Response to the Crisis of Flavian Propaganda.” In *Ancient Jewish and Christian Texts as Crisis Management Literature*, edited by David C. Sim and Pauline Allen, 9–28. Library of New Testament Studies. London: T. & T. Clark, 2012.

Alon, Gedaliah. “The Halacha in the Teaching of the Twelve Apostles.” Translated by Atalia Ben-Meir. In *The Didache in Modern Research*, edited by Jonathan A. Draper, 165–94. AGJU. Leiden: Brill, 1996.

———. “ההלכה שבתורת י״ב השליחים [דידאכי]” *Tarbiz* 11 (1940) 127–45.

Asano, Atsuhiro. *Community-Identity Construction in Galatians*. JSNTSup. Edited by Mark Goodacre. London: T. & T. Clark, 2005.

Audet, Jean-Paul. *La Didachè: Instructions des Apôtres*. Paris: Librairie Lecoffre, 1958.

———. “Esquisse Historique du Genre Littéraire de la “Bénédiction” Juive et de L’“Eucharistie” Chrétienne.” *RB* 65 (1958) 371–99.

———. “Affinités Littéraire Et Doctrinales Du «Manuel De Discipline».” *RB* 59 (1952) 219–38.

———. “Literary and Doctrinal Affinites of the ‘Manual of Discipline.’” In *The Didache in Modern Research*, edited by Jonathan A. Draper, 129–47. AGJU. Leiden: Brill, 1996.

Bammel, Ernst. “Pattern and Prototype of *Didache* 16.” In *The Didache in Modern Research*, edited by Jonathan A. Draper, 364–72. AGJU. Leiden: Brill, 1996.

Bar-Ilan, Meir. “Illiteracy in the Land of Israel in the First Centuries C.E.” In *Essays in the Social Scientific Study of Judaism and Jewish Society*, edited by S. Fishbane, S. Schoenfeld, and A. Goldschlaeger, 46–61. Hoboken, NJ: Ktav, 1992.

Barrett, C. K. “Jews and Judaizers in the Epistles of Ignatius.” In *Jews, Greeks and Christians: Religious Cultures in Late Antiquity*, edited by Robert Hamerton-Kelly and Robin Scroggs, 220–44. Leiden: Brill, 1976.

Barton, Stephen C. “Can We Identify the Gospel Audiences?” In *The Gospels for All Christians: Rethinking the Gospel Audiences*, edited by Richard Bauckham, 173–94. Edinburgh: T. & T. Clark, 1998.

Battifol, Pierre. *Studia Patristica: Études D’ancienne Littérature Chrétienne*. Paris: Leroux, 1889–90.

Bauckham, Richard. “For Whom Were the Gospels Written?” In *The Gospels for All Christians: Rethinking the Gospel Audiences*, edited by Richard Bauckham, 9–48. Edinburgh: T. & T. Clark, 1998.

Blue, Bradley. "Acts and the House Church." In *The Book of Acts in Its Graeco-Roman Setting*, edited by David W. J. Gill and Conrad Gempf, 119–22. The Book of Acts in Its First Century Setting. Grand Rapids: Eerdmans, 1994.

Bockmuehl, Markus. *The Remembered Peter: In Ancient Reception and Modern Debate.* Tübingen: Mohr Siebeck, 2012.

Botha, Pieter J. J. *Orality and Literacy in Early Christianity.* Biblical Performance Criticism. Eugene, OR: Cascade, 2012.

Bousset, Wilhelm. *Kyrios Christos: Geschichte des Christusglaubens von den Anfängen des Christentums bis Irenaeus.* Göttingen: Vandenhoeck & Ruprecht, 1913.

Brandon, S. G. F. *The Fall of Jerusalem and the Christian Church: A Study of the Effects of the Jewish Overthrow of A.D. 70 on Christianity.* London: SPCK, 1951.

Broadhead, Edwin K. *Jewish Ways of Following Jesus: Redrawing the Religious Map of Antiquity.* WUNT I. Tübingen: Mohr Siebeck, 2010.

Brock, Sebastian. "The Two Ways and the Palestinian Targum." In *A Tribute to Geza Vermes: Essays on Jewish and Christian Literature and History*, edited by Philip R. Davies and Richard T. White, 139–52. JSOTsup. Sheffield, UK: JSOT, 1990.

Brooks, E. Bruce. "Before and after Matthew." In *The Didache: A Missing Piece of the Puzzle in Early Christianity*, edited by Jonathan A. Draper and Clayton N. Jefford, 247–86. Early Christianity and its Literature 14. Atlanta: SBL, 2015.

Brown, David Michael. "The Didache and Traditioned Innovation: Shaping Christian Community in the First Century and the Twenty-First Century." PhD diss., Duke Divinity School, 2016.

Brown, Raymond E., and John P. Meier. *Antioch and Rome: New Testament Cradles of Catholic Christianity.* London: Geoffrey Chapman, 1983.

Bruner, Frederick Dale. *Matthew: A Commentary.* Vol. 2. Rev. and exp. ed. Vol. 2, Grand Rapids: Eerdmans, 2004.

Budge, E. A. Wallis. *The Book of the Dead: The Chapters of Coming Forth by Day: The Egyptian Text according to the Theban Recension in Heiroglyphic Edited from Numerous Papyri, with a Tranlation, Vocabulary, Etc.* London: Kegan, Trench, Trubner, 1898.

Butler, B. C. "The Literary Relations of Didache, Ch. XVI." *JTS* 11.2 (1960) 265–83.

———. "The 'Two Ways' in the Didache." *JTS* 12.1 (1961) 27–38.

Carrington, Philip. *Christian Apologetics of the Second Century in Their Relation to Modern Thought.* London: SPCK, 1921.

Carroll, Robert P. *Jeremiah: A Commentary.* The Old Testament Library. Philadelphia: Westminster, 1986.

Chester, Andrew. *Messiah and Exaltation: Jewish Messianic and Visionary Traditions and New Testament Christology.* WUNT. Tübingen: Mohr Siebeck, 2007.

Cheung, Alex T. *Idol Food in Corinth: Jewish Background and Pauline Legacy.* JSNTsup. Edited by Stanley E. Porter. Sheffield, UK: Sheffield Academic, 1999.

Clark, David. "Order and Chaos in the Didache." In *On Earth as in Heaven: The Lord's Prayer from Jewish Prayer to Christian Ritual*, 87–116. Minneapolis: Augsburg Fortress, 2017.

Clarke, Ernest G. *Targum Pseudo-Jonathan: Deuteronomy.* Aramaic Bible. 1987; v. 5B. Edinburgh: T. & T. Clark, 1998.

Cohen, Abraham. "Preface." In *Hebrew-English Edition of the Babylonian Talmud: Minor Tractates*, edited by Abraham Cohen. London: Soncino, 1984.

Cohen, Shaye J. D. "Judaism without Circumcision and 'Judaism' without 'Circumcision' in Ignatius." *HTR* 95.4 (2002) 395–415.

———. "Pagan and Christian Evidence on the Ancient Synagogue." In *The Synagogue in Late Antiquity*, edited by Lee I. Levine, 159–81. Philadelphia: ASOR, 1987.

Collins, John J. "Beyond the Qumran Community: Social Organization in the Dead Sea Scrolls." *Dead Sea Discoveries* 16.3 (2009) 351–69.

Connolly, Richard Hugh. "The Use of the *Didache* in the *Didascalia*." *JTS* 24 (1924) 147–57.

Corwin, Virginia. *St. Ignatius and Christianity in Antioch*. New Haven, CT: Yale University Press, 1960.

Craigie, Peter C. *The Book of Deuteronomy*. Grand Rapids: Eerdmans, 1976.

Cuvillier, Élian. "Torah Observance and Radicalization in the First Gospel. Matthew and First-Century Judaism: A Contribution to the Debate." *NTS* 55.2 (2009) 144–59.

Davies, W. D., and Dale C. Jr. Allison. *A Critical and Exegetical Commentary on the Gospel according to Saint Matthew*. The International Critical Commentary. Edited by J. A. Emerton et al. 3 vols. Vol. 3, Edinburgh: T. & T. Clark, 1997.

Davis, Cyprian. "The *Didache* and Early Monasticism in the East and West." In *The Didache in Context: Essays on Its Text, History and Transmission*, edited by Clayton N. Jefford, 353–67. NOVT*sup*. Leiden: Brill, 1995.

DeSilva, David Arthur. "The *Testaments of the Twelve Patriarchs* as Witnesses to Pre-Christian Judaism: A Re-Assessment." *JSP* 23.1 (2013) 21–68.

Deutsch, Celia. *Hidden Wisdom and the Easy Yoke: Wisdom, Torah and Discipleship in Matthew 11.25–30*. JSNTsup. Sheffield, UK: Sheffield Academic, 1987.

Dix, Gregory. "Didache and Diatessaron." *JTS* 34.135 (1933) 242–50.

Donahue, Paul J. "Jewish Christianity in the Letters of Ignatius of Antioch." *VC* 32 (1978) 81–93.

Donaldson, Terence L. *Judaism and the Gentiles: Jewish Patterns of Universalism (to 135 C.E.)*. Waco, TX: Baylor University Press, 2007.

Draper, Jonathan A. "Children and Slaves in the Community of the Didache and the Two Ways Tradition." In *The Didache: A Missing Piece of the Puzzle in Early Christianity*, edited by Jonathan A. Draper and Clayton N. Jefford, 85–121. Early Christianity and its Literature 14. Atlanta: SBL, 2015.

———. "A Commentary on the Didache in the Light of the Dead Sea Scrolls and Related Documents." PhD diss., University of Cambridge, 1983.

———. "Christian Self-Definition against the 'Hypocrites' in Didache Viii." In *The Didache in Modern Research*, edited by Jonathan A. Draper, 223–43. AGJU. Leiden: Brill, 1996.

———. "A Continuing Enigma: The 'Yoke of the Lord' in Didache 6.2–3 and Early Jewish-Christian Relations." In *The Image of Judaeo-Christians in Ancient Jewish and Christian Literature*, edited by Peter J. Tomson and Doris Lambers-Petry, 106–23. WUNT. Tübingen: Mohr-Siebeck, 2003.

———. "The Didache." In *The Writings of the Apostolic Fathers*, edited by Paul Foster, 13–20. London: T. & T. Clark, 2007.

———. "The Didache in Modern Research: An Overview." In *The Didache in Modern Research*, edited by Jonathan A. Draper, 1–42. AGJU. Leiden: Brill, 1996.

———. "Do the Didache and Matthew Reflect an 'Irrevocable Parting of the Ways' with Judaism?" In *Matthew, James, and Didache: Three Related Documents in Their Jewish and Christian Settings*, edited by Huub van de Sandt and Jürgen K. Zangenberg, 217–42. Symposium Series. Atlanta: SBL, 2008.

———. "Eschatology in the Didache." In *Eschatology of the New Testament and Some Related Documents*, edited by Jan G. van der Watt, 567–82. WUNT II. Tübingen: Mohr Siebeck, 2011.

———. "Mission, Ethics and Identity in the Didache." In *Sensitivity towards Outsiders: Exploring the Dynamic Relationship between Mission and Ethics in the New Testament and Early Christianity*, edited by Jacobus Kok, Tobias Nicklas, Dieter T. Roth, and Christine Hays, 462–82. WUNT II. Tübingen: Mohr Siebeck, 2014.

———. "Ritual Process and Ritual Symbol in 'Didache' 7–10." *VC* 54.2 (2000) 121–58.

———. "Social Ambiguity and the Production of the Text: Prophets, Teachers, Bishops, and Deacons and the Development of the Jesus Tradition in the Community of the Didache." In *The Didache in Context: Essays on Its Text, History and Transmission*, edited by Clayton N. Jefford, 284–312. NovTSup. Leiden: Brill, 1995.

———. "Torah and Troublesome Apostles in the *Didache* Community." In *The Didache in Modern Research*, edited by Jonathan A. Draper, 340–63. AGJU. Leiden: Brill, 1996.

———. "Torah and Troublesome Apostles in the Didache Community." *NovT* 33.4 (1991) 347–72.

———. "The Two Ways and Eschatological Hope: A Contested Terrain in Galatians 5 and the *Didache*." *Neot* 45.2 (2011) 221–51.

———. "Vice Catalogues as Oral-Mnemonic Cues: A Comparative Study of the Two Ways Tradition in the Didache and Parallels from the Perspective of Oral Tradition." In *Jesus, the Voice, and the Text*, edited by T. Thatcher, 111–35. Waco, TX: Baylor University Press, 2008.

———. "Wandering Charismatics and Scholarly Circularities." In *Whoever Hears You Hears Me: Prophets, Performance, and Tradition in Q*, edited by Jonathan A. Draper and Richard A. Horsley, 29–45. London: Bloomsbury, 1999.

———. "Weber, Thiessen, and 'Wandering Charismatics' in the *Didache*." *JECS* 6 (1998) 541–76.

———. "'You Shall Not Give What Is Holy to the Dogs' (Didache 9:5). The Attitude of the Didache to the Gentiles." In *Attitudes to Gentiles in Ancient Judaism and Early Christianity*, edited by David C. Sim and James S. McLaren, 242–58. Library of New Testament Studies. London: T. & T. Clark, 2013.

Draper, Jonathan A., and Clayton N. Jefford, eds. *The Didache: A Missing Piece of the Puzzle in Early Christianity*. Early Christianity and its Literature 14. Atlanta: SBL, 2015.

Dressler, Harold H. P. "The Sabbath in the Old Testament." In *From Sabbath to Lord's Day: A Biblical, Historical, and Theological Investigation*, edited by D. A. Carson, 21–42. Grand Rapids: Zondervan, 1982.

Dunn, James D. G. "The Rise and Expansion of Christianity in the First Three Centuries C.E.: Why and How Did Embryonic Christianity Expand beyond the Jewish People?" In *The Rise and Expansion of Christianity in the First Three Centuries of the Common Era*, edited by Clare K. Rothschild and Jens Schröter, 183–203. WUNT. Tübingen: Mohr Siebeck, 2013.

Easton, Burton Scott. "New Testament Ethical Lists." *JBL* 51.1 (1932) 1–12.

Esler, Philip F. *Galatians*. New Testament Readings. Edited by John Court. London: Routledge, 1998.

Evans, Craig A. *Matthew*. Edited by Ben Witherington III. Cambridge: Cambridge University Press, 2011.

Ferguson, Everett. *Baptism in the Early Church: History, Theology, and Liturgy in the First Five Centuries*. Grand Rapids: Eerdmans, 2009.

Finlan, Stephen. "Identity in the Didache Community." In *The Didache: A Missing Piece of the Puzzle in Early Christianity*, edited by Jonathan A. Draper and Clayton N. Jefford, 17–32. Early Christianity and Its Literature 14. Atlanta: SBL, 2015.

Fishbane, Michael. "Biblical Colophons, Textual Criticism and Legal Analogies." *CBQ* 42.4 (1980) 438–49.

Fitzgerald, J. *Teaching of the Twelve Apostles*. New York: Alden, 1884.

Flusser, David. "Paul's Jewish-Christian Opponents in the *Didache*." In *The Didache in Modern Research*, edited by Jonathan A. Draper, 195–211. AGJU. Leiden: Brill, 1996.

Fonrobert, Charlotte Elisheva. "The Didascalia Apostolorum: A Mishnah for the Disciples of Jesus." *JECS* 9.1 (2001) 483–509.

Fox, Michael V. *Proverbs 1–9: A New Translation with Introduction and Commentary*. The Anchor Bible. Edited by William Foxwell Albright and David Noel Freedman. New York: Doubleday, 2000.

Fraade, Steven D. "Interpretative Authority in the Studying Community at Qumran." *JJS* 44.1 (1993) 46–69.

———. "Literary Composition and Oral Performance in Early Midrashim." *Oral Tradition* 14.1 (1999) 33–51.

Fredriksen, Paula. "Why Should a "Law-Free" Mission Mean a 'Law-Free' Apostle?" *JBL* 134.3 (2015) 637–50.

Frey, Jörg. "Flesh and Spirit in the Palestinian Sapiential Tradition and in the Qumran Texts: An Inquiry into the Background of Pauline Usage." In *The Wisdom Texts from Qumran and the Development of Sapiential Thought*, edited by Charlotte Hempel, A. Lange and H. Lichtenberger, 367–404. Bibliotheca Ephemeridum Theologicarum Lovaniensium. Leuven: Leuven University Press, 2002.

Galinsky, G. Karl. *The Herakles Theme: The Adaptations of the Hero in Literature from Homer to the Twentieth Century*. Lanham, MD: Rowman & Littlefield, 1972.

Gardiner, Professor, and Cyrus Carpenter Camp. *The Teaching of the Twelve Apostles, with an Introduction and Notes*. Oxford: J. Vincent, 1884.

Garrow, Alan J. P. "The Didache and Revelation." In *The Didache: A Missing Piece of the Puzzle in Early Christianity*, edited by Jonathan A. Draper and Clayton N. Jefford, 497–514. Early Christianity and its Literature 14. Atlanta: SBL, 2015.

———. "The Eschatological Tradition Behind 1 Thessalonians: *Didache* 16." *JSNT* 32.2 (2009) 191–215.

———. *The Gospel of Matthew's Dependence on the Didache*. JSNTSup. London: T. & T. Clark, 2004.

Gehring, Roger W. *House Church and Mission: The Importance of Household Structures in Early Christianity*. Peabody, MA: Hendrickson, 2004.

Gero, Stephen. "The So-Called Ointment Prayer in the Coptic Version of the Didache: A Re-Evaluation." *HTR* 70.1/2 (1977) 67–84.

Giambrone, Anthony. "'According to the Commandment' (*Did*. 1.5) Lexical Reflections on Almsgiving as 'the Commandment.'" *NTS* 60 (2014) 448–65.

Gibbins, H. J. "The Problem of the Liturgical Section of the Didache." *JTS* 36.144 (1935) 373–86.

Giet, Stanislas. *L'énigme de la Didachè*. Publications de la Faculté des Lettres de L'université de Strasbourg. Vol. 149, Paris: Éditions Ophrys, 1970.

Ginsberg, M. "Derek Ereș Zuṭa: Introduction." In *Hebrew-English Edition of the Babylonian Talmud: The Minor Tractates*, edited by Abraham Cohen 58a. London: Soncino, 1984.

Glover, Richard. "The Didache's Quotations and the Synoptic Gospels." *NTS* 5 (1959) 12–29.

Golb, Norman. *Who Wrote the Dead Sea Scrolls? The Search for the Secret of Qumran.* London: O'Mara, 1995.

Goodman, Martin. *The Roman World, 44 BC–AD 180.* Routledge History of the Ancient World. London: Routledge, 1997.

Gordon, Alexander. *Teaching of the Twelve Apostles.* London: Reveirs, 1884.

Granitz, Nicholas. "Heracles and the Foundings of Sparta and Rome." B.A. dissertation, Ashland University, 2011.

Grant, Robert M. "The Decalogue in Early Christianity." *HTR* 40.1 (1947) 1–17.

Hakola, Raimo, and Adele Reinhartz. "John's Pharisees." In *In Quest of the Historical Pharisees*, edited by Jacob Neusner and Bruce D. Chilton, 131–47. Waco, TX: Baylor University Press, 2007.

Halleux, André de. "Ministers in the *Didache*." Translated by Jonathan A. Draper. In *The Didache in Modern Research*, edited by Jonathan A. Draper, 300–20. AGJU. Leiden: Brill, 1996.

Hare, Douglas R. A., and Daniel J. Harrington. ""Make Disciples of All the Gentiles" (Mt 28:19)." *CBQ* 37.3 (1975) 359–69.

Harnack, Adolf von. *Die Apostellehre und die Jüdischen beiden Wege.* Leipzig: Hinrichs, 1896.

Harnack, Adolf von, and Oscar von Gebhardt. *Die Lehre der zwölf Apostel: nebst Untersuchungen zur ältesten Geschichte der Kirchenverfassung und des Kirchenrechts.* Leipzig: Hinrichs, 1884.

Harrington, Daniel J. *The Gospel of Matthew.* SP. Collegeville, MN: Liturgical, 1991.

———. "Matthew's Christian-Jewish Community." In *Introduction to Messianic Judaism: Its Ecclesial Context and Biblical Foundations*, edited by David J. Rudolph and Joel Willitts, 159–67. Grand Rapids: Zondervan, 2013.

Harris, J. Rendel. *The Teaching of the Apostles and the Sibylline Books.* Cambridge: Wallis, 1885.

———. *The Teaching of the Apostles: Newly Edited with Facsimile Text and a Commentary.* Cambridge: Cambridge University Press, 1887.

Harris, William Vernon. *Ancient Literacy.* London: Harvard University Press, 1989.

Hartin, Patrick J. "Ethics in the Letter of James, the Gospel of Matthew, and the Didache: Their Place in Early Christian Literature." In *Matthew, James, and Didache: Three Related Documents in Their Jewish and Christian Settings*, edited by Huub van de Sandt and Jürgen K. Zangenberg, 289–314. Symposium Series. Atlanta: SBL, 2008.

Hartman, Lars. *"Into the Name of the Lord Jesus": Baptism in the Early Church.* Edinburgh: T. & T. Clark, 1997.

Hempel, Charlotte. "Interpretative Authority in the Community Rule Tradition." *DSD* 10.1 (2003) 59–80.

Henderson, Ian H. "Didache and Orality in Synoptic Comparison." *JBL* 111.2 (1992) 283–306.

Hendriksen, William. *Exposition of the Gospel according to Mark.* New Testament Commentary. Grand Rapids: Baker, 1975.

———. *Exposition of the Gospel according to Matthew.* New Testament Commentary. Grand Rapids: Baker, 1973.

Heron, James. *The Church of the Sub-Apostolic Age: Its Life, Worship, and Organization, in the Light of "the Teaching of the Twelve Apostles."* London: Hodder & Stoughton, 1888.

Hézser, Catherine. *Jewish Literacy in Roman Palestine*. Texts and Studies in Ancient Judaism. Tübingen: Mohr Siebeck, 2001.

Hitchcock, Roswell D., and Francis Brown. Διδαχη Των Δωδεκα Ἀποστολων. Teaching of the Twelve Apostles. Recently Discovered and Published by Philotheos Bryennios, Metropolitan of Nicomedia. New York: Scribner's Sons, 1884.

———. Διδαχη Των Δωδεκα Ἀποστολων. Teaching of the Twelve Apostles. Recently Discovered and Published by Philotheos Bryennios, Metropolitan of Nicomedia. 2nd ed. London: Nimmo, 1885.

Hodge, Caroline Johnson. "The Question of Identity: Gentiles as Gentiles—but Also Not—in Pauline Communities." In *Paul within Judaism: Restoring the First-Century Context to the Apostle*, edited by Mark D. Nanos and Magnus Zetterholm, 153–74. Minneapolis: Fortress, 2015.

Hoffman, Yair. "The Status of the Decalogue in the Hebrew Bible." In *The Decalogue in Jewish and Christian Tradition*, edited by Henning Graf Reventlow and Yair Hoffman, 32–49. Library of Hebrew Bible/Old Testament Studies. London: Bloomsbury, 2012.

Holladay, Carl R. *Acts: A Commentary*. The New Testament Library. Louisville, KY: Westminster, 2016.

Holladay, William L. *A Commentary on the Book of the Prophet Jeremiah, Chapters 1–25*. Hermeneia - a Critical and Historical Commentary on the Bible. Edited by Paul D. Hanson. 2 vols. Vol. 1, Philadelphia: Fortress, 1986.

Horner, George W. "A New Papyrus Fragment of the "Didaché" in Coptic." *JTS* 25.99 (April, 1924) 225–31.

———. *The Statutes of the Apostles or Canones Ecclesiastici: Edited with Translation and Collation from Ethiopic and Arabic MSS; Also a Translation of the Saidic and Collation of the Bohairic Versions; and Saidic Fragments*. London: Williams & Norgate, 1904.

Horrell, David G. "The Label Χριστιανός: 1 Peter 4:16 and the Formation of Christian Identity." *JBL* 126.2 (2007) 361–81.

Horsley, Richard A. "The Historical Context of Q." In *Whoever Hears You Hears Me: Prophets, Performance, and Tradition in Q*, edited by Jonathan A. Draper and Richard A. Horsley, 46–60. London: Bloomsbury, 1999.

———. "Introduction." In *Whoever Hears You Hears Me: Prophets, Performance, and Tradition in Q*, edited by Jonathan A. Draper and Richard A. Horsley, 1–14. London: Bloomsbury, 1999.

———. "The Oral Communication Environment of Q." In *Whoever Hears You Hears Me: Prophets, Performance, and Tradition in Q*, edited by Jonathan A. Draper and Richard A. Horsley, 123–49. London: Bloomsbury, 1999.

———. *Sociology and the Jesus Movement*. 2nd ed. New York: Continuum, 1994.

Janicki, Toby. *The Way of Life: The Rediscovered Teachings of the Twelve Jewish Apostles to the Gentiles*. Marshfield, MO: First Fruits of Zion, 2017.

Jefford, Clayton N. "Authority and Perspective in the Didache Community." In *The Didache: A Missing Piece of the Puzzle in Early Christianity*, edited by Jonathan A. Draper and Clayton N. Jefford, 33–58. Early Christianity and its Literature 14. Atlanta: SBL, 2015.

———. *Didache: The Teaching of the Twelve Apostles*. Early Christian Apocrypha. Edited by Julian V. Hills et al. Vol. 5. Salem, OR: Polebridge, 2013.

———. "Did Ignatius of Antioch Know the *Didache*?" In *The Didache in Context: Essays on Its Text, History and Transmission*, edited by Clayton N. Jefford, 330–51. NovTSup. Leiden: Brill, 1995.

———. "Introduction: Dynamics, Methodologies, and Progress in Didache Studies." In *The Didache: A Missing Piece of the Puzzle in Early Christianity*, edited by Jonathan A. Draper and Clayton N. Jefford, 1–13. Early Christianity and Its Literature 14. Atlanta: SBL, 2015.

———. "The Milieu of Matthew, the Didache, and Ignatius of Antioch: Agreements and Differences." In *Matthew and the Didache: Two Documents from the Same Jewish-Christian Milieu?* edited by Huub van de Sandt, 35–47. Minneapolis: Fortress, 2005.

———. *The Sayings of Jesus in the Teachings of the Twelve Apostles*. Edited by A. F. J. Klijn, J. Den Boeft, G. Quispel, J. H. Waszink and J. C. M. Van Winden. VC*sup*. Leiden: Brill, 1989.

Jefford, Clayton N., ed. *The Didache in Context: Essays on Its Text, History and Transmission*. Leiden: Brill, 1995.

Jeremias, Joachim. *Infant Baptism in the First Four Centuries*. Translated by David Cairns. London: SCM, 1960.

Jervell, Jacob. "The Law in Luke-Acts." *HTR* 64.1 (1971) 21–36.

Jewett, Robert. *A Chronology of Paul's Life*. Philadelphia: Fortress, 1979.

Jewett, Robert, and Roy Kotansky. *Romans: A Commentary*. Minneapolis: Fortress, 2007.

Jones, F. Stanley, and Paul A. Mirecki. "Considerations on the Coptic Papyrus of the *Didache*: (British Library Oriental Manuscript 9271)." In *The Didache in Context: Essays on Its Text, History and Transmission*, edited by Clayton N. Jefford, 47–87. NovTSup. Leiden: Brill, 1995.

Jonge, M. de. "The Transmission of the Testaments of the Twelve Patriarchs by Christians." *VC* 47.1 (1993) 1–28.

Katz, Steven T. "Issues in the Separation of Judaism and Christianity after 70 C.E.: A Reconsideration." *SBL* 103.1 (1984) 43–76.

Khomych, Taras. "The Admonition to Assemble Together in Didache 16.2 Reappraised." *VT* 61.2 (2007) 121–41.

———. "Perfection in the *Didache*: Ethical Objective or Eschatological Hope?" *StPatr* 51 (2011) 3–13.

Kinzer, Mark S. "Epilogue Postmissionary Messianic Judaism, Three Years Later: Reflections on a Conversation Just Begun." In *Israel's Messiah and the People of God: A Vision for Messianic Jewish Covenant Fidelity*, edited by Jennifer M. Rosner, 175–95. London: Lutterworth, 2011.

———. "The Nature of Messianic Judaism: Judaism as Genus, Messianic as Species." *Hashivenu* (2000) 1–44.

———. *Postmissionary Messianic Judaism: Redefining Christian Engagement with the Jewish People*. Grand Rapids: Brazos, 2005.

Kline, Meredith G. *The Structure of Biblical Authority*. 2nd ed. Reprint, Eugene, OR: Wipf & Stock, 1989.

Kloppenborg, John S. "The Transformation of Moral Exhortation in *Didache* 1–5." In *The Didache in Context: Essays on Its Text, History and Transmission*, edited by Clayton N. Jefford, 88–109. NOVTsup. Leiden: Brill, 1995.

Knopf, D. Rudolph. *Die Lehre der zwölf Apostel; die zwie Clemensbriefe*. Tübingen: Mohr, 1920.

Knox, Wilfred L. "Περικαθαίρων (*Didache* III 4)." *JTS* 40.2 (1939) 146–49.

Konradt, Matthias. *Israel, Church, and the Gentiles in the Gospel of Matthew*. [Israel, Kirche und die Völker im Matthäusevangelium]. Translated by Kathleen Ess. Studies in Early Christianity. Edited by Wayne Coppins and Simon Gathercole. Waco, TX: Baylor University Press, 2014.

Köstenberger, Andreas J. "Response: Progress and Regress in Recent Johannine Scholarship—Reflections upon the Road Ahead." In *What We Have Heard from the Beginning: The Past, Present, and Future of Johannine Studies*, edited by T. Thatcher, 105–7. Waco, TX: Baylor Univ. Press, 2007.

———. *A Theology of John's Gospel and Letters: The Word, the Christ, the Son of God*. Biblical Theology of the New Testament. Grand Rapids: Zondervan, 2009.

Kraft, Robert A. *Barnabas and the Didache*. The Apostolic Fathers. Edited by Robert M. Grant. London: Nelson, 1965.

Langer, Ruth. *Cursing the Christians? A History of the Birkat Haminim*. New York: Oxford University Press, 2012.

Lanier, Gregory R. "Scriptural Inspiration and the Authorial 'Original' amid Textual Complexity: The Sequences of the Murder-Adultery-Steal Commands as a Case Study." *JETS* 61.1 (2018) 47–81.

Larsen, Matthew David, and Michael Svigel. "The First Century Two Ways Catechesis and Hebrews 6:1–6." In *The Didache: A Missing Piece of the Puzzle in Early Christianity*, edited by Jonathan A. Draper and Clayton N. Jefford, 477–96. Early Christianity and its Literature 14. Atlanta: SBL, 2015.

Lawrence, Jonathan David. *Washing in Water: Trajectories of Ritual Bathing in the Hebrew Bible and Second Temple Literature*. Academia Biblica. Edited by Steven L. McKenzie. Leiden: Brill, 2006.

Layton, Bentley. "The Sources, Date and Transmission of Didache 1.3b–2.1." *HTR* 61.3 (1968) 343–83.

Levinson, Bernard M. "Esarhaddon's Succession Treaty as the Source for the Canon Formula in Deuteronomy 13:1." *JAOS* 130.3 (2010) 337–47.

Lindemann, Andreas. "Die Taufe in der Didache, bei Justin und in der Didaskalia." In *Ablution, Initiation, and Baptism*, edited by David Hellholm, Tor Vegge, Øyvind Norderval, and Christer Hellholm. Beihefte Zur Zeitschrift Für Die Neutestamentliche, 767–816. Berlin: de Gruyter, 2011.

Lockett, Darian R. "Structure or Communicative Strategy? The 'Two Ways' Motif in James' Theological Instruction." *Neot* 42.2 (2008) 269–87.

López, René A. "A Study of Pauline Passages with Vice Lists." *BSac* 168 (2011) 301–16.

Luedemann, Gerd. *Opposition to Paul in Jewish Christianity*. Translated by M. Eugene Boring. Minneapolis: Fortress, 1989. [*Paulus, der Heidenapostel*, vol. 2: *Antipaulinismus im frühen Christentum*.]

Luz, Ulrich. *Matthew: A Commentary*. Translated by Wilhelm C. Linss. Hermeneia. A Critical and Historical Commentary on the Bible. 3 vols. Minneapolis: Augsburg, 2005. [*Das Evangelium nach Matthaus*.]

Magness, Jodi. "Sectarianism before and after 70 CE." In *Was 70 CE a Watershed in Jewish History?* edited by Daniel R. Schwartz and Zeev Weiss, 69–89. Ancient Judaism and Early Christianity. Leiden: Brill, 2012.

Martyn, J. Louis. *History and Theology in the Fourth Gospel*. The New Testament Library. Edited by C. Clifton Black et al. 3rd ed. Louisville: Westminster John Knox, 1979.

———. "A Law-Observant Mission to Gentiles: The Background of Galatians." *SJT* 38.3 (1985) 307–24.

Matthews, Shailer. "The Council at Jerusalem." *The Biblical World* 33.5 (1909) 337–42.

McEleney, Neil J. "The Vice Lists of the Pastoral Epistles." *CBQ* 36.2 (1974) 203–19.

McKenna, Margaret Mary. "The 'Two Ways' in Jewish and Christian Writings of the Greco-Roman Period: A Study of the Form Repentance Parenesis." Philadelphia: University of Pennsylvania Press, 1981.

McNamara, Martin, Kevin J. Cathcart, and Michael Maher. *The Aramaic Bible: The Targums*. 22 vols. Edinburgh: T. & T. Clark, 1986–.

Meeks, Wayne A., and Robert L. Wilken. *Jews and Christians in Antioch in the First Four Centuries of the Common Era*. Sources for Biblical Study. Vol. 13, Missoula, MT: Scholars, 1978.

Meier, John P. "Nations or Gentiles in Matthew 28:19?" *CBQ* 39.1 (1977) 94–102.

Metzger, Bruce M. "The Formulas Introducing Quotations of Scripture in the NT and the Mishnah." *JBL* 70.4 (1951) 297–307.

Milavec, Aaron. *The Didache: Faith, Hope, and Life of the Earliest Christian Communities, 50–70 C.E.* Mahwah, NJ: Newman, 2003.

———. *The Didache: Text, Translation, Analysis, and Commentary*. Collegeville, MN: Liturgical, 2003.

———. "Distinguishing True and False Prophets: The Protective Wisdom of the *Didache*." *JECS* 2.2 (1994) 117–36.

———. "The Pastoral Genius of the Didache: An Analytical Translation and Commentary." In *Religious Writings and Religious Systems, Volume 2: Systemic Analysis of Holy Books in Christianity, Islam, Buddhism, Greco-Roman Religions, Ancient Israel, and Judaism*, edited by Jacob Neusner et al., 89–125. Brown Studies in Religion. Atlanta: Scholars, 1989.

———. "The Purifying Confession of Failings Required by the Didache's Eucharistic Sacrifice." *BTB* 33.3 (2003) 64–76.

———. "Synoptic Tradition in the Didache Revisited." *JECS* 11.4 (2003) 443–80.

———. "The Two Ways as a Rabbinic Training Manual Such as the Derek Zuta (1991)." Lecture, The Atheneum of Ohio. Academia. Jan 20, 2017. https://www.academia.edu/29785028/The_Two_Ways_in_the_Didache_as_a_Rabbinic_Training_Manual_Such_as_the_Derek_Erez_Zuta_1991_.

Mimouni, Simon Claude. *Early Judaeo-Christianity: Historical Essays*. Translated by Robyn Fréchet. Interdisciplinary Studies in Ancient Culture and Religion. Leuven: Peeters, 2012.

Mitchell, Nathan. "Baptism in the *Didache*." In *The Didache in Context: Essays on Its Text, History and Transmission*, edited by Clayton N. Jefford, 226–55. NovTSup. Leiden: Brill, 1995.

Moule, C. F. D. "A Note on Didache Ix.4." *JTS* 6.2 (1955) 240–43.

Murphy-O'Connor, Jerome. *Paul: A Critical Life*. Oxford: Clarendon, 1996.

Myllykoski, Matti. "Without Decree: Pagan Sacrificial Meat and the Early History of the Didache." In *The Didache: A Missing Piece of the Puzzle in Early Christianity*, edited by Jonathan A. Draper and Clayton N. Jefford, 429–53. Early Christianity and Its Literature 14. Atlanta: SBL, 2015.

Nautin, Pierre. "La Composition De La «Didachê» Et Son Titre." *Revue de l'Histoire des Religions* 155.2 (1959) 191–214.

Nessim, Daniel F. J. "Didache and Trinity: Proto-Trinitarianism in an Early Christian Community." Presentation at the Annual Meeting of the Evangelical Theological Society, San Antonio, TX, Nov. 16, 2016.

Newport, Kenneth G. C. *The Sources and Sitz im Leben of Matthew 23*. JSNTSup. Sheffield, UK: Sheffield Academic, 1995.

Niederwimmer, Kurt. *Die Didache*. Kommentar Zu Den Apostolischen Vätern. Edited by N. Brox, G. Kretschmar and K. Niederwimmer. Göttingen: Vandenhoeck & Ruprecht, 1989.

———. "Der Didachist und Seine Quellen." In *The Didache in Context: Essays on Its Text, History, and Transmission*, edited by Clayton N. Jefford, 15–36. NovTSup. Leiden: Brill, 1995.

———. *The Didache: A Commentary*. Translated by Linda M. Maloney. Hermeneia. Minneapolis: Fortress, 1998.

———. "An Examination of the Development of Itinerant Radicalism in the Environment and Tradition of the *Didache*." Translated by Jonathan A. Draper. In *The Didache in Modern Research*, edited by Jonathan A. Draper, 321–39. AGJU. Leiden: Brill, 1996.

Nikander, Perttu. "The Sectio Evangelica (Didache 1.3b–2.1) and Performance." In *The Didache: A Missing Piece of the Puzzle in Early Christianity*, edited by Jonathan A. Draper and Clayton N. Jefford, 287–310. Early Christianity and its Literature 14. Atlanta: SBL, 2015.

Nongbri, Brent. "The Use and Abuse of P52: Papyrological Pitfalls in the Dating of the Fourth Gospel." *HTR* 98.1 (2005) 23–48.

O'Loughlin, Thomas. *The Didache: A Window on the Earliest Christians*. London: SPCK, 2010.

———. "The Missionary Strategy of the Didache." *Transformation: An International Journal of Holistic Mission Studies* 28.2 (2011) 77–92.

Paget, James Carleton. *The Epistle of Barnabas: Outlook and Background*. Tübingen: Mohr, 1994.

———. *Jews, Christians and Jewish Christians in Antiquity*. WUNT. Tübingen: Mohr Siebeck, 2010.

Pardee, Nancy. "The Didache and Oral Theory." In *The Didache: A Missing Piece of the Puzzle in Early Christianity*, edited by Jonathan A. Draper and Clayton N. Jefford, 311–33. Early Christianity and its Literature 14. Atlanta: SBL, 2015.

———. *The Genre and Development of the Didache: A Text-Linguistic Analysis*. WUNT. Tübingen: Mohr Siebeck, 2012.

Parker, Pierson. "Once More, Acts and Galatians." *JBL* 86.2 (1967) 175–82.

Patterson, Stephen J. "Didache 11–13: The Legacy of Radical Itineracy in Early Christianity." In *The Didache in Context: Essays on Its Text, History and Transmission*, edited by Clayton N. Jefford, 313–29. NovTSup. Leiden: Brill, 1995.

Peradse, Gregor. "*Die Probleme Der Georgischen Evangelienübersetzung*." *ZNW* 29.1 (1930) 304–9.

Petersen, Emil. *Die Lehre Der Zwölf Apostel*. Leipzig: Dreicher, 1884.

Powell, Mark Allan. "Do and Keep What Moses Says (Matthew 23:2–7)." *JBL* 114.3 (1995) 419–35.

Reed, Jonathan. "The Hebrew Epic and the *Didache*." In *The Didache in Context: Essays on Its Text, History and Transmission*, edited by Clayton N. Jefford, 213–25. NovTSup. Leiden: Brill, 1995.

Regev, Eyal. "Moral Impurity and the Temple in Early Christianity in Light of Ancient Greek Practice and Qumranic Ideology." *HTR* 97.4 (2004) 383–411.

Reich, Ronny. "The Synagogue and the *Miqweh* in Eretz-Israel in the Second-Temple, Mishnaic, and Talmudic Periods." In *Ancient Synagogues: Historical Analysis and Archaeological Discovery*, edited by Dan Urman and Paul V. M. Flesher, 289–97. Leiden: Brill, 1995.

Rendsburg, Gary A. "The Inclusio in Leviticus Xi." *Vetus Testamentum* 43.3 (1993) 418–21.

Rhodes, James N. "The Two Ways Tradition in the *Epistle of Barnabas*: Revisiting an Old Question." *CBQ*.73 (2011) 797–816.

Riesner, Rainer. "Pauline Chronology." In *The Blackwell Companion to Paul*, edited by Stephen Westerholm, 9–29. Oxford: Blackwell, 2011.

Rivkin, Ellis. *A Hidden Revolution*. Nashville: Abingdon, 1978.

Robinson, Joseph Armitage. *Barnabas, Hermas and the Didache*. London: SPCK, 1920.

———. "The Problem of the Didache." *JTS* 51.3 (1912) 339–56.

Robinson, Thomas A. *Ignatius of Antioch and the Parting of the Ways: Early Jewish-Christian Relations*. Peabody, MA: Hendrickson, 2009.

Romestin, Augustus Henry Eugene de. *The Teaching of the Twelve Apostles. Διδαχη Των Δωδεκα Ἀποστολων. With Translation*. 2nd ed. Oxford: Parker, 1884.

Rordorf, Willy. "An Aspect of the Judeo-Christian Ethic: The Two Ways." Translated by Jonathan A. Draper. In *The Didache in Modern Research*, edited by Jonathan A. Draper, 148–64. AGJU. Leiden: Brill, 1996.

———. "Baptism according to the *Didache*." Translated by Jonathan A. Draper. In *The Didache in Modern Research*, edited by Jonathan A. Draper, 212–22. AGJU. Leiden: Brill, 1996.

Rordorf, Willy, and André Tuilier. *La Doctrine des Douze Apôtres (Didachè) Introduction, Texte, Traduction, Notes, Appendice et Index. Sources Chrétiennes*. Paris: Cerf, 1978.

———. *La Doctrine des douze Apôtres (Didachè) Introduction, Texte, Traduction, Notes, Appendice et Index*. Sources Chrétiennes. Paris: Cerf, 1998.

Rudolph, David J. *A Jew to the Jews: Jewish Contours of Pauline Flexibility in 1 Corinthians 9:19–23*. WUNT. Tübingen: Mohr Siebeck, 2011.

———. "Paul's "Rule in All the Churches" (1 Cor 7:17–24) and Torah-Defined Ecclesiological Variegation." Paper presented at the American Academy of Religion Conference, November 3, 2008.

Sabatier, Paul. Διδαχη Των Ιβ' Ἀροστολων. *La Didachè ou l'enseignement des douze Apôtres*. Paris: Librairie Fischbacher, 1885.

Saldarini, Anthony J. *Matthew's Christian-Jewish Community*. Chicago: University of Chicago Press, 1994.

Salmon, George. *A Historical Introduction to the Study of the Books of the New Testament: Being an Expansion of Lectures Delivered in the Divinity School of the University of Dublin*. London: Murray, 1894.

Sanders, Jack T. *Schismatics, Sectarians, Dissidents, Deviants: The First One Hundred Years of Jewish-Christian Relations*. London: SCM, 1993.

Sandmel, Samuel. "Parallelomania." *JBL* 81.1 (1962) 1–13.

Sandt, Huub W. M. van de. "'Bearing the Entire Yoke of the Lord': An Explanation of Didache 6:2 in the Light of Matthew 11:28–30." In *The Scriptures of Israel in Jewish and Christian Tradition: Essays in Honour of Maarten J. J. Menken*, edited by Bart J. Koet, Steve Moyise and Joseph Verheyden, 331–44. NovTSup. Leiden: Brill, 2013.

———. "James 4,1–4 in the Light of the Jewish Two Ways Tradition 3,1–6." *Bib* 88.1 (2007) 38–63.

———. "Law and Ethics in Matthew's Antitheses and James's Letter: A Reorientation of Halakah in Line with the Jewish Two Ways 3:1–6." In *Matthew, James, and Didache: Three Related Documents in Their Jewish and Christian Settings*, edited by Huub van de Sandt and Jürgen K. Zangenberg, 315–38. Symposium Series. Atlanta: SBL, 2008.

———, ed. *Matthew and the Didache: Two Documents from the Same Jewish-Christian Milieu?* Minneapolis: Fortress, 2005.

Sandt, Huub W. M. van de, and David Flusser. *The Didache: Its Jewish Sources and Its Place in Early Judaism and Christianity.* Assen: Van Gorcum, 2002.

Sandt, Huub W. M. van de, and Jürgen K. Zangenberg, eds. *Matthew, James, and Didache: Three Related Documents in Their Jewish and Christian Settings.* Symposium Series 45. Atlanta: SBL, 2008.

Sansone, David. "Heracles at the Y." *JHS* 124 (2004) 125–42.

Schaff, Philip. *The Oldest Church Manual Called the Teaching of the Twelve Apostles.* London: Jerrard, 1885.

———. *The Oldest Church Manual Called the Teaching of the Twelve Apostles.* 3rd ed. New York: Funk & Wagnalls, 1889.

Schermann, Theodor. *Eine Elfapostelmoral oder die X-Rezension der "Beiden Wege."* München: Lentner, 1903.

Schmid, Ulrich. "Old Testament and New Testament Versions of the Mosaic Law: The Intersection of Oral and Written Tradition." In *XIV Congress of the International Organization for Septuagint and Cognate Studies, Helsinki, 2010*, edited by Melvin K. Peters, 587–604. Septuagint and Cognate Studies. Atlanta: SBL, 2013.

Schoedel, William R. *Ignatius of Antioch: A Commentary on the Letters of Ignatius of Antioch.* Hermeneia. Philadelphia: Fortress, 1985.

Schöllgen, Georg. "The Didache as a Church Order: An Examination of the Purpose for the Composition of the *Didache* and Its Consequences for Its Interpretation." In *The Didache in Modern Research*, edited by Jonathan A. Draper, 43–71. AGJU. Leiden: Brill, 1996.

Schröter, Jens. "Jesus Tradition in Matthew, James, and the Didache: Searching for Characteristic Emphases." In *Matthew, James, and Didache: Three Related Documents in Their Jewish and Christian Settings*, edited by Huub van de Sandt and Jürgen K. Zangenberg, 233–55. Symposium Series. Atlanta: SBL, 2008.

Schürer, Emil. *The History of the Jewish People in the Age of Jesus Christ (175 B.C.–A.D. 135).* Vol. 3.1. Edinburgh: T. & T. Clark, 1986.

Schütz, John Howard. *Paul and the Anatomy of Apostolic Authority.* Cambridge: Cambridge University Press, 1975.

Segal, Alan F. "Jewish Christianity." In *Eusebius, Christianity, and Judaism*, edited by Harold W. Attridge and Gohei Hata, 326–51. Detroit: Wayne State University Press, 1992.

Sigal, Phillip. *The Halakhah of Jesus of Nazareth according to the Gospel of Matthew.* Studies in Biblical Literature. Rev. ed. Atlanta: SBL, 2007.

Sim, David C. *Apocalyptic Eschatology in the Gospel of Matthew.* Monograph Series. Cambridge: Cambridge University Press, 1996.

———. "Fighting on All Fronts: Crisis Management in the Gospel of Matthew." In *Ancient Jewish and Christian Texts as Crisis Management Literature*, edited by David C. Sim and Pauline Allen, 62–78. Library of New Testament Studies. London: T. & T. Clark, 2012.

———. *The Gospel of Matthew and Christian Judaism.* Studies of the New Testament and Its World. Edinburgh: T. & T. Clark, 1998.

———. "Reconstructing the Social and Religious Milieu of Matthew: Methods, Sources, and Possible Results." In *Matthew, James, and Didache: Three Related Documents in Their Jewish and Christian Settings*, edited by Huub van de Sandt and Jürgen K. Zangenberg, 13–32. Symposium Series. Atlanta: SBL, 2008.

Skarsaune, Oskar. *In the Shadow of the Temple: Jewish Influences on Early Christianity.* Downers Grove, IL: Inter-Varsity, 2002.

Slingerland, Dixon. "Suetonius "Claudius" 25.4 and the Account in Cassius Dio." *JQR* 79.4 (1989) 305–22.

Smith, Murray J. "The Lord Jesus and His Coming in the Didache." In *The Didache: A Missing Piece of the Puzzle in Early Christianity*, edited by Jonathan A. Draper and Clayton N. Jefford, 363–407. Early Christianity and its Literature 14. Atlanta: SBL, 2015.

Spivak, Eugene (Jeff). "A Christian-Jewish School: Didache, Doctrina, Matthew." PhD diss., University of Aberdeen, 2007.

Stempel, Hermann-Ad. "Der Lehrer in 'Der Lehre der zwölf Apostel.'" *Vigiliae Christianae* 34.3 (1980) 209–17.

Stewart, Alistair C. *On the Two Ways: Life of Death, Light or Darkness: Foundation Texts in the Tradition.* Translated by Alistair C. Stewart. Popular Patristics Series. Yonkers, NY: St Vladimir's Seminary Press, 2011.

Stewart, David Tabb. "Leviticus 19 as Mini-Torah." In *Current Issues in Priestly and Related Literature: The Legacy of Jacob Milgrom and Beyond*, edited by Roy E. Gane and Ada Taggar-Cohen, 299–323. Resources for Biblical Study. Atlanta: SBL, 2015.

Streeter, Burnett Hillman. "The Much-Belaboured Didache." *JTS* 37.147 (1936) 369–74.

Stuiber, A. "Das ganze Joch des Herrn" (*Didache* 6,2–3)." *StPatr* 4 (1961) 323–29.

Suggs, M. Jack. "The Christian Two Ways Tradition: Its Antiquity, Form, and Function." In *Studies in New Testament and Early Christian Literature: Essays in Honor of Allen P. Wikgren*, edited by David Edward Aune, 60–74. NovTSup. Leiden: Brill, 1972.

Tajfel, Henri. "Social Categorization, Social Identity and Social Comparison." In *Differentiation between Social Groups: Studies in the Social Psychology of Intergroup Relations*, edited by Henri Tajfel, 61–76. London: Academic Press, 1978.

Taylor, Charles. *The Teaching of the Twelve Apostles: With Illustrations from the Talmud.* Cambridge: Deighton Bell and Co., 1886.

———. "Tracings of a Saying of the Didache." *JTS* 8.29 (1906) 115–17.

Telfer, William. "The *Didache* and the Apostolic Synod of Antioch." *JTS* os–40.2 (1939) 133–46.

———. "The 'Plot' of the *Didache*." *JTS* 45 (1944) 141–51.

Thiessen, Matthew. "Abolishers of the Law in Early Judaism and Matthew 5,17–20." *Biblica* 93.4 (2012) 543–56.

Tomson, Peter J. "Transformations of Post-70 Judaism: Scholarly Reconstructions and Their Implications for Our Perception of Matthew, Didache, and James." In *Matthew, James, and Didache: Three Related Documents in Their Jewish and Christian Settings*, edited by Huub van de Sandt and Jürgen K. Zangenberg, 91–121. Symposium Series. Atlanta: SBL, 2008.

Tuckett, Christopher M. "Synoptic Tradition in the *Didache*." In *The Didache in Modern Research*, edited by Jonathan A. Draper, 92–128. AGJU. Leiden: Brill, 1996.

Tuilier, André. "La Didachè Et Le Problème Synoptique." In *The Didache in Context: Essays on Its Text, History and Transmission*, edited by Clayton N. Jefford, 110–30. NovTSup. Leiden: Brill, 1995.

Turner, David L. *Matthew.* Baker Exegetical Commentary on the New Testament. Grand Rapids: Baker, 2008.

Unnik, W.C. van. "De La Regle Μήτε προσθεῖναι μήτε ἀφελεῖν dans L'histoire du Canon." *Vigiliae Christianae* 3.1 (1949) 1–36.

Vahrenhorst, Martin. "The Presence and Absence of a Prohibition of Oath in James, Matthew, and the Didache and Its Significance for Contextualization." In *Matthew, James, and Didache: Three Related Documents in Their Jewish and Christian Settings*, edited by Huub van de Sandt and Jürgen K. Zangenberg, 361–78. Symposium Series. Atlanta: SBL, 2008.

Varner, William C. "The Didache's Use of the Old and New Testaments." *The Masters Seminary Journal* 16.1 (2005) 127–51.

———. *The Way of the Didache: The First Christian Handbook.* Lanham, MD: University Press of America, 2007.

Vaux, Roland De. *Archaeology and the Dead Sea Scrolls: The Schweich Lectures of the British Academy 1959.* London: Oxford University Press, 1973.

Verme, Marcello Del. *Didache and Judaism: Jewish Roots of an Ancient Christian Work.* London: T. & T. Clark, 2004.

Viljoen, Francois P. "Jesus' Teaching on the 'Torah' in the Sermon on the Mount." *Neot* 40.1 (2006) 135–55.

Vokes, Frederick Ercolo. *The Riddle of the Didache: Fact of Fiction, Heresy or Catholicism?* London: SPCK, 1938.

Vööbus, Arthur. *Liturgical Traditions in the Didache.* Stockholm: ETSE, 1968.

Warfield, Benjamin Breckinridge. "Text, Sources, and Contents of 'the Two Ways' or First Section of the Didache." *BSac* 43.169 (1886) 100–161.

Webb, Robert L. *John the Baptizer and Prophet: A Socio-Historical Study.* JSNTSup. 62. Sheffield, UK: JSOT, 1991.

Welch, John W. "From the Sermon on the Mount to the Didache." In *The Didache: A Missing Piece of the Puzzle in Early Christianity*, edited by Jonathan A. Draper and Clayton N. Jefford, 335–61. Early Christianity and its Literature 14. Atlanta: SBL, 2015.

Wengst, Klaus. *Didache (Apostellehre), Barnabasbrief, Zweiter Klemensbrief, Schrift an Diognet.* Schriften des Urchristentums. Darmstadt: Wissenschaftliche Buchgesellschaft, 1984.

Wibbing, Siegfried. *Die Tugend- und Lasterkataloge im Neuen Testament und ihre Traditionsgeschichte unter besonderer berücksichtigung der Qumran-Texte. BZNW.* Berlin: Töpelmann, 1959.

Wilhite, Shawn Joseph. *The Didache: A Commentary.* Apostolic Fathers Commentary Series. Eugene, OR: Cascade, 2019.

———. "'One of Life and One of Death': A Critical Assessment of Apocalypticism in the Didache's Two Ways." PhD diss., Southern Baptist Theological Seminary, 2017.

Wilson, Stephen G. *Luke and the Law.* Cambridge: Cambridge University Press, 1983.

Zangenberg, Jürgen K. "Reconstructing the Social and Religious Milieu of the Didache: Observations and Possible Results." In *Matthew, James, and Didache: Three Related Documents in Their Jewish and Christian Settings*, edited by Huub van de Sandt and Jürgen K. Zangenberg, 43–69. Symposium Series. Atlanta: SBL, 2008.

Zetterholm, Magnus. "The Didache, Matthew, James-and Paul: Reconstructing Historical Developments in Antioch." In *Matthew, James, and Didache: Three Related Documents in Their Jewish and Christian Settings*, edited by Huub W. M. van de Sandt and Jürgen K. Zangenberg, 73–90. Symposium Series. Atlanta: SBL, 2008.

Author Index

Subject Index

Index of References

Ancient Eastern Documents

Hebrew Bible

Ancient Jewish Writers

Josephus

Against Apion

Antiquities of the Jews

Jewish War

Philo

On the Cherubim (De Cherubim)

Decalogue

The Special Laws (De Specialibus Legibus)

Every Good Man Is Free (Quod Omnis Probus Liber Sit)

Sacrifices

On the Unchangeableness of God

Who Is the Heir

New Testament

Matthew

Clement

1 Clement to the Corinthians

2 Clement to the Corinthians

Clement of Alexandria

Protrepticus

Stromateis

Quis dives salvetur

Cyprian

On Jealousy and Envy

Didache

Didache (*continued*)

* 9 7 8 0 7 1 8 8 9 6 6 2 1 *
BV - #0026 - 260623 - C0 - 229/152/16 - PB - 9780718896621 - Matt Lamination